Contents at a Glance

Table of Contents

Introduction

*T*he examinations for the PRINCE2 (PRojects IN a Controlled Environment – Version 2) project management method have proved popular. That popularity has reached the point that having a PRINCE2 qualification is sometimes a pre-requisite to getting a contract, new job or promotion. Even where it isn't a pre-requisite, it usually helps.

If you're reading this having already started your studies, then you'll already know that PRINCE2 is a project *methodology*. That simply means that it contains useful information and a clear structure to help you as you progress through a project. When I am teaching PRINCE2 on training courses, people often tell me at the start, 'I know about project management, but I'm looking for some structure to help me run my projects.' Well, with PRINCE2 you've got it.

The exams are to show that you understand what's in the method and that you understand how to apply the method to a project. And, yes, it's 'exams'. To make your joy complete, you have two chances to show how good you are. The Foundation exam covers the bit about understanding the method. The Practitioner exam is focused on checking that you know how to apply PRINCE2 to a project. You need to pass the Foundation before you can take the Practitioner exam, but that doesn't stop you taking the two exams close together, because the Foundation is very fast to mark – just a minute or so.

About This Book

PRINCE2 should be about delivering projects better, and indeed *PRINCE2 For Dummies* will help you do that as well as help you learn the method. This workbook, however, has a different objective and it is solely focused on the two PRINCE2 exams.

You'll find help here as you plan your revision for the exams and check out what you know and also where you're not so clear and need to do a bit more revision. Here you'll find:

- ✔ **Checklists** for both the Foundation and the Practitioner exams. You can tick off the items where you're confident, and put any remaining ones on your revision hit list. The checklists cover the official exam syllabus, but also some key background points.

- ✔ **Clarification** on particular points in each subject area where you may be finding PRINCE2 tricky, or you may have misunderstood something.

- ✔ **Quick quizzes** to rapidly check your knowledge of particular areas or points, such as whether something is a benefit and can go in a Business Case or not.

- ✔ **Foundation-level practice questions** grouped by subject so you can have a go as you learn PRINCE2. The official practice papers aren't a lot of help until the end, because the subjects come up on those papers in random order.

✔ **Practitioner-level practice questions** so you can get used to the different formats of these multiple-choice questions. That way, when you come to your Practitioner exam, you'll be focused clearly on PRINCE2, not struggling with the mechanics of the question style.

In this book, cross references to a section in the PRINCE2 manual are shown like this: [**Manual** 3.2.1]. Cross references to a section in *PRINCE2 For Dummies* are shown like this: [**P2FD** Ch11 Justifying the Project].

What You'll Need Alongside This Book

This book is targeted at revision and exam practice, not explaining the method or learning it, so you'll need some things alongside to complete your set of PRINCE2 materials.

The manual and PRINCE2 For Dummies

The PRINCE2 exams aren't a pushover by any means, and success requires both hard work in learning then effective exam preparation with revision and practice with exam style questions. The first of those, learning the method, is covered by a companion book *PRINCE2 For Dummies* and, of course, by the official manual for the PRINCE2 method, *Managing Successful Projects with PRINCE2* (The Stationery Office).

This workbook covers the second area, which is revision and practice with exam questions. You'll find some help between the covers on the content of PRINCE2, but that help is targeted at things that people often misunderstand or find hard to understand in the first place. For full details, you'll need to refer to the manual; for a more friendly explanation then try *PRINCE2 For Dummies*. This workbook has lots of cross references to both of these other publications. For clear and helpful explanation, *PRINCE2 For Dummies* has been extremely well received, but you'll also need the manual. The *For Dummies* books are a supplement to the official manual, not a replacement for it, to help with effective learning and exam preparation.

The official practice papers

There's one other thing you'll need, and that's the official exam practice papers. This book doesn't reproduce the official practice questions, because you can get those for free anyway. If you're on a training course as you read this book, then your training provider should provide you with a set. If you're not, then ask the exam authority. The exams are currently managed by APMG Ltd on behalf of the Cabinet Office, part of the UK Government, which owns PRINCE2. APMG's website and UK address are below.

The practice papers will always be readily available, because there are no past papers but the exam authority must let people see what the papers look like. Because the exam is run just about every week, it's not possible to produce a new paper every time. Questions are drawn from a pool from which past papers were made up. For that reason, past papers cannot be made available. When you sit an exam, you'll find that your question paper is very carefully collected in at the end.

APMG's UK address is APMG-UK, Number 12, The Valley Business Centre, Gordon Road, High Wycombe, Buckinghamshire, HP13 6EQ. APMG does have offices in other countries too. Its website at the time of writing is www.apmgroupltd.com.

Foolish Assumptions

I assume that you:

✔ Want to give yourself the very best chance of passing the exams, so you've set time aside for learning and revision as well as having bought this book

✔ Have a copy of the official PRINCE2 manual, which you can use to prepare for the exams and – because the exam is open book – take into the Practitioner exam with you

✔ Have some other explanation to help you learn PRINCE2; that may be the companion book, *PRINCE2 For Dummies*, or material from a training provider, or both

How This Book Is Organised

This book is divided into five parts. This section gives you an idea of what lies ahead – apart from some hard work, but then you knew that!

Part I: Explaining the Exams

The first couple of chapters give you some background to the exams and, importantly, explain the question formats used in the exams and throughout the rest of the book. There's also a chapter on what to do if things go wrong and you don't pass your exam. Some of you reading this may actually have bought this book to give you a better chance the next time around.

This section also gives a short project scenario of a project that will be the subject of Practitioner level practice questions throughout the rest of the book.

Part II: Revising the Processes

The chapters in Part II cover the PRINCE2 processes one at a time. You can go through these chapters as you are learning the method or use them to brush up at the end.

Part III: Revising the Themes

The theme-based chapters are to help you revise the seven PRINCE2 themes, such as Risk and Change. As with the processes in Part II, you can read these chapters as you learn about each theme or use them to check your understanding at the end.

Part IV: Revising the Method as a Whole

When you're learning PRINCE2, it can be hard to see how everything fits together. But you need to know how it all fits together before you sit the exams, because there are questions based on that integration. Part IV is designed to be used after you've done Parts II and III, to check your understanding across the whole method – for example, how the themes and processes support each of the seven PRINCE2 principles.

Part V: The Part of Tens

Here you'll find some hints on getting ready for the exams, and also some key points for understanding the product-based planning technique which PRINCE2 uses – and which a lot of training courses don't teach too well, so you may need a bit of extra help.

Icons Used in This Book

The theme chapters include some 'quick quiz' panels to rapidly check your understanding of particular areas. Have a go at answering these blocks of questions; in each case, you'll find the answers at the end of the chapter containing the quiz.

Most 'remember' points are when you're learning the method, so you'll find lots of them in the companion book, *PRINCE2 For Dummies*. In this one, there are a just a few, so watch out for this icon.

This icon indicates either a real-world example from my many years of involvement with PRINCE2, or a hypothetical instance which illustrates a key point.

This icon introduces a shortcut to help you get to grips with the complexities of the method as quickly as possible.

In the world of PRINCE2, there are plenty of Ways Not To Do Things. This icon flags them up.

Where to Go from Here

The great thing about the *For Dummies* books is that you don't have to read them all the way through. You can simply turn to the bit you want. That's especially true of Parts II and III, where you can turn to the process or theme that you're learning about at the moment. Within the chapters though, there's no need to read everything. Where a point is clarified, if you already understand that point just skip the rest of the explanation and move on.

Part I
Explaining the Exams

The 5th Wave · By Rich Tennant

EXAM ROOM

TRUE   FALSE

In this part . . .

Part I sets the scene for the PRINCE2 exams. It explains the format and also the style of questions. In the Foundation exam the style is 'classic' multiple choice, but even here there are strategies that you will find useful. The Practitioner exam is also multiple-choice, but here you find different styles such as matching questions. This section goes through each style to help you understand them quickly.

Hopefully you will succeed in both exams after reading this book. However, if something goes wrong – as it can in any exam – you'll also find some advice in this section on handling exam failure. That may be especially important to you if the reason you have bought this book is because you've already failed an exam and want to give yourself a better chance next time around.

Chapter 1

Understanding the PRINCE2 Exams

Good news! You've probably bought this book to give yourself the best chance of passing either or both of the PRINCE2 exams. Well, the good news is that the exams are passable and although good preparation won't guarantee success, it will give you a very good chance. Most people who understand the method well and who have prepared thoroughly pass. It's great for me in the 'trainer' part of my job to have an exam sitting with a 100 per cent pass rate. With a recent series of four large in-house courses with a prestigious client – actually a royal institute – in London, two had 100 per cent pass at Practitioner in the exam sittings, and only a couple of people missed in the other two, and one only narrowly. I hope that the high pass rate reflects the quality of my training, but what it also reflects is the candidates' determination and very hard work.

Grasping the Exam Basics

At Foundation, it's rare indeed for anyone to fail, provided they've prepared properly, and most pass with strong marks. The exam authority intends that nearly everyone should pass this exam, but don't imagine that means the questions will be easy. The acceptance of a high pass rate is in the context of everyone preparing thoroughly.

If you're a bit worried about the exams, then be comforted by the knowledge that they're a concern for nearly everyone, daunting for many, and a severe problem to a few. Part of the problem is that it may be quite some time since you took an exam and you may feel 'rusty' about the whole process. These things are all thrown into sharp relief if your future – such as a new job, a new contract or a promotion – hangs in the balance and depends, at least in part, on your success. If you do suffer from exam nerves, you'll find a bit of help in the section 'Managing Exam Nerves' later in this chapter.

The not-so-good news – sorry, but I need to warn you – is that the PRINCE2 exams are a bit . . . er . . . awkward. They are not the same as exams at school or university where papers have been written by academic specialists. The PRINCE2 exams are written and controlled by people in the PRINCE2 community who wanted to become involved but who were not required to have a specialist background in the educational psychology of testing. Instead, the people have largely learned on the job. Inevitably that means that the exam has seen more than its fair share of problems.

The non-specialist background is often visible in the papers where questions are not well phrased or are simply strange. I have often heard candidates say after the exam that it was 'hard to see what they were getting at' in some of the questions. Sadly, this factor occasionally leads to failure. The exams have been criticised by some PRINCE2 trainers over the years, too; one who does have a qualified educational background (but not me this time) said at one trainer conference, 'We are supposed to be testing PRINCE2 knowledge and understanding, not language comprehension.' Now this negative slant isn't included here to depress you, but rather to make you aware of the nature of the exams that you'll face.

Going back to the good news again, practice with the question styles will be a real help, and this book has lots of practice questions. If you can get really good marks overall, then losing one or two on any poorly worded questions won't be too much of a concern for you.

Taking exams on a training course – or not

If you're not on a training course as you read this book, and haven't already booked on one, you may be asking yourself whether a course is necessary. The answer is no, you don't need a course. You can learn PRINCE2 by yourself from books and by getting hold of practice papers from the exam authority. For many people a training course is preferable, though, for a couple of reasons. First of all, you put time aside and focus on learning PRINCE2. Second, you can ask questions if you don't understand something and, hopefully, you'll get a knowledgeable answer from a course tutor who does understand the method properly. On the other hand, if you don't go on a course, you can fit in your study of the method around other things, and work at your own speed.

Face-to-face training and distance-learning packages usually include the exams in the cost. If you're learning on your own though, you can take the exams at an open centre – there's more about that in a moment.

If you're thinking of booking a training course, you need to be a bit careful. In the UK there are now a lot of PRINCE2 Accredited Training Organisations (ATOs). You might imagine that if companies are all accredited then the courses are pretty much the same. In reality, there's a wide spectrum ranging from those training companies that only teach what they think you need to know to pass the exams to those that set out to give you a solid practical understanding of the method in addition to preparing you for the exams. Accreditation is a minimum standard, not a uniform standard. In terms of tutors' experience there are those who bring many years of practical PRINCE2 project experience into the training room through to those who have only recently qualified themselves and have hardly ever use the method in practice (if at all). I know this to be true having turned away many accredited PRINCE2 trainers over the years who were already doing some work for other ATOs and wanted to deliver Practitioner courses for my company. Trainers with little or no experience don't add much value, and sometimes when you ask a question they can only tell you what's in the PRINCE2 manual; you can read that for yourself anyway.

In short, be careful out there. If you opt to take a course, choose it with care and find a company that can help you really understand the method so that you can tackle the exams from a position of strength. Don't pick one that will merely rehearse you in exam answers. If you do, you're then likely to feel very vulnerable in the exams, because you don't really understand what the method is all about. Instead, you just end up hoping that you can associate the answers that the company taught you with relevant questions in the exam. Even if you get through the exams, you'll then have trouble applying PRINCE2 intelligently during projects, when with better training you could have done both well.

Taking exams at a public centre

As indicated in the previous section, you can learn PRINCE2 independently using a distance-learning course or just by studying on your own. Distance-learning courses often include exam provision as part of the package, but in any case there's an option to sit exams at public centres.

The organisation currently contracted to run exams is APMG, and you should contact it to find out where the current centres are and when the exams will be running. APMG can also advise on taking the exams outside the UK should you need to do that. APMG's contact details are in the Introduction to this book.

Unlocking Exam Success

The three main keys to success are:

✔ Knowing the method well

✔ Revising thoroughly

✔ Practising with sample questions

If you're unclear on any part of the method and can't fathom that bit of the manual, you might like to get a copy of the companion to this book, *PRINCE2 For Dummies*. Lots of people have commented very kindly that *PRINCE2 For Dummies* makes the method easier to understand and they've found it a real help when learning. It explains the method in a much more practical way than a manual can. For thorough exam preparation . . . well that's where this book fits right in. To help you find relevant explanations in *PRINCE2 For Dummies* and the appropriate section of the PRINCE2 manual, cross references are included in the text of the book.

Practising with questions is essential. You'll find practice questions throughout this book, but in addition sample papers are available from the PRINCE2 exam board. If you're attending a training course or have purchased a distance-learning package, the practice papers should be given to you by your course provider. If you're studying on your own, you should contact the exam administrators, APMG, for sample papers, because they can't let you take an exam without you knowing what you'll be facing. Again, APMG's contact details are in the Introduction to this book.

If you think that you're at a disadvantage with the exams because you don't have significant project management experience, don't worry. Having such experience can be a help, but remember that the exams are about PRINCE2 not project management. Many people who learn PRINCE2 and are successful in the exams work in areas such as project support or are managers who supervise staff running projects but don't actually run them themselves. Strangely, perhaps, extensive project management experience can actually be a drawback if that experience has been with an approach that is significantly different to PRINCE2. Such people often have to do some 'unlearning' before they can take on board the detail of PRINCE2. When learning PRINCE2 then, you'll find things easier if you forget the past and focus on how the method works.

A second point for learning the method well, and related to the point made in the last paragraph, is to temporarily forget about your own projects. The human brain works powerfully by trying to relate everything new to something that is already familiar. That can really work against you here. While you're learning PRINCE2, try not to work out how to apply the method to past projects or indeed your current project. Over the years, I've seen a few people fail to heed that warning only to lose the thread completely and become thoroughly confused. At the point that they've reached, it seems the method won't work well on their projects and they get distracted from learning as they try to think through how they might fix it. Actually, things later in the method resolve the apparent problems. It's a much better strategy for learning to focus first on learning PRINCE2. Later, when you thoroughly understand the method and how it all fits together, you can go on to consider how you'll apply it to your live projects, adjusting it if necessary.

Understanding the Exams and Levels

There are two main exams: the Foundation and the Practitioner. Then there's the Re-registration exam which you need to take at intervals of from three to five years to keep your Practitioner qualification up to date. Foundation and Practitioner exams are aimed at slightly different things, although there's an overlap.

The Foundation Certificate is intended to show that you understand the terminology of the method and the how all the elements of PRINCE2 work, for example how themes are used during projects, and also how the elements work together. For example, how does the principle of 'manage by exception' fit into the processes?

The Practitioner Certificate, as the name suggests, is intended to show that you can apply the method to a project. The Practitioner level overlaps with Foundation in that the exam also checks for understanding of how the method is used. The Practitioner exam then goes on to test your ability to apply the method to a project by giving you a description of a project (the project 'scenario') and basing many, but not necessarily all, of the Practitioner questions on it. The same project scenario is used throughout a particular Practitioner paper. To put your mind at rest a bit, the pitch of the exam is that you can apply the method to a non-complex project.

The Re-registration exam is, obviously enough, at Practitioner level.

Understanding the Foundation exam

The PRINCE2 Foundation Certificate, then, is intended to show that the holder understands the principles and terminology of the method. The questions are fact based, not opinion based, so the 'right' answer will have been taken from the manual. The logistics of the exam are set down in the panel.

Understanding the structure of the paper

The 75 questions cover all parts of the method and are not in any particular order; they're not grouped by subject, for example, or project sequence.

Checking that you've covered everything

As you use this book, you'll see that each subject chapter has a revision checklist for Foundation. The list will help you make sure that you've got to grips with the areas in that subject that are significant for the Foundation exam, including those which appear on the exam syllabus. If you feel a bit uneasy about any item in the list, that's a prompt to go and have another look at that area.

Avoiding timing out

You may be concerned that you'll not have enough time to answer all the questions, particularly if it's been a while since you last sat an exam. Time management is significant in the Foundation exam, but timing isn't usually a big problem. You should have enough time to answer all the questions. In all the years I've been teaching PRINCE2, I've only ever known four or five people time out in the Foundation exam. If you end up being another one though, in Chapter 2 you'll find some advice about managing your time in the closing minutes of the exam.

Foundation exam

One hour.

Seventy-five questions, of which 70 are live, with the remaining 5 being questions that the exam board is testing. You won't know which five are the experimental questions, and they won't affect your mark in either direction; they simply don't count.

Questions are all the classic style of multiple choice, usually with four options: a, b, c and d. The style is explained in Chapter 2.

There's only one right answer to each question – allegedly – but there's more on this point later in this section.

The pass mark is 50 per cent. So of the 70 live questions you need to score 35 or more to pass.

No levels of pass. You'll be told your mark, but the official result is simply a pass or a fail, and there are no 'honours' or 'you only just scraped it' levels.

Your result can be given to you immediately by your training company, but the result is provisional. The paper will be re-marked by the exam authority for the final result.

There are no trick questions – allegedly. If there's a poor question, then it may cause you a problem, but there is no deliberate intention to trip you up.

Going on to Practitioner

In order to sit the Practitioner exam, you need to have passed Foundation. If you've booked both exams in the same course event, don't worry that the result of the Foundation exam won't be available in time. The Foundation is marked immediately, and you'll be given your result. Although that result is provisional, it's accepted by the exam authority; if you pass, you can go on to the Practitioner exam.

You may wonder what happens if your provisional mark is a pass but when the paper is machine marked it throws up a miscount and you fail. Well, you've got to be right on the boundary for a miscount of a mark or two to make a difference. As explained in the next section, if you don't score good marks in the Foundation and you're not well clear of the pass mark, then it's not looking good for the Practitioner anyway.

Building a firm foundation for the Practitioner level

If you're planning to take the Practitioner exam, you need to be aware that there's a strong correlation between good Foundation marks and success at Practitioner level. In my company, Inspirandum, we did some checks and found that those with fewer than 50 marks out of the 70 in the Foundation exam are very unlikely to pass the Practitioner. That's a high pass mark of around 70 per cent.

You may think that this correlation sounds a little odd, since the two exams are targeted at rather different things. However, it makes more sense when you think it through. Although you can look at your manual in the Practitioner exam, unlike the Foundation where you can't, you don't have time to refer to it a lot. Put simply, you can look at the manual to confirm something, but you don't have time to start reading lots of it in order to find answers. You need to be fluent in the method to pass the Practitioner, and if you need to look up lots of detail because you don't know it, then you're not fluent. That flows on nicely to the next section, 'Leaving a gap between a PRINCE2 training course and sitting the Practitioner level'.

Leaving a gap between a PRINCE2 training course and sitting the Practitioner level

Many people who take both exams as part of a training course sit the exams in the same training event run in the same week. However, there's an option to delay taking an exam. For the Practitioner exam in particular, you may want to think about leaving a gap for three reasons:

- ✔ **Some people learn more quickly than others; however, those who learn more slowly often remember better and keep their knowledge for much longer.** If you take things on board more slowly, then you may find it an advantage to leave a gap between the exams to give you more time to absorb PRINCE2 and be sure that you understand it before you go on to take the Practitioner. That's often much better than taking it too soon only to fail, then having to do it a second time knowing that you've already failed once.

- ✔ **The Practitioner Exam is getting steadily harder.** There's an unfortunate mechanism whereby the exam authority has focused, at least in the past, on having the 'right' number of people pass. As training companies have put more effort into preparing people for the exams (sadly usually at the expense of training them how to run projects well with PRINCE2), the pass rate has risen. To compensate for that, the exam has been made more difficult. Whereas it used to be fine for most people to sit the Foundation and Practitioner exams in the same week, there's now a distinct advantage for many in leaving a gap to allow more time to check things over and, even more significantly, get in more practice with sample Practitioner questions.

✔ **You really need to have reached the right level.** If you didn't get about 50 marks or above in the Foundation, although you passed, then you aren't quite fluent enough in PRINCE2 and you'll benefit from having more time to brush up before you attempt the Practitioner paper.

Leaving a gap between the exams doesn't mean you need to leave a gap in your learning though. If you're attending a course, then you may find it better to learn the method to its full extent in one go and take the Foundation. Then go away and practise with Practitioner questions before tackling the Practitioner exam. In my company, we've always made it possible for people to do that. We used to find that about 10 per cent of people found it helpful to leave a gap, but the number is now much greater for the reason I've already explained in this section: the exam is tougher, and you also need to be familiar with the different multiple-choice question styles. When I had the superb results mentioned earlier in this chapter, I put part of the success down to the fact that the Practitioner exam followed on a week after the main training event.

Judging the gap between a course and the exam

If you're considering a gap, how long should it be? Well, about a week is ideal. A month is fine. But after a couple of months, you'll start to be at a disadvantage rather than having a benefit. After about two months, although you'll have had more time to revise and practise, your speed of recall of information from the course will start to diminish. If you need to start looking a lot of things up in the manual because you can't quite remember them, you're in for timing problems in the exam and are more likely to fail.

Getting your certificate (s)

If you pass the Foundation and go on in the same course event to take Practitioner and you pass that too, then you'll only get a single certificate, which is the Practitioner Certificate. You don't need a Foundation Certificate in that case, because everyone knows that if you hold the Practitioner qualification then you must also have passed Foundation.

If you do both exams in the same training event and pass the Foundation but fail the Practitioner, then you'll, predictably enough, get a Foundation Certificate. When you take the Practitioner again and hopefully pass this time, you'll get a Practitioner Certificate. If you leave a gap between the exams and don't do them at the same event, you'll end up with a Foundation Certificate when you pass the Foundation and then a Practitioner Certificate when you pass that exam – one certificate for each end of your bookshelf.

Understanding the Practitioner Exam

The Practitioner is to test your understanding of how to use PRINCE2 and whether you can apply it to a project, as explained in the previous section.

Practitioner exam

Two and a half hours.

Eight sections, each with ten questions. Unlike the Foundation, there are no 'experimental' questions in this exam, so all questions are live ones.

Each question is worth 1 mark, so the whole paper is 80 marks.

The pass mark is 55 per cent, so you need 44 marks to pass.

You don't have to pass each section, just achieve 55 per cent across the whole paper.

Questions are different styles of multiple choice, such as matching questions and sequence questions. I explain the styles in Chapter 2.

There's only one right answer to each question unless you're specifically asked to give more than one answer.

As with the Foundation exam, there are no levels of pass. The result is simply a pass or a fail.

Your training company may give you your result very quickly, or it will follow within about two weeks – after the paper has been marked centrally.

There are no deliberate trick questions and there's no intention to try to catch you out.

Understanding the structure of the Practitioner paper

Six of the eight sections in the exam are each based on one theme. The remaining two sections are each based on one set of process groups. The groups are Starting Up a Project with Initiating a Project, then Managing a Stage Boundary with Closing a Project and Directing a Project, then Controlling a Stage with Managing Product Delivery.

To check that you can apply the method to a project, the exam provides details of a particular project and then bases the questions on that project scenario. Don't worry that the project example will be some obscure branch of rocket science of which you have no knowledge. It will be about something you can understand easily enough. The example used in this book is about preparing a set of offices in a headquarters building for staff who are in a new business unit. Even if you're not a building expert, you can understand about the need for new phone lines, carpeting and furniture.

The Practitioner exam uses some strange terminology to describe the sections. Currently each of the eight sections is termed a question, and each question has ten bits, each of which is also referred to as a question. That's confusing to just about everyone other than PRINCE2 examiners! For clarity in this book, the eight major parts of the Practitioner paper are referred to as sections, and the ten component elements within each one, and which score a mark, are referred to as questions.

Referring to scenario information

The whole paper uses a single project scenario, and that scenario is in a physically separate part so you can have that section open alongside the question paper. The good news here is that you only have to get your head around one project and not several. There's some initial scenario information, typically taking up about two-thirds of a side. Then for some of the sections, but not all, there's additional information that relates just to that section. For example, it's common to have some additional information about a project risk to go with the 'risk' section of the paper. In the exam, you need to take into account any extra information for the section you're working on, but also the overall scenario information for the project.

The additional information for a section is often about half a page. However, it may be longer, and a notable example is with Organization, where there can be as much as one and a half pages describing a range of people who may be involved in the project, and from whom you'll then be asked to select suitable people to fill project management team roles.

Keeping to time

Time management is absolutely critical. Let's say that again for emphasis. Time management is critical for success in the Practitioner exam.

Happily the Practitioner exam, like the Foundation, lends itself to clear time management by its very structure. There are 9 sections, each worth 12 marks, so you need to distribute your answer time evenly between the 9. You won't complete particular sections to the exact second, but you really can't afford to slip by very much.

In my company, Inspirandum, we inevitably get some people who fail the Practitioner. Because of the practical nature of our course, such failure is very rarely because of a problem with PRINCE2 knowledge. It's almost always down to exam technique, and within that by far the most common problem is timing out.

You'll find advice in Chapter 2 on how to structure your time in the Practitioner exam. It isn't as simple as dividing the two and a half hours by the eight sections, because there's project scenario information to read first. There's the main scenario, but then some sections will have extra project information. You'll need to allow time for reading the main scenario and then, for each section as you come to it, any additional scenario for that section. With a bit of contingency time – good risk management – that leaves you with about 15 minutes to answer each of the sections of 10 questions.

It's a bad mistake to 'steal' time from later sections if you're struggling with one or two questions within a section. Rather than let the timing slip, take a guess at the probable answers and move on. If you spend 15 minutes extra on questions that you're having trouble with early on in the exam, you may find you haven't got time to do the last section, where, in the same 15 minutes, you may have scored many more marks. That can, and sometimes does, make the difference between a pass and a fail.

Guarding your feelings

The Practitioner exam is pretty tough, so most people find it a bit nerve-wracking. Bear in mind that most people pass the exam, although that involves a lot of hard work and good preparation. Try to have a positive outlook, based on your preparation, and try not to let over-concern become an additional burden. If you suffer from exam nerves and this is likely to be a particular problem, have a look at the section later in this chapter, 'Managing Exam Nerves'.

Also be prepared for a feeling that you've failed after you've handed in your Practitioner paper. Relatively few people think that they've passed, although all hope it. In my company, we get a constant stream of inbound emails after we've sent out the results. People say some very nice things about our course and their confidence that they can now go out and use PRINCE2 well on their projects, but when reflecting on a successful exam outcome they often say 'I was really surprised, because I was sure I'd failed.'

Understanding the Re-registration exam

Your PRINCE2 Practitioner qualification lasts forever, but it's dated. You're only considered up to date if you regularly top up with a Re-registration exam. This must be done at intervals of between three and five years. If you do top up within this window, you need only take the Re-registration exam, which is shorter than the full Practitioner. If you leave it longer than five years, then to get up to date again you have to face a full Practitioner paper.

Preparing for the Re-registration exam

You don't necessarily have to attend a training course to go for the Re-registration exam. However, it's worth considering to get back up to exam speed, and especially if there has been a new edition of the PRINCE2 manual since you last did the exam. On a training course, you can be shown where the method has changed since the previous edition of the manual.

You must allow sufficient time for preparing for the Re-registration. As with the full Practitioner exam, that means both revision and practice with exam questions. If you haven't used all of the method for a while on projects, you'll probably be well aware of the need to prepare. But if you're using PRINCE2 regularly, you can be lulled into a false sense of security that you know what you're doing on projects so you don't need to revise too much. Remember that you need to be really fluent in the method to be successful. On a project, you can spend a few minutes reading something up in the manual if you need to. In the exam, you can't keep doing that, because you're under time pressure; you have to know it already and be able to recall the information quickly and accurately.

You need to put time aside to revise and practise for the Re-registration exam. Don't try to slot in a bit of revision in the evenings, after long days on a busy project, in the few days leading up to the exam. If possible, take two or three days out before the exam so you can really focus. That's likely to be much more time-efficient than doing a bit of revision, travelling to and from the exam, and taking the exam only to fail and have to do it all over again.

Re-registration exam

One hour.

Three sections, each with 10 questions. There are no 'experimental' questions in this exam, so all of the questions are live ones.

Each question is worth 1 mark, so the whole paper is 30 marks.

The pass mark is 55 per cent, so you need 17 marks to pass.

You don't have to pass each section, just achieve 55 per cent across the whole paper.

Questions are at Practitioner level. In fact, currently the practice is to build the paper using three of the nine sections of the full Practitioner exam running on the same day. I explain the question styles in Chapter 2.

There's only one right answer to each question, unless you're specifically asked to give more than one answer.

There are no levels of pass. The result is simply a pass or a fail.

Your result may be given to you by your training company on the day, or will follow within about two weeks, after the paper has been marked centrally.

There are no deliberate trick questions and there's no intention to try and catch you out.

Practising with questions

Probably the most important part of your preparation for Re-registration is practice with the Practitioner-level questions. If you're up to speed on each of the question styles, you'll find the exam that much less daunting. Buying this book is a good start to getting up to speed with the question styles, but do also get the practice papers from the exam authority or the training company where you'll be taking the exam. That gives you even more opportunity to practise against the clock.

Don't be fooled that because you've been using PRINCE2 for some years on live projects, the exam will be that much easier for you. Sadly perhaps, the PRINCE2 exam is about passing the PRINCE2 exam, not running live projects with the method. Be warned that the exam authority did some checking a while ago and found that the pass rate for Re-registration was no higher than the pass rate for Practitioner. In other words, practical experience of applying the method doesn't seem to offer any advantage when it comes to the Practitioner exam.

Managing Exam Nerves

If you're nervous about exams, then you're in good company because a lot of people are in the same position. It may be that you just don't like exams (like me!) or are nervous because it's a long time since you last sat one. Here are some hints and tips for handling exam nerves. You won't find that everything helps you, but you may find some things that do.

If you have big problems with exam nerves, as opposed to 'butterflies in the stomach' that most people have, it can be useful to try and find out why. This can help to focus your thoughts on how best to handle the problem. For many, the problem is the fear of failure.

Handling exam nerves

Try the following to help you cope with exam nerves:

1. **Think briefly about the consequences of failure. Would it be that terrible?**

2. **Can you simply take the exam again if it all goes wrong?**

3. **Is it likely that you'll fail – how well do you know the method? If you think there's a likelihood of failure, use that energy to learn more; try not to waste it in worry.**

4. **Are your thoughts dominated by pictures of someone telling you that you've failed? If so, spend a bit of time visualising someone telling you that you've passed.**

5. **Visualise success, not failure. Develop a strong mental picture of you passing and having the certificate in your hand with your name on it. Attach other dimensions such as how you'll feel and what others will say. This can work to build confidence and help you to be positive.**

6. **If you tend to think of the exam as a test of your weakness, work on your thinking and try to approach the exam as a chance to prove that you know the method.**

Handling Special Requirements

To make the exams fair, time allowances are available to those with special difficulties, and sometimes other special provision is available, such as for those with eyesight difficulties.

Taking the exams in your second language

If you're taking the exam in English but you have a different first language, then ask your training provider for a PRINCE2 glossary in your first language. A lot of glossaries are now available, and there may well be one which translates English PRINCE2 terminology into your first language. You may find a glossary helpful while you're learning the method, not just in the exams.

Irrespective of whether you're taking in the exam in English, you can also ask to take in a dictionary to help with translation. In most cases you won't need the dictionary, because you'll already be familiar with the PRINCE2 terms from your course, but even so you might like one there as a comfort factor just in case something isn't clear or your mind goes blank.

Depending on your exact language abilities and where you're taking the exam, you may be allowed extra time. The allowance is for the extra time you'll spend in translating the English of the question to your first language in order to think it through, then working back into English to identify the answer.

It's hard in this book to set down the exact circumstances in which extra time will be allowed, since the rules and guidelines keep changing. If you're booked on a training course, the best advice is to contact your training provider well before the course and talk it through. If you're taking exams in a central exam location, then contact the exam organisation, APMG, again well before the time of the exam.

There's one final provision to consider. If the PRINCE2 exams are available in your first language, see whether you can take them in that instead.

I had a Project Manager from Holland on one of my courses a while ago. After taking the course and Foundation exam in English, he actually sat a Dutch exam paper for Practitioner. Everyone else on the course was jealous because, from his description afterwards, it sounded like the Dutch paper was more straightforward than the English one that day.

Taking the exams if you're dyslexic

In my company, Inspirandum, we find that about 5 per cent of people attending our PRINCE2 courses are dyslexic. So the first thing to say here is: don't worry, the whole exam process is well set up to meet your needs. Provision ranges from an extra time allowance to working in an adjacent room and having someone read the paper out to you. The extra time allowance is typically 30 minutes for the Practitioner and a smaller amount for Foundation.

You need to provide evidence of your dyslexia. Acceptable forms of evidence include a medical statement, a report from an authorised dyslexia assessment or something like a university statement acknowledging your dyslexia in the context of university exams.

If you need someone to read out the questions to you, it's very important to get the arrangements in place early – such as booking an extra room – and to make sure that the reader is suitable. One delegate told me about two exams he sat on a different subject. The reader for the first one was fine and did a good job, but for the second, a different person was involved and read out the text in a flat, expressionless way. The lack of intonation made the meaning as difficult to grasp as if the candidate had read the text for himself.

Dealing with special physical needs

If you have other needs, then do ask – whether you have a permanent issue such as an eyesight limitation, or a temporary one such as a recent injury. As with dyslexia, you'll need some form of evidence to confirm that the need is genuine, so that unscrupulous people can't get extra time. Don't take it as a personal slight when you're asked for evidence. If your need is genuine, then you'll find the exam organisation is extremely understanding and helpful and will work with you, and your training provider if you go on a course, to give you as fair a chance as possible in the exams.

If you need extra-large print because of eyesight limitations, then provision includes preparing a double-size (A3) paper for you. If you have had an injury preventing use of your writing hand, it's possible for someone to sit with you to fill in the ovals on the answer sheet according to your instructions.

In one training course, I had a delegate with an ongoing medical condition which gave her severe pain. At regular intervals throughout the course she needed to stand and walk around a bit – which was fine. She also needed special provision for the exam: she said she would find it easier to stand throughout the exam. We arranged with the exam authority for a time allowance to offset the breaks she needed to walk around, and we got a high table from the bar in the hotel in which we were running the course so she could stand up to do the papers. Other course delegates were most understanding and weren't distracted by her quietly walking up and down at the back of the room from time to time. She passed with great marks and went on to run projects and programmes for a major UK children's charity.

Applying for special provision

If you're attending a training course, then in most cases your training provider won't have the discretion to decide on a time allowance or other special provision. Instead, the provider will need to get permission from the exam authority. The important thing in all instances is to talk to your training provider, or APMG in the case of central exams, in good time. Good time means at least four weeks before you're due to take the exam.

Where you need to supply medical evidence, you must allow time for that to be checked and, if it isn't quite suitable, for the exam authority to come back to you saying what it does need and for you to then have sufficient time to get it. Clearly, in the case of provision of double-size exam papers, these need to be prepared in advance – so again you need to be in communication early. You can't say on the morning of an exam that you need a large-print paper; it will be far too late.

Having a problem on the day

If you have a problem on the day of your exam, such as a severe headache or you feel ill, you must tell the exam invigilator before the start of the exam. You then have two choices: to call it a day and arrange to sit the exam when you're feeling better, or to go for it anyway. If you decide to go for it, the invigilator can note down on the exam form that you were unwell; if your result is borderline, your circumstances may just be taken into account.

The important thing to remember is that you must report any problem up front, before the exam has started. It's no good having a bad exam then deciding at the end that you didn't feel too well and asking for it to be reported then; it will be too late.

Chapter 2

Revising and Preparing for the Exams

In This Chapter

▶ Planning for effective revision

▶ Keys to success

▶ Getting ready to take the exams

▶ Strategies for dealing with exam questions

▶ The formats of the questions

▶ The Practitioner project scenario used in this book

The wise say that success often hinges on the three Ps: preparation, preparation and preparation. The PRINCE2 exams are no exception, and if you're to be successful in them, you must prepare well and put the time aside to do that. The advice in this chapter reinforces the point that you really need to understand the method. This chapter then, focuses on your revision and how to set about practice with exam-style questions.

If you aren't sure about how some or all of the method works, then you may like to invest in a copy of the companion book, *PRINCE2 For Dummies*, which explains everything in a rather more practical way than a manual can do. You'll also need a copy of the official manual, *Managing Successful Projects with PRINCE2*.

Planning Your Revision

At the end of the day how you revise is, of course, down to you. You may already be very clear on what works best for you. Having said that, it normally helps to revise in two ways:

✔ **Revise the different areas of PRINCE2, such as the themes and processes, as you go along.** After you've studied each part, revise it thoroughly to be sure you've understood it well and know it. If you're attending a training course, each evening try to lock in the areas that you've covered during the day. Approaching detailed revision in this way has two benefits:

  • If you're really clear on one area of the method, it helps you with learning subsequent related areas. For example, it can be a bit tricky getting to grips with the exact responsibilities of the different roles at end stage if you haven't thoroughly taken on board what the roles are and are still unsure of them.

- The method is large – as you probably already appreciate. Breaking up the detailed revision in this modular way reduces the load just before the exam. Clearly, spreading the revision load is particularly important if you're attending a training event where the exams are included at a fixed time in the course.

✔ **Go over the method again just before the exams.** Revise generally, but with a particular focus on any areas where you still don't feel too confident. However, don't focus solely on the areas where you're unsure. You need to go over everything again at a high level to be sure that you have the whole method in your mind now, not isolated and unconnected islands of information on the different parts.

The chapters in Parts II, III and IV of this book are to help you with your revision. I've written one chapter on each of the processes and themes, and then a couple on management products and how the whole method fits together. You can use these chapters to check your learning during a training course or as you work through the manual, subject area by subject area. Each chapter has practice questions in both Foundation and Practitioner styles. For more on the differences between the two, read the specific information on each exam and its question styles later in this chapter.

Putting Time Aside for Revision

Whichever way you've chosen to learn PRINCE2, whether by self-study, distance-learning course or through a face-to-face training course, make sure you put sufficient time aside for it. Putting time aside means time for revision as well as for the actual learning itself.

Keeping your evenings free during a course

If you're attending a course held within reach of your home – perhaps held on site within your own organisation – then cancel your evening commitments for the duration of the course. A full course covering the method and both exams typically takes five full days.

Before people attend one of my PRINCE2 courses, I always ensure that I point out very clearly that they need to keep the evenings free for revision. Before running a course for a particular local authority, I gave the usual warning in good time. When I arrived to start the training, I reinforced the importance of revising each evening. The response from almost all attendees was that they couldn't possibly do that. One person had a cookery class one evening a week, badminton club on another and other regular appointments on other nights and couldn't miss them. I was rather alarmed and pointed out the intensity of the PRINCE2 course. She remained adamant that she couldn't cancel anything – and she didn't. Another person kept quiet but came up to me on the second morning, after he was unable to answer basic questions in the morning review, to explain that he worked in a bar each evening. He assured me that he had read some of the manual, though, because he had the book under the counter and managed to look at a few pages before the bar got busy. I reported the problem immediately to managers within the organisation, but they weren't interested and said that their staff would do their best. The exam results for that group were, predictably, disastrous. By the way, I'm not criticising local authorities in general. Another course that I taught at around the same time had staff who were incredibly dedicated and professional. It was a large course and everyone took both the Foundation and Practitioner exams as part of the week-long event. We had a 100 per cent pass rate in both exams.

Keeping your days free during a course

The heading of this section may sound a little strange, and if it's caught your attention because of that, good. If you're attending a course, then your days *are* free to learn PRINCE2 . . . aren't they? You may realise that I'm talking about the influence of your mobile phone. You really need to concentrate on learning, and you can't do that if you keep nipping out to take a call or you're busy texting a colleague about some key work issue (I trust that you're not merely tweeting to your friends) while your course tutor is explaining some essential part of the method.

Try to clear the decks before you go on the course, so that you won't be interrupted with matters that you could have dealt with beforehand. You should also explain to colleagues – and managers – that you're going on a course that will be taking all of your attention. Ask them not to contact you unless it really is essential.

On training courses, I always ask people to keep their phones switched right off unless they are expecting a really urgent call. I said this at the start of one event, as usual, but one guy kept his phone on and had a stream of incoming calls each day. He had his phone on silent but kept grabbing it and going out of the door to take a call. He was frequently gone for ten minutes, and sometimes more. On the first morning, I warned him that he was missing essential material and that the phone calls were a real problem. The phone calls were still happening in the afternoon, so I talked to him about it again. It turned out that he was trying to run a project while attending the course, and hadn't delegated any of the work to others. It was a critical time in the project, and he needed to be in control. I advised him to leave the course and come back on a later one when he had more time available, but he insisted on staying and said he could manage. I tried again a day later, with the same response. He'd booked for Foundation and Practitioner exams as part of the event, but didn't get as far as the Practitioner exam because he failed the Foundation – and he failed it spectacularly.

Using an email auto-responder

Try to cut down on the volume of emails you're likely to receive by explaining to people that you're going to be away for a few days. Set up an auto-responder message to say that a delay will occur before you answer an email – or better still that you're out of the office for the week – and give the details of a colleague who can be contacted if someone needs to take action.

You may think that emails are less of a problem because you can deal with them at the end of the day. However, remember the advice in the previous section about keeping your evenings free for revision. It's not good to have an intensive day of training followed by an hour and a half answering emails, because you'll start your revision late in the evening when you're really tired.

Attending a course that's on site

If your PRINCE2 course is being held as an organisational event in or near your own building, then beware of the temptation to go back to your desk in the morning and afternoon breaks or at lunchtime to check on things. Two problems arise with trips back to the office:

 ✔ **You lose the focus on PRINCE2, because you get involved again in the hustle and bustle of your day-to-day job.** You're also likely to still be thinking about work issues as you start the next course session and not be concentrating fully on the material, which may be important.

> ✔ **You're bound to be spotted, and one or two people will find something vitally urgent they need to discuss with you.** Almost always that will make you late returning to the training room and you'll have missed important content in the course. In turn, that can lead to misunderstandings and difficulty in taking on board subsequent information.

The answer is to try your hardest to be 'away' during the course. If you or your colleagues think that's impractical, consider what happens when you go on holiday or you're off sick with some nasty bug. You can't nip back to your desk three or four times a day then.

You may be tempted to think, 'Oh I know it can be a problem, but I can handle it,' but please take the warning seriously. It can undermine your learning with consequent impact on your PRINCE2 projects as well as your chances of success in the exams.

Including revision in distance learning

If you're learning PRINCE2 with a distance-learning package, remember to set aside time for personal revision before your exams, not just time to work through the package. The package should include questions and reinforcement material, but that material is based on what the author thinks you'll need to know. With personal revision, you can spotlight the things that you're finding awkward or difficult to understand. Remember also that you need to learn the method, not merely work through the training material.

Different people have different learning styles, and your personal revision can be in a style that you know works effectively for you. For example, those with an auditory learning style lock on to words and like the course tutor to explain things with examples and analogies. Is that you? If so, you may well have found that the best way of locking information into your memory during revision is to pace up and down and repeat things out loud.

Calculating the revision time you need

People often ask how much time is needed for revision, and that question is probably in your mind too. It's a difficult question to answer because the answer depends on a range of factors. Some people learn faster than others, particularly if they've recently done other learning such as a college or university course. Familiarity with the content of the method is also a factor. If the whole of the method is entirely new to you, it can take up to an hour to revise each subject area, such as a theme or process, and some people need a bit more even than this on some parts of the method. If you've some project experience, then you may find you can learn PRINCE2 in much less time. Perhaps the approach to projects that you've already used is different to PRINCE2, but nevertheless some of the underlying concepts will be the same; perhaps it's just the terminology that's different. If that's the case for you, you'll be able to get to grips with the detail of the method much more rapidly.

When planning your time, don't forget that it's important to practise with exam questions as part of your revision, so schedule in some time for that too. See what I mean about putting enough time aside for learning the method?

Preparing for the Exams

The best preparation for the exams is to know the method well. On PRINCE2 training courses run by my company, Inspirandum, I always encourage delegates to aim for excellence, not merely to pass. That means hard and dedicated work while you're learning, but if it pays off with exam success then it will have been worth the effort. One person I taught said at the end of the course, 'It was like my life was on hold for a week!' True. And she passed both exams with great marks.

Here are a few tips for the exams themselves:

✔ **Get plenty of sleep:** No, not during the exams, because that can seriously reduce the number of marks you score. Do, however, get a good night's rest before the day of an exam. You'll be at a disadvantage and likely to misread questions if you've been revising hard until 3.30 a.m. and have then gone into the exam room tired.

✔ **Arrive in good time:** If you're travelling to the exam, set off in plenty of time. Currently the rules say you should be there 30 minutes before the start of the exam, so aim for quite a bit earlier than that. Don't rush into the exam room hassled and right on the 30-minute limit because there was a travel delay and you didn't allow sufficient contingency; you need good project management skills! If you do make the deadline by the skin of your teeth, you'll still be shaken up by the rush and all the concern that you might miss the exam, and that isn't a good start. If you live some way from the exam location, consider staying somewhere nearer overnight if you can afford it or if your organisation will pay – or if you can persuade a willing friend or relative to take you in.

✔ **Eat well:** Especially if your exam is in the morning, do have breakfast. An empty stomach does not help with exam nerves. Equally, if your exam is in the afternoon, have a light lunch and not a heavy one. Be especially careful if you're on a training course and your course provider has hired a hotel or conference centre which automatically provides a three-course hot dinner at lunch time. You could pay dearly for that meal if you end up sleepy in the exam.

✔ **Carry the right gear:** You don't need much for the PRINCE2 exams, but make sure you have everything to hand that you actually do need. Have a couple of HB or B pencils (wooden ones are rather better for shading in the ovals on the answer sheets, as the leads are thicker than with automatic pencils and are less likely to break). Have a pencil sharpener, a decent eraser and, for the Practitioner exam only, your PRINCE2 manual. You might like to have a few sweets and a bottle of water as well. If you take sweets, make sure they don't have noisy wrappers that will annoy other candidates as well as embarrass you in the silence of the exam room.

✔ **Take photo ID:** Registration for the exam currently requires a photo ID such as a passport, photocard driving licence or official photo security card if you work in a large organisation such as a government department. Be careful not to forget your ID, as you can't sit the exams without it. The idea is to make it harder for someone to attend a course pretending to be another person and then sit the exams for that person. Personally I'm not convinced, since most people don't look much like the ancient photo on their ID!

✔ **Avoid last-minute cramming:** It's not usually helpful to cram information in the minutes before the exam. Instead, walk about, breathe deeply and try to relax. It can be a good idea to avoid other candidates if you're a bit nervous. If you talk to others and they mention something you didn't revise too well, it will only increase your tension.

Gearing Up for the Foundation Exam

For the Foundation exam, you can't have any reference material to hand at all, not even the PRINCE2 manual. It's a closed-book exam, so everything needs to be in that fluffy space between your ears! You may think you'd like to have some clean paper to hand to make notes during the exam, but actually you won't need it.

Marking up your answers

The exam consists of a question paper and an answer sheet. The answer sheet has printed ovals on it, and you use a pencil to fill in completely the oval you choose, or to put a very thick bar across the middle, to show your answer to a question. Figure 2-1 shows the format.

Figure 2-1:
The answer
sheet
format.

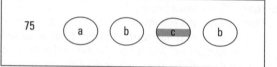

Be sure to put a very thick bar across the oval or fill it in completely, since the paper will be cross-checked by a machine, and the optical reader can fail to see thin lines, ticks, crosses, circles and spots. You must use only pencil on the answer sheet, and if you change your mind on an answer, make sure that you rub out the previous pencil marking very thoroughly. If the machine detects pencil in two ovals, you will not receive any marks for that question.

Understanding the Foundation question style

All Foundation questions are the classic style of a question and then four possible answers. The following example shows the classic format used in the Foundation exam.

> Which of the following is a PRINCE2 principle?
>
> a) Manage by roles
>
> b) Manage by products
>
> c) Manage by wishful thinking
>
> d) Manage by exception

The correct answer is d), although, like me, you may be aware of many organisations where everyone is convinced the right answer should be c).

Sometimes a paper contains more than 75 questions. There may appear to be 75, but some questions are comprised of up to four 'true or false' questions, and you need to get all of them right to score the single mark. The following simple example illustrates the multiple true/false format.

Read the following four statements about days of the week.

A. The day after Monday is Tuesday.

B. Friday is the only day of the week beginning with the letter F.

C. The day after Thursday is Sunday.

D. Two days of the week begin with the letter S.

Which of the statements are correct?

a) A, B and C

b) A, C and D

c) B, C and D

d) A, B and D

Because Sunday isn't the day after Thursday, statement 'C' is false. The answer is therefore 'd', because statements A, B and D are correct.

You need to appreciate two important points for this sort of question:

✔ **Be careful to pick the right answer from the list.** Having done all the hard work and decided correctly, in the example above, that Sunday doesn't come straight after Thursday, don't go and pick the wrong option from the answer list because you're under pressure and get careless.

✔ **Remember that this type of question can be put in the negative.** For example, 'Which item on the list is *NOT* . . . ?' Be careful not to lose track of the negative. Again, if you're feeling under pressure of time, you can forget that you're dealing with 'not'. You see a correct statement and go for it without really looking at the rest, only to lose the mark.

To help keep track of what's true and what's false as you're working through the list on the question paper, it's sensible to write 'T' or 'F' against each item. If you rely on your memory, you run the risk of forgetting what you thought was right, and so can end up picking the wrong option, even though your initial thinking was correct, or wasting time because you need to check the first items all over again.

Writing on the question paper

Although you can only use pencil on the answer sheet, you can write all over the question paper with anything you like. So that can be pencil again, or pen, or coloured pencils or a highlighter. A lot of people find marking up the paper helpful to emphasise things as they are reading.

Developing a strategy for Foundation

It helps to have a strategy, so you know how you'll approach the Foundation paper. This is down to you and what you know works well for you, but this section gives some overall advice and also some specific pointers on the nature of the exam and a few pitfalls to avoid. This section also covers one or two problems you may encounter in the exam, for which it pays to decide in advance what you'll do if you come across them.

Getting some marks in the can

Some questions in the exam can have difficult wording. Over the years the wording has improved, but at the time of writing it's still a problem occasionally. In addition, you're going to find questions in some subject areas easier to answer than others. For this reason, it often makes sense to deal first with the questions that you can answer immediately or with a bit of thought, and put more difficult ones on hold and come back to them later.

As I pointed out earlier, in the section 'Writing on the question paper', you can mark up the question paper so, if a question is causing you problems, you can put a big star by it on the question paper and come back and have another look at it later.

There are three reasons why putting difficult questions on hold can help:

- ✔ **You build confidence.** If you press ahead with questions you can answer, you get some confidence because you have some marks in the can. If the first few questions on the paper are hard (and I've seen papers like this), you can become very disheartened. If you decide not to move on until you've got to grips with the questions you find difficult and answered them, you see the time slipping by, and it can get to you. You imagine that the whole paper will be like this, and the mounting pressure makes it even harder to concentrate.

- ✔ **You warm up.** Even if you've done some recent practice with Foundation-level questions, you still warm up during the exam itself. Sometimes when you return to an apparently difficult question, you quickly see what it's getting at and you can answer it.

- ✔ **Your memory is jogged.** Sometimes a question later in the paper on the same subject jogs your memory, and you recall the right answer to the earlier one.

Although I've just said that you should put a difficult question on hold, do guess at the answer before you move on; you can always change it later, because your answer on the answer sheet is in pencil. If you don't have time to return to the question, who knows, your guess may have been right. If you don't answer it at all, then you've no chance of scoring a mark.

Expecting some tough questions

Some people think that multiple choice means easy. If you haven't already realised, the multiple-choice questions in the PRINCE2 exams can be far from easy. I always think that the questions break down into two basic categories of 'easy' and 'difficult'. Easy questions are where you happen to know the right answer, and difficult questions are where you don't. The difficult questions break down into two subcategories of tough and awful. Tough ones are where you know you read something about that in *PRINCE2 For Dummies* last Tuesday, but you can't quite remember what it was. Awful ones are where you didn't even know that point is in the method!

Don't be put off by the fact you're almost certain to encounter a few questions where you simply don't know the answer. You'll find advice later in this section on how to deal with such questions. But the fact is that even if five of the 70 live questions come under the category of 'awful', you'll still have 65 questions to get the 35 marks you need in order to pass.

Avoiding 'structure' tactics

Don't play 'structure' games with this exam – they don't work. Don't imagine, for example, that about 25 per cent of the answers will be 'a', 25 per cent 'b' and so on. The danger arises where you're in doubt about the answer to a particular question and, since there have been very few 'd' answers in the exam so far, you conclude that it's more likely to be 'd' than any of the other three options.

The PRINCE2 Foundation exam isn't built around an even distribution of answer letters. There's a large pool of questions and these are grouped in topic bands. A few questions are taken from each band, then the rest of the paper is topped up at random out of all of the bands. This is to prevent you getting 75 questions all on, say, processes. Of the questions selected for a paper, there can then be an uneven distribution of 'a', 'b', 'c' and 'd' answers, because the questions were drawn from the pool by subject, not by answer letter. I saw a paper some years ago where 'd' was the correct answer for relatively few questions in the paper. It was just chance, not design.

Equally, don't be thrown by runs of the same letter as the correct answer. Again this is just chance. The danger here is that you've already answered 'a' for a run of four questions and you think it may be 'a' for the next. However, you determine that 'a' is probably not right because the examiners surely wouldn't have put yet another 'a' answer. Remember the structure of the pool and it's not that the examiners did or didn't do anything. Of the questions selected from the pool, as it happened there was a run of the same letter for the answers in that part of the paper.

Again, I saw a paper some years ago where the same letter was the correct answer for six questions in a row. The next question had a different letter as the correct answer, but then it went back to the original letter for another two questions after that. It was just chance.

In short, there's no structural connection between one Foundation question and any other question on the paper. If you think that the correct answer to a question is 'a', then select it, no matter what has gone before and no matter how often that letter has been the right answer so far in the exam.

Reading the question

Yes, it's what they told you at school: RTFQ – Read The Flipping Question! You need to read the exam questions very carefully to be as sure as you can that you've properly understood them. If you misread a question, you're obviously likely to pick the wrong answer.

Guessing answers

Surprisingly, perhaps, this tip is to encourage you to guess. Well, at least to guess where you don't know what the answer is. There's no negative marking in the exam, so you won't be penalised for a wrong answer. Because of that, don't leave any questions out, and if you don't know the answer, guess. If there are four possible answers, you have a 25 per cent chance of hitting the right one by guessing.

Life can be hard as a trainer and exam invigilator. I ran a course where one person attending was a Project Manager from New Zealand who had a great sense of humour as well as being technically excellent. During the exam, I caught movement out of the corner of my eye, and turned to look at him. He had his head up and his eyes closed while he circled his pencil over a question on the exam paper. He stabbed the pencil onto the paper then looked down, nodded and filled in that answer. How I managed not to explode laughing and disrupt the exam I really don't know. His approach though was exactly right. He got very high marks because of his high level of competence, but on that one question he really didn't have a clue, so he let his pencil choose. Unfortunately I don't know which question it was, so I can't tell you the outcome.

Thinking before you guess

Following on from the last point, before you guess, think. Sometimes it's possible to rule out one or two of the answers by logic. For example, you know this question has got nothing whatever to do with Start Up and it certainly hasn't got anything to do with closure. That leaves only two options, and you don't know which is the right one. So guess! You've now increased your chances of hitting the right answer to 50 per cent.

Avoiding talking yourself out of the right answer

When writing something by hand where you haven't got a spellchecker kicking in, have you ever looked at a correctly spelled word and wondered whether it was right? The more you look at it, the more sure you become that it's actually spelled wrongly. You can't think how it should be spelled, but you're now convinced that the perfectly correct spelling is wrong. The same psychological mechanism comes into play in multiple-choice exams. Having finished the Foundation questions, most candidates go back over them to check their answers, and that's good practice. Agonising over the answers, however, isn't good practice. It often happens that someone going over a question again and again ends up changing the initial right answer for a wrong one. So don't talk yourself out of the right answer.

Before machine marking was introduced for the Foundation exam, candidates marked up their answers in ink. That meant any last-minute changes remained visible. One person I taught was, once again, very good technically and passed the Foundation exam with high marks. However, he could have scored more than he did. Towards the end of the exam, when going back over questions he'd been a bit unsure of, he altered six of his answers. In every instance, he changed the answer from a correct one to a wrong one.

Taking account of your gut reaction

Sometimes, people just feel that a particular answer is right, or say that their initial gut reaction is that one particular answer is correct. Having studied education and learning, I'm a huge fan of the human brain; it's incredible. Before the exams, you'll have studied PRINCE2 intensively, and in that process you'll have internalised more than you might imagine. When you have a gut reaction, it obviously isn't your gut at all but your brain. Your subconscious has put things together and flashed to the answer, while your conscious brain is still struggling with the details of the question.

Now please note this carefully: gut reactions can be wrong, so I'm not saying to follow them mindlessly. But if you really don't know the answer to a question, do consider what your initial reaction was, because surprisingly often it's right.

Slowing down on negatives

The Foundation exam often includes a number of negative questions. For example, 'Which one of these is *not* part of the purpose statement for the Change theme?' Where the answer options are quite lengthy and need thinking about, it's easy to lose track of the fact that the question is negative. Three of the four options will actually be correct, because it's the wrong one you're looking for. It helps here to slow down, and you might like to underline the word 'not' on the question paper if you find during practice that you tend to lose track in this way.

Managing your time

You must manage your time during the Foundation exam so that you don't time out. In one sense, that's not difficult, because with 75 questions you have clear milestones to show your progress. In another sense it's not so easy, because you're going to find some questions harder than others, and you'll need more time to deal with them.

During the main part of the exam, don't get bogged down on a question that you're finding very difficult. As suggested earlier in this section, if you're getting really stuck, then it's better to take a guess at that question, put a big star or question mark against it on the question paper so you can find it again, and move on. If you have some spare time at the end of the exam, you can come back and look at it again. That's a much better strategy than spending a long time trying to solve what is, to you, an insoluble question, and then not having time to answer the last ten questions in the exam – and so risking failing the whole paper.

 Even if you do find yourself short of time and unable to finish the paper, don't leave any questions out. In the last minute or two of the exam, simply guess the remaining answers – if you're really pushed for time, that can be without even looking at the question paper. For each guess, you have a 25 per cent chance of hitting the right answer, so for every four guesses at the end of the exam, by rights you should get a mark.

 One person I taught some years ago failed the Foundation by one mark. He didn't answer the last six questions, and said afterwards that he hadn't had time. So why didn't he select the 'a' option for the last six questions? Surely at least one of them would have been 'a', and in that case he would have passed. I gave that example when teaching a course in the Channel Islands some time afterwards. As it happened, someone there also timed out, and again it was the last six questions that she didn't have time to answer. Remembering my advice, she simply guessed the answers to the six questions. However, she didn't pick the same letter each time, but rather one at random for each. At the end of the exam she told me what she'd done, and when I came to mark the paper I found that she'd got four out of those six correct. I told her that if she was that fortunate, she should have spent 5 minutes answering the whole paper like that and gone for an extended tea break for the remaining 55 minutes of the exam!

 If you can, though, before you resort to outright guesses on unanswered questions, scan through to see whether there are any that you find easy and where you know the right answer immediately. In other words, if you're facing a time out, your trigger point for emergency action should be about five minutes from the end of the exam.

Finding more than one correct answer

There should only be one right answer to each question, but occasionally a question slips through where more than one answer is correct. Such a situation is not intentional, though, and those setting the question didn't appreciate that there was a problem.

 If you do find two correct answers, then often while one isn't exactly wrong, another is clearly right. Or, of the two answers, you can see that one is better than the other.

    Cat – dog – rabbit

Which animal is listed to the left of rabbit, is it cat or dog? You may answer 'both of them', but if you did then you're wrong and you didn't read the question. The question said cat *or* dog. So the answer is dog. Both of the other animals are to the left of rabbit, but dog is immediately to the left of it and so is a better answer than cat. So, in the exam, if you get two answers that seem to be right for a particular question, which is the most 'right'? You may think even now that cat is a better answer, because cat is further to the left than dog; if so, you've hit on another problem, which is where your view doesn't quite coincide with that of the person who set the question. Actually, that second problem tends to be more of an issue in the Practitioner exam, where a question can include an element of judgement on applying the method to a project. In cases like this, just go with the answer that you think is the best or the most 'right'.

Gearing Up for the Practitioner Exam

If you skipped the earlier section 'Gearing Up for the Foundation Exam' because you already hold a Foundation Certificate, the first advice in this section is to nip back and read it. The general approach to questions in Foundation applies also to Practitioner. The Foundation approach holds good because the Practitioner questions are also multiple choice, although in the Practitioner there are different styles of multiple choice. Actually the official name for the approach to the Practitioner exam is 'objective testing', and you may hear this term used in the context of the exam. However, since the questions are written by fallible human beings, you may think that 'objective' is perhaps not quite the best description. You may think that but, of course, I can't possibly comment.

The Practitioner exam went over to a multiple-choice format some years ago to facilitate machine marking. The previous format with an essay-style response was taking too long to mark. The essay style had the disadvantage that you were writing with a pen for three hours (the previous time allowance for the exam). Few people these days write for that length of time with a pen, and candidates with aching wrists after just one hour had become a real problem. However, the format did have the advantage that you could explain yourself. If you made a convincing point, even if it was not in the marking scheme, an examiner could award you a mark. The advantage of the multiple-choice format is that you're shading in ovals rather than writing many pages of script, so you don't get an aching hand. The downside, though, is that you can't explain yourself. If you don't give the exact answer that has been programmed into the machine, then no matter how right you are, you won't get the mark.

A further downside of the multiple-choice format is that while there's considerably less writing to do, there's considerably more reading. For that reason alone, if you have dyslexia or an eyesight limitation you should take steps to get an extra time allowance. How you should set about that is described in Chapter 1 in the section about handling special requirements.

Understanding the meaning of 'open book'

The Practitioner exam is *open book*, but that book is only the official PRINCE2 manual. You cannot use any other reference information in the exam. The only exception is if you're taking the exam in your second language, in which case you're allowed to have a dictionary to help with translation, and a copy of the PRINCE2 glossary in your first language, if one is available for that language.

Here are a few 'cans' in the context of the open book rules:

- ✔ You can make your own notes on the surface of the pages of your copy of the manual before taking it into the exam. That includes the blank pages such as the endpapers of the book.

- ✔ You can highlight key points in the book, or use underlining, arrows, stars or anything else you like to draw attention to a particular passage.

- ✔ You can have index tabs fixed to the page edges, so you can find things quickly.

Here are a few 'cant's' in the open book rules:

- ✗ You can't write notes on a sheet of paper and slip the sheet into your manual.

- ✗ You can't stick notes into the manual, such as information cut out from your training course material or other reference books.

- ✗ You can't write reference information onto locational tags, only location information. For example, you can write 'Risk Register' on a tag and stick it onto the edge of the appropriate page in Appendix A of the manual. But you can't add the words 'created during Initiation'.

You may think that the open book rules are a bit weird. Why is it that you can write notes into the book and so spoil it, but you can't write the same notes on a bit of paper and slip it into the book just for the exam? The idea is that it stops training companies mass-producing crib sheets with guidance on how to handle known questions in the pool, and giving them out at the start of the exam.

Be careful not to break the open book rules. The exam authority can and does check on exam sessions. If there's a snap visit and you're found with reference material that's not permitted, the whole exam can be suspended for everyone in the room, and your exam invigilator can be in for big trouble too. So, play by the rules and pass because you know your stuff anyway.

Marking up your answers

The Practitioner exam uses the same approach to answer sheets as the Foundation exam, with ovals where you put a thick pencil bar through the shape or fill it in completely. See Figure 2-1, earlier in the chapter. The difference with the Practitioner exam is that there are usually many more than four options for each question.

Developing a strategy for Practitioner

It helps if you've thought through in advance what will help in the exam and how you'll tackle particular problems if you hit them. This section gives you some tips on preparing before the exam, and what to do during it.

Tabbing your manual

Coloured index tabs are great for finding your way around the manual quickly. You may only save a few seconds turning to a page, but if you do that each time you need to find something it soon mounts up into a worthwhile time saving. You can use that time for scoring marks rather than finding things in the manual.

A tab can only have locational information written on it, such as 'Quality Review'. You mustn't add additional information.

Writing notes in your manual

Although you can't insert extra paper into the book with notes on, you can, under the present rules, write notes onto the surface of the page. If something isn't very clear in the manual and you think you might forget the meaning if you need to refer to it in the exam, make a quick pencil note. There's a balance here with making notes though. It's helpful to have notes on key points, but you don't want so many that you then can't find the points you need among a mass of detail now covering the pages.

Knowing what's in the book

Be sure you know what's in the manual, and where. It makes no sense to struggle to remember something, or try and work it out, when actually it's printed somewhere in the book and, with a flick of the wrist, you could be looking right at it.

Referring to Appendix A

If you get questions on the detail of a management product, immediately flick the manual open to the appropriate page in Appendix A. It will only take a moment, but then you can glance at it if you need to while answering.

I was invigilating a Practitioner exam in a company at the end of a week-long training course. As I was collecting the papers in at the end, one candidate told me 'I did the section on the Business Case last, and I only opened the manual at the end. I'd completely forgotten that the Business Case includes the benefits.' I controlled my reactions really well, despite thinking incredulously 'You *forgot* that the Business Case includes *benefits*!' I smiled and said through gritted teeth, 'Well let's hope you've done enough in the rest then.' Actually, she did extremely well in the rest and passed the exam comfortably. But why did she run the risk of trying to remember what's in a Business Case when she could have had the manual open at Appendix A, right above her answer sheet?

Managing your time

Time management is absolutely critical for success in the Practitioner exam. There are eight sections, each carrying ten marks, so you need to divide up your answer time evenly between the eight sections. It doesn't pay to spend extra time on some questions that you're finding difficult and score the odd mark – or perhaps not scoring any – and then leave out the last section of the paper because you didn't have time for it. In the additional time that you spent on the difficult questions, you could probably have scored many more marks in the last section.

Don't steal time from later sections of the paper by overrunning on earlier sections.

Calculating the answer time

To work out the answer time for each section, remember that there's a project scenario to read and understand. To be safe, you should allow around 25 minutes to read the various bits of scenario information. Of the 150 minutes (two and a half hours) of the exam, that now leaves you 125 minutes. A 5-minute contingency takes you down to 120 minutes. That's precisely 15 minutes for answering the ten questions in each of the eight sections

The main project scenario covers the whole exam, then some of the sections will have further information about the project that applies just to that exam section. Your 25 minute scenario allocation includes time to read section specific information, but of course when answering questions you'll often need to refer back to the detail.

Getting into the project scenario

The last section included a tip about allowing enough time to read the project scenario. The length of the overall scenario information is usually between about a half and three-quarters of a page of A4. It's a good investment of time to read the overall scenario information carefully and get 'into' the project, so you have a good feel for it. Be careful to note any points of detail that seem important. You won't necessarily remember them all, but you can highlight them to draw your attention to them later.

Where additional scenario information is provided for particular sections of the exam, it's not worth reading this until you're ready to tackle the associated questions. That's because you'll only need that information for that single section and, if you read it up front, you may have forgotten the detail when you get to that section an hour or two later.

Bearing the scenario in mind

During the exam, you can make two equal and opposite errors with the scenario. The first and most common error is to refer to the additional scenario information for the section you're working on, but forget to check the main scenario information that covers the whole exam. The second, but less common, is to remember to consult the main scenario, but forget to check the additional project information for that section.

Be systematic, then. At the start of a section, be sure to check for additional scenario material. Then during questions, check both the main project information as well as the additional material.

You must hand in all the papers at the end. However, there's no rule against taking the scenario paper to bits by removing the staple. If you do take it to bits, you can have the additional scenario for the section and the main scenario side by side in front of you. Now, perhaps I shouldn't have said that, because it gives your invigilator a much harder job to make sure that everything has been collected at the end. But it's too late: I've said it now, and anyway the invigilator's been sitting there daydreaming for two and a half hours while you've been slaving away, so don't feel too bad.

Remembering to RTFQ and ATFQ

Yes, it's the advice from school exams to Read The Flipping Question and Answer The Flipping Question. Be careful to read the questions thoroughly and then stay on track as you answer. It's all too easy be in a hurry and misread the question or, in your haste, forget the detail of the question and start answering something different.

Make sure that you keep the question clearly in mind as you answer; underlining key words in the question may help. A common cause of missing marks isn't lack of knowledge of PRINCE2 but misreading the questions. Sometimes a single word can make all the difference, such as whether a product is 'created' or 'updated'.

You can write all over the question paper and scenario paper with anything you like, such as a pen or highlighter. Only the answer sheet has to be completed in pencil.

Be especially careful towards the end of the exam if you're under pressure of time. Reading questions in a hurry is a recipe for misreading and then not scoring any marks at all on them. If you do that, you may as well have put your pencil down and had a relaxed doze for the last few minutes of the exam. Well, that may be a slight exaggeration, but you get the point. If you're under pressure of time, be all the more careful to focus hard on the question and the exact wording of the answer options.

Guessing again

One especially relevant point from the Foundation advice earlier in this chapter is to guess the answer to the question if you don't know it. The Practitioner exam, like the Foundation, has no negative marking. If you don't know the answer to a question, you've nothing to lose from guessing. The bad news is that there are usually more than four possible answers to each question, so your percentage chance of hitting the right one by guessing is proportionately lower.

Here's a passing thought. If you have enough monkeys, answer sheets and pencils, sooner or later one of the monkeys will become a qualified PRINCE2 Practitioner. Come to think of it, I think I met him on a failing project.

Getting to grips with Practitioner question styles

The Practitioner exam has different styles of multiple-choice question. This section explains each.

Classic style

This is the same overall style to the one used in the Foundation exam, but with a couple of possible twists.

In the company offices, staff are usually provided with several basic items of furniture. On which two items of furniture could a staff member normally place a computer to write a report?

    a) Desk

    b) Hatstand

    c) Sidetable

    d) Filing cabinet

    e) High-backed executive chair

    f) Low-backed guest chair

Please note that in this particular example of a classic question, you're being asked for two answers not one. The correct response for the example would be 'a' and 'c'. You can put a computer on a desk or sidetable, but you wouldn't *normally* (and that word is significant in the question) put a computer on a chair or filing cabinet, and balancing one on a hatstand would be just about impossible. Note here also that there are six possibilities in the list. There can be different numbers of answers in the list, unlike in the Foundation exam where there are usually four and never more than that.

You need to read classic-style questions carefully and take particular note of the number of answers you're asked to give. Unlike the Foundation exam where there is, allegedly, only ever one correct answer, in the Practitioner there can be two. You need to get them both right in order to score the mark. Where you're asked for two answers, you may find it helpful to underline the word 'two' in the question, so you keep it clearly in mind. It's essential, obviously enough, to get the right number of answers. If you're asked for one answer and you mark in two, then the question will be disqualified and you'll get nothing. Similarly, if you're asked for two answers and you only put in one, then you'll get nothing. Just occasionally there are more right answers than the number you're being asked for.

Identify two objects which are round.

a) Football

b) Sugar cube

c) Globe

d) Wheel

e) Westminster Bridge

In the example above, three of the objects are round. So if you selected any two out of football, globe and wheel, you'd be right and get the mark. If you put all three, you'd be wrong because the question said to identify two objects, not three.

Critique style

Describing critique as a separate style to classic style isn't quite right, but the question approach is substantial enough to deserve special attention in its own subsection. A critique question is where a product, or part of one, is set down in the additional scenario for the section, along with a warning that it isn't necessarily correct. Don't be fooled, because if you see that warning then there are going to be errors in the product, and your task is to try to identify them.

The sort of question involved in a critique approach tends to be the classic style, where the answer options are either to give different replacement sections for a part of the product, or to say that actually the part of the product is correct and doesn't need replacing.

Twinkle, twinkle little star,

How I wonder what you are.

Up above the world so high,

Like a hotdog or a pie.

Warning. There may be errors in this extract from a well-known nursery rhyme.

The words 'Like a hotdog or a pie' in the last line should be:

a) Left in place because they are correct

b) Replaced with the words 'Unlike a hotdog or a pie'

c) Replaced with the words 'Like a sandwich – cheese on rye'

d) Replaced with the words 'Like a diamond in the sky'

e) Removed altogether and entered into the Risk Register

So it would seem that d is the correct answer, in case you're not sure or can't remember that far back.

Bear in mind that critique questions:

✔ **Can involve a substantial amount of reading.** Sometimes the suggested replacements are paragraphs of text, so the whole question can be quite lengthy.

✔ **Can get confusing when the alternative answers look similar.** The best advice here is to get clear first on what the product should be. So have a look at Appendix A in the manual and quickly focus on what the product is and what it's for. Then look at the possible answers, and often you'll find the wrong ones are now much easier to spot.

A second approach when you're unclear is to put a cross by those answers that you know to be wrong. This helps you focus on the remainder rather than being boggled by a whole page full.

Critique questions are not only used for textual problems, but can also be applied to diagrams. Obviously you can't be asked to draw something like a Product Flow Diagram in a multiple-choice-format exam with only ovals on the answer sheet. However, you may get a diagram with some problems buried in it and then have to select an option which identifies an error at a particular point, or say that no error exists. This may be extended so that the options are replacement fragments of diagram and you need to say which should be inserted in place of the erroneous part.

Sequence style

Sequence questions can have their own style, as in the following example, or can be in the form of a matching question, as explained in the next section, or even a classic one.

Sometimes you may go to a restaurant for a meal. Your visit will include:

1. Eating the food

2. Going into the restaurant

3. Making a selection from the menu

4. Leaving the restaurant

5. Ordering the food

Which of the following sequences represents the correct order of these things?

      a) 5, 4, 3, 1, 2

      b) 2, 3, 5, 1, 4

      c) 2, 3, 5, 4, 1

      d) 1, 2, 5, 3, 4

      e) 5, 1, 3, 2, 4

So, in the example, it's clearly 'b'. Some of the sequences may look very similar, as in options 'b' and 'c' in the example. Be very careful to select the right one. If you've established the right sequence, it's a great shame to lose the mark because you didn't notice two numbers were reversed in two similar-looking answers.

There are three ways of tackling a sequence question, depending on whether you're very brave, a bit brave or not brave at all:

- ✔ **Being very brave:** You'll know you have the right answer once you've established that only one answer has the correct sequence up to the point you're at. So in the above example, once you've got 2, 3, 5 and 1, you know that b must be correct.

- ✔ **Being a bit brave (me when I'm doing these questions):** You'll then go on to check the remainder of that one answer to ensure that the rest of the sequence is right. So, is the final action indeed 4?

- ✔ **Not being brave at all:** You'll check all of the sequences.

How you answer sequence questions is, of course, up to you, but the 'a bit brave' approach does have an advantage. It's worth checking the rest of the sequence that you've now decided is right, because if one of the remaining items is clearly wrong, it warns you that you misread the first part. By spending a few moments to check that one sequence, you won't miss a mark for making a mistake. For some question styles, you'll have to work very much harder to get a mark, so the extra effort to ensure you don't miss out on a mark in a sequence question is worthwhile.

While you're reading this book, you may think that you're unlikely to get the early part of a sequence wrong, but remember that things are a bit different when the exam is for real and you may be under time pressure.

Matching style – including true/false and sequence

In this type, a statement is made then there are two columns. For each entry in the column 1, you're asked to identify the appropriate answer from the column 2. It isn't always a case of one-to-one matching like a children's puzzle though. An entry in the column 2 may be the right answer to more than one question, and some entries in the column 2 may never be used at all. So, you may find that the option A in the column 2 is the correct answer for three of the ten questions. But equally you may find that the option B isn't the right answer for any of the questions.

The matching style can also appear in two other ways. The first is for true/false questions. With true/false, there are only two options in column 2, and these are . . . you've guessed it! So for each statement in column 1, you're simply matching to A = true or B = false.

A second variant on the matching format is for sequence questions. The sequence may have its own format, as explained in the previous section, but often the matching style is used. So, column 1 is the list of events and column 2 is the order of A = first, B = second, C = third, D = fourth, and so on. You simply match the event to the right part of the sequence.

In the case of matching to a sequence, you may find that one of the entries in column 1 isn't part of the sequence at all – so stay awake, you need to be very careful. If an item doesn't belong in the sequence, you'll match it with an entry in column 2 that says something to the effect of 'not part of the sequence'.

Assertion–reason

The final style is the one that most people find the most awkward. However, it's a good job that you bought this book, because there are some steps which really help with this style of question. I can't promise that the steps will make the questions easy, but they'll certainly make them easier.

Assertion–reason questions take the form of a statement then the word 'because' and then a second statement. So . . .

The moon looks white **because** it's lit up by the sun.

That looks straightforward enough, and it is if you follow a three-step approach. However, you don't always do the third step. If either of the statements is false, or both are, you stop after Step 2. Ask yourself:

1. **Is the first statement correct?**

2. **Is the second statement correct?**

3. **If *both* statements are correct, is the second statement the reason why the first one is true?**

In the example above, yes the moon does look white, so the first statement, the assertion, is right. The moon is indeed lit by the sun, so the second statement is also correct. Given that both statements are both right, the last step is to ask whether the second statement is the reason that the first one is right. Here, that's the case. The moon does look white because it's lit up by the sun.

It may be that two statements are correct but the second one isn't the reason why the first one is right.

Berlin is a city **because** PRINCE2 is a project management method.

Both statements are true, but the 'because' link fails. Although PRINCE2 is a project management method, that's not the reason that Berlin is a city.

You can get confused with this question format if you don't appreciate that the word 'because' simply doesn't apply unless both statements are true. That's a problem with the layout of the question. You can struggle to see how the 'because' can be right if the assertion statement or the reason statement is wrong. Stay with the three-step approach and you'll be just fine.

There are five possible answers to choose from in an assertion–reason question.

Selection	Assertion	Reason	
A	True	True	And the reason is why the assertion is true.
B	True	True	But the reason statement isn't why the assertion is true.
C	True	False	
D	False	True	
E	False	False	

Taking each of the five possible answers, here are questions that would give those answers. The first repeats one of the earlier examples.

The moon looks white **because** it's lit up by the sun.

The answer is A (true–true). Both the 'assertion' and 'reason' statements are true, and the second statement is indeed the reason that the first statement (the assertion) is correct.

The moon looks white **because** it's round.

The answer is B (true–true). Again both statements are true. The moon looks white and it's also round. However, this time the second statement isn't the reason that the first one is right. The moon looks white, but this isn't because it's round, so it's B, not A.

The moon looks white **because** it's made of cheese.

The answer is C (true–false). The moon isn't made of cheese (unless you believe Wallace and Gromit), so there's no need to go on to the third step of seeing whether there's a link between the two statements.

The moon looks square **because** it's lit up by the sun.

The answer is D (false–true). The first statement is false and the second one is true. Because one of the statements is false, again there's no need to go on to the third step to see whether there's a link between the two statements.

The moon looks square **because** it's made of cheese.

The answer is E (false–false). Again, no need for the third step to look for a link. You only look for a 'because' link if both statements are true.

A key to tackling these rather complex questions successfully is to get into a rhythm of answering using the three-step approach described earlier in this section. The good news – if there's any at all with this question style – is that the answer letters are always the same for that combination of true and false. So across all assertion–reason questions in the Practitioner exam, a true–false will always be option C and false–false will always be option E.

More bad news with the style is that clearly you have to get all of it right to get the mark. You could have correctly identified that both statements are true, but if you then get the third step wrong, you end up selecting the wrong letter. In turn, that means you lose the whole mark, despite having worked hard and got two-thirds of the question right. So, dangerous huh? Work carefully and systematically, then.

As with other question styles, marking up your question paper can help enormously. As you check a statement to see whether it's true or false, write 'T' or 'F' against it on your question paper. When you've checked both statements, it's then mechanical to pick the correct answer letter. If you don't mark up the paper in this way and you find that you need to consult the manual to make quite sure of the second statement, you may lose track of what you thought for the first statement. That either means you need to check the first statement again, wasting valuable time, or that you remember incorrectly, select the wrong letter and lose the mark, despite the fact you initially made the right decision about the first statement.

The Practitioner Scenario For This Book

Like in the Practitioner exam, many but not quite all of the Practitioner-level questions in this book are based on a project. This last section gives you information on the project that I will use throughout the book, but some chapters may also have extra, subject specific, information. You'll need to refer back to the project scenario in this last section when you're tackling the practice Practitioner questions in later chapters.

In the Practitioner exam, as well as in the book, be careful to refer to both sources of information: the information in the main scenario and also any additional project information provided just for that subject area, such as quality.

Preparing the new business unit

Princess Projects Plc is planning to redecorate and refurnish a suite of four offices for staff to move into to form a new e-commerce business unit. One office is already empty, staff are currently in the process of moving out of the second office, and the other two are due to be vacated in two weeks' time. The offices will then be empty apart from old carpets, window blinds and a few items of usable furniture left behind by the previous occupants. The carpets are old and worn and will need replacing as part of the project. The project will also involve some minor structural alterations to make four new doorways to link the rooms, buying some new furniture, and installing new phone lines, an extra power circuit and some extra power points. The rooms will then be decorated in line with the company colour scheme and re-carpeted. After carpeting the room, the new furniture can be put in place, alongside the usable existing items of furniture.

The requirements for phones, electrical circuits and the position of furniture will be set down in the final office plan. That final plan will be developed from a draft plan which will be circulated to all the staff who will work in the business unit so that they can comment. Staff are coming from different parts of the company to form the new business unit, but the Human Resources Department has a list of them. The position of new doorways has already been decided, because planning permission was needed as well as the consent of a heritage agency. Both permissions have been obtained already.

Structural alterations can start as soon as the final office has been vacated by staff, but work on other aspects of the project will only start once the final office plan is complete and agreed by the new head the unit. Paint will be bought from a local supplier, and the office can be repainted as soon as the modification work and cabling is complete. The structural alterations, painting and carpeting will be done by the company's own works team, who will form part of the project. New phone lines will be installed by our telecoms provider (the telecoms engineers are external to the project), with the position of the phone sockets as shown in the final, approved, office plan. Phone sockets will all be installed above desk level for easy access.

A furniture list will be drawn up from the approved office plan, and this will show what existing furniture is in place as well as what new furniture will be required. The new furniture will be ordered online from an Internet-based office furniture supplier. Once the four offices are completely ready for staff to move in, the project will be complete.

Chapter 3

Dealing with Disappointment

*I*t would be easy to publish this book without ever mentioning failure, but the *For Dummies* series is about practicality and reality, so dodging the issue wouldn't be right, and anyway it wouldn't be fair if you've hit a problem and need some advice. Sometimes exams just don't go well on the day despite the best preparation, and you just don't get enough marks. Perhaps you've already had a go at a PRINCE2 exam and failed, and that's why you bought this book.

Handling Failure

Candidates who fail a PRINCE2 exam tend to have one of two reactions. The first is to be incensed and ask 'How could that possibly have happened to me?' They wonder whether the exam was marked correctly. The second reaction, and overwhelmingly the more common, is to say with resignation that they're not surprised and at the end of the exam they already knew deep down that they'd failed.

To pick up on the question about whether the paper was marked fairly, well of course the answer is yes. Even where the Foundation exam is marked by hand at first, it's cross-checked using machine marking – so there's no space for human error in the final result. You may disagree with some of the 'right' answers if you see them, but, like in many other exams, that goes with the territory.

Putting the exams in context

If you've failed, the best thing to do is to come to terms with the outcome and accept it. If you try to see the situation as a setback rather than a disaster, it may help to put the exam results into context. The important thing in project management is running projects well, and the important thing in PRINCE2 is using the method knowledgeably and intelligently to do that. After putting in all the work to learn PRINCE2, it's really good to have a piece of paper to put on the wall (or to shove in your filing cabinet), but pieces of paper don't run projects.

At the end of the day, does it really matter that you failed? Worse things happen to people every moment of every day. It may be disappointing not to have passed and it may be inconvenient, but it isn't life-threatening.

If you were relying on an exam pass to get a new job or contract, then things are a bit tougher and there's no easy answer to that. Instead, all I can do is to encourage you to go for it again and, provided you have a good grip of PRINCE2, to do so quickly.

It's rare indeed to see someone I've taught fail the Foundation exam. But I do see occasional failures at Practitioner. One manager failed the Practitioner and never took it again, much to my disappointment. However, he's been responsible for setting up the use of PRINCE2 within his large company, and it's one of the most intelligent and effective implementations of the method that I've seen. Another person I taught decided that he wasn't ready to take the Practitioner exam, although he was booked in to do it as part of the week-long course. He never did feel ready and never did sit the exam. However, he's been hugely successful in running projects with PRINCE2 and has used the extremely powerful product-led planning approach in new ways that would blow your socks off if you saw it; he's done so on substantial projects, too. If you want to see a bit of what he's come up with, read *PRINCE2 For Dummies*!

Having a bad time with a Foundation paper

If you know PRINCE2 well and just have a bad day with a particular exam paper and fail, you can probably take the exam again immediately. Currently, it's normal practice for a spare paper to be included in the Foundation exam pack. If something goes badly wrong and you fail, you'll probably find that you can stay on for an extra hour and sit another paper.

Deciding on whether to take the spare paper depends what you think caused the problem. It rather depends on whether you thought your initial failure was just a paper going wrong for you or whether it confirmed what you already suspected: that you hadn't really got things clear yet.

If it was just that the paper went wrong, then taking it again immediately is a good idea. If you thought you had a good chance and are only planning to do Foundation, another shot straight away is a good option. Also, if you're attending a training course and were planning to do the Practitioner paper during the same training event, then it's probably better to take the Foundation again straight away and move on through to the Practitioner.

If, however, you don't feel that you're knowledgeable enough in your answers, it may be better to go away and hit the books for some more revision before trying again. Perhaps, for example, you're one of those people, like me, who tends to learn more slowly than some but then remembers the information for years and years. If there's an issue with your knowledge and understanding, going away for a bit more study first is probably a better idea.

I had an aeronautical engineer on a full PRINCE2 course who asked intelligent, relevant questions throughout the event and who clearly understood things well. He was equally good in reviews during the week. However, when he took the Foundation he failed. He was a bit surprised, but I was in shock. I've only seen a few people fail Foundation over the years, and I can usually see it coming. I marked his paper twice more to make sure I hadn't miscounted or put the plastic overlay sheet in slightly the wrong position. I talked to him about it and offered the back-up paper, and he decided to go for it. He was an intelligent man but said he had struggled with the wording on that particular paper and had difficulty seeing what the questions were getting at. He thought that a second go might do the trick, and it did. He not only passed at the second attempt, but passed with a strong mark which was in line with my evaluation of his understanding of the method.

Looking forward, not back

If you've failed an exam and it's not the sort of quickly fixed Foundation problem described in the last section, then rather than spending time and emotional energy being disappointed about the past, turn your attention instead to the future. Focus on what you can do to pass next time and pass well. Remember that if you failed you were, obviously enough, under the pass mark, so that even if you'd got a few more marks, and just enough to pass, you'd only have scraped through. What you need to concentrate on now is passing strongly.

If you failed by only one or two marks, it's easy to keep dwelling on it and thinking, 'If I'd just got two more, I'd have passed.' You can turn that negative around to a positive by thinking instead, 'I'm very nearly there and I only need to do slightly better next time to get through.'

Finding Out What Went Wrong

Before going on to prepare for another attempt, it pays to do some analysis of what went wrong last time, so you can avoid falling into the same hole again. If you attended a training course, do talk to your course tutor. Your tutor may be able to indicate problem areas based on an assessment of your understanding and recall during the course.

In my company, Inspirandum, we almost never get failures at Foundation, and we've looked very carefully at those – usually few – instances where we get Practitioner failures. The cause is nearly always exam technique problems rather than technical knowledge, despite the exam preparation we put alongside practical teaching of the method. If you think that exam technique is part or all of the reason why you had difficulties, check out the following list to try to pinpoint one or more specific issues:

- Did you read the questions carefully or did you do them in a rush – in other words, do you think you may have missed part of what a question was getting at or misunderstood part of it? You may have been reading too quickly because you felt under pressure of time or because you were a bit nervous.

- Did you start looking for the answers to questions before you really understood what was being asked?

- Did you work systematically through all the answers given? Even if you're pretty sure you've hit on the right answer immediately, a glance at the other answers is worthwhile. If you've made a mistake, you're likely to spot it if you check and see a second answer that's right even though you're only being asked for one. Finding a second right answer makes you go back and look at your first response again.

- Did you pick up on negatives: 'Which one of these is *not* a reason to escalate an issue to the Project Board?' Or did you forget the negative perspective of such questions and latch on to a right answer, which was actually incorrect because it was a wrong one that you were supposed to be looking for?

- Did you answer in line with a standard 'PRINCE2 manual' approach to the questions, or according to how your organisation has used the method in a non-standard way to meet particular project needs?

- For the Practitioner exam, did you remember to refer to the main project scenario as well as the extra scenario for particular sections?

- Again for the Practitioner exam, did you answer questions related to the scenario but without looking closely enough at the scenario? In other words, do you think you might have missed key information about the project, and that's why you got answers wrong?

- Did you manage your time well across the whole paper, or were you in a rush in the last questions, where you might have made mistakes and so failed to score marks?

- Do you know that you missed some questions out and didn't have time to go back to do them later?

Finding holes in your knowledge

You can do a couple of things to find gaps in your knowledge. The first you can tackle now and the second you can do as you work through this book revising the different subject areas.

A first check is to think systematically through the method and ask yourself whether you really understand that area. Usually you'll realise that you don't understand it, or that you had an inkling you don't. Ask yourself whether you went into the exam hoping that certain things wouldn't come up. If you did, then this fact alone indicates you were unsure of those areas.

Using the revision checklists in this book

In each of the theme and process chapters in Parts II and III of this book, you'll find revision checklists. As well as the lists providing a structure for revision, you may find them helpful for checking quickly to see whether you are unsure of any areas.

 Do be wary of the Quality theme. It's a strange part of the PRINCE2 manual, being very focused on definitions rather than on the implementation of quality management throughout the method. As a result, a lot of people feel unhappy about it even when their knowledge is fine for the exams.

Looking out for questions where you can't see why you're wrong

The second thing to do to find gaps in your knowledge is to watch out for questions that you get wrong when practising. If, when you see the answer, you say to yourself 'Oh yes, of course,' then you know PRINCE2 well enough and it isn't a problem – you probably just misread the question. But if you can't immediately see why you're wrong, then it indicates a gap in either your knowledge or understanding.

Finding holes in your understanding

Gaps in your understanding of PRINCE2 will cause you a problem in both the Foundation and Practitioner exams. This is trickier than a hole in knowledge. If you really don't understand the 'whys' and you've been on a training course, it indicates that perhaps the training course wasn't as good as it was cracked up to be. It isn't always easy to spot a sub-standard course in advance, since you take it on trust that your trainer will know the subject. Some people spot a problem during the course though, and realise that they haven't learned the method properly despite the assurances of their trainer.

In my company, we always teach a full Practitioner course, even if someone only wants to take the Foundation exam; they just leave the course after we've done the Foundation exam session and don't stay on for the Practitioner exam. Personally, I don't see the point of a 'training' course if you can't then apply what you've learned. Lots of wasted effort in creating PRINCE2 paper mountains in projects demonstrates that often people don't really know what they're doing. One guy I taught already had the Foundation Certificate, having taken a course with another training company. He wasn't happy, though, and searched around for a more practically focused company to do the whole of Foundation again as well as tackle the Practitioner. On attending my company's event he said, 'In the last course they just taught me the right answers to the questions. Sitting your course, I now understand _why_ they're the right answers.'

If that's you, then you're going to have to think the method through some more. You may also find the explanations in the companion book to this one, _PRINCE2 For Dummies_, helpful.

Hitting difficulties with question styles

If it was the style of the questions that threw you in your exam, then the answer is to practise a lot to gain familiarity with the formats. The formats are a particular issue at Practitioner level, where there are a number of different styles of multiple choice, not just the classic style as it appears in the Foundation paper. You'll find lots of help with understanding the question styles in Chapter 2.

Timing out

If your problem is with time management and you simply didn't have time to do all the questions, then don't feel lonely. Timing out is a common cause of failure in the Practitioner paper, although occasionally in the Foundation as well. The good news is that you can do things about it.

If you have dyslexia or some physical limitation that makes taking exams difficult, you really should apply for the extra time allowance. You can find information in Chapter 1 on how to do this. Some people are a bit reluctant to apply for extra time, because they think it gives them some advantage. It doesn't; the extra time is just to offset – at least partly – the effect of the limitation you have and to give you a fairer chance in the exam.

Everybody can do two other things to help tackle timing problems:

- **Milestoning.** Watch the time carefully during the exam and stick to your schedule. Both exams have a set number of questions and a fixed time in which to answer them, so it's relatively easy to monitor how you're doing using the questions as progress milestones.

- **Practise against the clock.** A really helpful idea is to practise exam questions within a time constraint, but pushing yourself harder to complete in less than the time allowed for the exam itself. For the Foundation paper, instead of allowing yourself the full hour to do 75 questions, set your timer for 45 minutes. For the Practitioner, instead of allowing yourself 15 minutes a section, set your timer to 12 minutes.

If you still find you're unable to answer the questions in time as you get into your question practice, try to identify why that is. For Practitioner, are you looking up rather too much in the manual? If so, you need to do more revision to get more familiar with the method. Or are particular subjects causing you difficulty, such as the Quality theme or the Managing a Stage Boundary process? If so, target them for more revision. Or perhaps it's the integration of the method that you find hard to deal with, and the fact that although you know the component parts of PRINCE2, you don't understand how they fit together. In that case, head for Chapter 19 in this book and also read *PRINCE2 For Dummies*, to get a better overview of the method as a whole.

Struggling With Exam Nerves

Suffering with exam nerves is really tough, and Chapter 1 has some general advice on managing them. However, if you have a major problem, you'll probably already know those things anyway from previous experience. There's little I can say here apart from to encourage you to keep going and try again. If you know your PRINCE2 but failed because of nerves, then you really do deserve the certificate.

For some, taking the exam a second time proves less of an ordeal than the first time around, because the whole process has become familiar. In addition, the gap between your attempts means you'll have additional time to revise, so you'll feel even more prepared and your ability to score more marks means that you're more likely to pass anyway.

A student who sat one of my courses was technically excellent but had terrible exam nerves. She managed the Foundation because of her extensive knowledge, but not the Practitioner. She sat the Practitioner again a few weeks later, only to fail again. Undaunted she tried again, only to fail again. I offered to provide any help that she thought would contribute, and indeed she started to send me practice answers to comment on. I did comment on the answers, but she was doing really well with them. The problem wasn't her ability to answer questions, it was the exam itself. She tried again, and failed again. She was absolutely fine going into the exam. She had her pencils in front of her and a few sweets, together with her manual. But as soon as the printed exam paper was put down in front of her, she went to bits. She finally passed the exam at the sixth attempt. She has my huge admiration, and I think she deserves a medal.

Deciding About a Re-take

If you've a good grasp of PRINCE2, the best advice is to simply sit the examination again as soon as possible. You should give yourself time to prepare but not leave such a big gap that you lose the level of recall you had when you'd first finished learning the method. Don't forget that you'll usually be busy in that long gap doing your job: you won't be spending all day and every day revising PRINCE2 (unless you have an unusual employer or a lot of free time).

You'll need to revise all the parts of the method because, of course, the questions may be on different aspects next time. Don't just revise the bits that you think led to your failure before. Just because Quality Review didn't come up in the 'quality' section of the Practitioner paper last time around doesn't mean that it won't come up next time. And just because the detail of the Senior Supplier role wasn't questioned in the last Foundation paper doesn't mean that there won't be two questions on it next time you sit the exam.

If you feel that you don't have a good enough understanding of PRINCE2, then there's no point in sitting the exam again until you do. If you've been learning the method on your own, then you might consider attending a face-to-face training course if you have funds and time available. If you do decide on a training course, then choose carefully – as I advise in Chapter 1.

Preparing for the Next Shot

If you've failed a PRINCE2 exam, you need to prepare for your next shot by revising the whole method as well as focusing on those areas where you think you're below par. In particular, make sure you're clear on each of the following areas:

- **Roles and responsibilities:** Make sure you know what each role is responsible for within the project management team [**Manual** Appendix C, **P2FD** Ch10 and Ch11] and what the roles are doing in a PRINCE2 project.

- **Processes:** Check you know the sequence in which the processes are used, who is primarily responsible for the activities within each process, and who else is involved. Practise 'locating yourself' when looking at a particular activity, to be clear on what is going on at that point, what products are in use and where you are in the project. So, for example, when you 'Authorize a Stage or Exception Plan' in the process Directing a Project, you're a Project Board member in a Project Board meeting at the end of a stage (End Stage Assessment), or you're part way through a stage after an Exception Plan has been produced by the Project Manager (Exception Assessment).

- **Themes:** Go through them all again to be sure you have a clear understanding. Make sure that you know what each theme is for and what it contains and, for the Foundation exam, make especially sure that you're familiar with the 'purpose' statements at the start of each theme and process chapter in the PRINCE2 manual.

✔ **Principles:** Make sure you understand what each one means and check that you know how it's built in to the method. For example, exception management is used in Controlling a Stage when the Project Manager escalates an issue, but it's also used at project level and again at team level in Managing Product Delivery, because a Team Manager may be working within tolerances on a Work Package.

✔ **Management products:** Make sure you know what each product is used for and when, who produces it and what the sections in each one are all about.

✔ **Product planning (for Practitioner level):** Make sure you understand the diagrams and the Product Description, and practise drawing some diagrams. Although you're not required to draw answers in a multiple-choice format exam, if you've practised you'll be well used to the techniques and you'll find it easier to answer questions about them. [**P2FD** Ch14]

Getting the Right Mindset

The good news is that provided your technical knowledge is okay, you'll almost certainly pass the second time around. That good news is related to the point I made earlier in this chapter that many people fail because of exam strategy problems such as timing out, rather than because they don't understand PRINCE2 and how to use it.

I read on the back of a matchbox once, 'Experience is what you get when you're looking for something else.' I like that, because often it's so very true. If you've failed a PRINCE2 exam, you were indeed looking for something else: you were looking to pass. You didn't pass, but don't underestimate the value of that experience when tackling the exam again. You'll be in a better position next time and have a significantly increased chance of success.

Part II
Revising the Processes

The 5th Wave   By Rich Tennant

PROJECT MGMT
1. DIRECT
2. MANAGE
3. SQUEEZE 'EM WHERE IT HURTS

"Can we go over step 3 again?"

In this part . . .

Part II of this book works systematically through the PRINCE2 processes with a chapter on each. You'll find useful information here such as revision checklists, clarification on points that those learning PRINCE2 often misunderstand or find hard to get to grips with, and then practice questions so you can get up to exam speed.

The practice exam questions are designed to help you in three ways. First, they're grouped by subject with a set of questions at the end of each chapter. That means that you can test yourself even as you're learning PRINCE2, not just in final revision at the end. Second, they give you the chance to get familiar with the styles of question that you'll get in the exams, so when you finally sit the paper you'll be focused solely on the PRINCE2 and not struggling with the question style. Third, the questions do test your knowledge and help you find any gaps where you need to revise a bit more, but they also point out elements of practical exam strategy to give you an edge and perhaps a few extra marks.

Chapter 4

Starting Up a Project

Start Up or, to give it the full process title, Starting Up a Project, is fairly straightforward provided that you have a clear idea of what it's all about.

Many people misunderstand Start Up and think it's some lengthy part of PRINCE2 that delays the start of the project. Start Up isn't lengthy at all and in fact should happen quickly. It's to sketch out the idea for a project and ensure that it's worth proceeding to full planning – Initiation. The Project Brief, produced in Start Up, should indeed be brief. If you get the sketch of an idea into your head, you should then find the process much easier to understand. Start Up is very much a high level view of the project idea, so doesn't, for example, contain fine detail such as plans, specific costings and detail of staff resourcing. A key word that may help you lock on to the nature of the process is 'roughly'. Roughly, what will the project cost if it goes ahead? Roughly, what are the benefits likely to be? Roughly how long is it all likely to take?

A key phrase from the PRINCE2 manual which is a focus for testing your understanding of Start Up in the exams is, 'Do we have a viable and worthwhile project?'

Getting to Grips With the Process Model

If you're reading this book while you're learning PRINCE2, as opposed to reading it after learning the method, before taking the exams, then you may get a little boggled by the process model. As Starting Up a Project is the first process and you're likely to be revising it first, it's worth checking that you understand how the models work.

The process models, each with its activity boxes, are simply sets of steps. Now the concept of having steps in each process is generally unpopular, because many people assume that you have to complete every step or use the steps in a strict order. In fact, using the process model isn't like that at all, and the activities act as a helpful checklist, not a sequence to follow slavishly; you can leave things out if they aren't needed in a particular project. When you come to consider what you need to think through and prepare before starting a project, then the whole of the Start Up process with its checklist of activities and a suggested sequence for them comes across as fairly sensible and logical.

Revising the Start Up Process

In your revision for the process, be sure that you understand the areas covered in the following checklists. If you can't tick any item with confidence, you need to go and look at that subject area again.

At Foundation level, you're not required to know all the activities in every process, but you're required to know them in some. Watch out, because Start Up is one of the processes where you do need to be familiar with the activities.

Revision checklist – Foundation

❑ The purpose statement for the process – make sure you can recognise it to be able to identify missing words and know which process the statement belongs to.

❑ The place of the mandate as a trigger to Start Up, and who provides it – corporate or programme management.

❑ The management products in use in the stage: the logs, Project Brief, Project Product Description (PPD) and Outline Business Case within the brief and the Initiation Stage Plan. Make sure you know what they are.

❑ The activities making up the process, so you can recognise them as belonging to Starting Up a Project, know what is going on in each and are aware of the overall sequence of activities.

❑ The definition of a stakeholder in PRINCE2, and the point that the Executive is appointed from among the stakeholders.

❑ Where in the process people are appointed to project management team roles.

❑ The use of the project management team structure to record who's doing what in the project (which person has which role or roles).

❑ Who's responsible for what in the process. For what is the Executive responsible, and for what is the Project Manager responsible, for example.

❑ What comes immediately after Start Up: the Project Board will consider the brief and decide whether to authorise the start of the project and run the Initiation Stage (the first activity in the process Directing a Project).

Revision checklist – Practitioner

❑ The contents of the Project Brief, including the component parts, and why they are needed at this point in the method.

❑ Why stage planning is needed at the end of Start Up: to produce the Stage Plan for the Initiation Stage.

❑ The purpose and use of the management products used in Start Up, and the sections within each one, so you can quickly spot where something is wrong with faulty examples provided in the exam in critique-style questions.

❑ How the activities within Start Up will be varied to meet the needs of a particular project. For example, if good information has come in on the mandate, there's less work to do to produce the Project Brief.

❑ The roles in the project management team (although there's more on organisation in Chapter 12).

Clarifying Some Key Points

This section contains a few notes on some of the items in the checklist, to help you revise. Here I focus on a few of the areas which can be the source of misunderstanding or concern. If you scan a section and you're confident that you already know that point well, move on to the next one.

Getting an overview of Starting Up a Project

You can get lost in the detail a bit when studying the different parts of PRINCE2. In case you're not absolutely clear on what *Start Up* is about, then in a nutshell it:

✔ Happens before the project, and happens quickly

✔ Sketches out the proposed project

✔ Checks that the proposed project looks justified

✔ Filters out a bad project idea early, rather than rushing into full planning (Initiation) straight away only to discover later on that it's a bad idea and the planning work was all a waste of time and resources

✔ Appoints people to project management team roles to make the decision on whether to initiate the project, and decides who will control the project if it does go forward

Going fast with Start Up

Start Up should happen rapidly. You may not even do all of the Start Up process for a particular project. The whole thrust of the process is to check that the project looks worthwhile, on the sketchy information currently available, and that it's worth investing in the much more detailed work of Initiation (the full planning).

Two specific phrases in the PRINCE2 manual spell out this sketchy nature of Start Up and the main purpose of the process. The first is that the process 'prevents poorly conceived projects from ever being initiated'. That, perhaps, is wishful thinking, but it certainly helps reinforce the idea of checking out a potential project before diving into the detailed, and more expensive, work of Initiation. The second phrase that's significant in the manual is that Start Up is about doing the 'minimum necessary' to decide whether to go forward to Initiation. In other words, you don't have to do everything in the process on every project. [**Manual** 12.1]

Being clear that Start Up isn't a stage

It's a common mistake to think Starting Up a Project is a stage. It isn't. It comes before the project and so before any project stages. For that reason there's no Stage Plan for it. The PRINCE2 lifecycle is longer than the project lifecycle. PRINCE2 finishes when the project finishes but it starts earlier than the project, and that earlier part is Start Up.

Figure 4-1 shows the position of Start Up relative to the project, and may help you get clear on this point if you still find it a bit confusing.

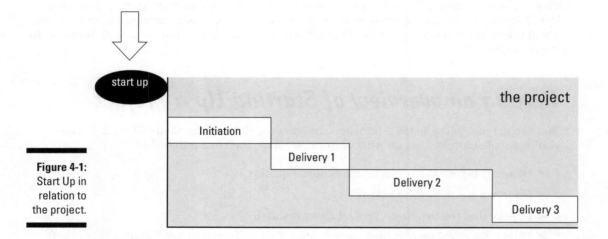

Figure 4-1:
Start Up in
relation to
the project.

Knowing your brief from your PID

When you're learning PRINCE2, sometimes the products all seem to swim around in your head, and it's easy to get confused, particularly where headings are similar. There's a similarity between the brief and the Project Initiation Documentation (PID), and you need to be clear on what each is.

A helpful analogy is with having a house built for you. As a highly paid PRINCE2 expert (well, soon anyway), if you go to an architect to ask for your new house to be designed, the architect will sketch out an idea first. When you've approved the sketch and agreed that that's pretty much what you want for the house, the architect will go away and produce detailed plans which conform to planning and building regulations. The architect doesn't start with full drawings then, but with a sketch. That's the difference in concept between the *brief*, which is a 'sketch' of the project, and the *PID*, which is the equivalent of the scale drawings. Both the sketch and the scale drawings will show a kitchen. It's just that the scale drawings show it in much more detail than the sketch did. The detailed drawings will also show more things, such as the electrical circuits. In the same way, some of the content of the PID is the same as in the brief, but it's in more detail, and there are some new things which were just too detailed for a sketch.

Understanding nesting – the brief as a folder

Another common cause of confusion is how management products fit together and what higher-level products they fit into. For example, where does the Business Case come? Does it belong in the brief or is it in the PID? The answer is that the Business Case is in both, but at different times in its development. When the Business Case is first written, it's sketchy (the *Outline* Business Case). After the brief is approved, that Business Case is worked into full detail, at which point it goes into the PID. The PID, including the Business Case inside it, is then maintained throughout the project. In fact, the minimum that the Business Case can be updated is at the end of each stage; in the process Managing a Stage Boundary there's an activity 'Update the Business Case'.

Going back to how products fit together, it may help you to think of both the Project Brief and the PID as folders containing other things.

Being clear on roles and job descriptions

PRINCE2 stresses that appointments are to roles rather than to jobs because one person may have more than role, and most roles can be shared by more than one person. Both of these facts bring great flexibility. For example, one person may be both the Project Manager and a team member. This person is running the project but also doing some of the work of the project. The Senior User role on the Project Board may be shared between two people whose staff are both affected by the project. One Senior User comes from Department A and the other from Department B in the organisation. The allocation of roles can then be backed up with job or role descriptions. So, a job description may say that one person on the project is covering two roles or part of a role.

The full detail of roles and responsibilities is in the Organization theme. Don't worry about this detail too much if you haven't yet learned about that theme, because it will make more sense when you have.

Practising With Some Questions

On the following pages you'll find some questions to have a go at. The answers are on the grey-edged pages at the end of the chapter.

The questions in this chapter are samples for you to practise with, preferably to time. They don't cover everything that you're likely to be asked. To prepare for the exam, you need to be confident in all areas of the subject, and not just learn the answers to these particular questions.

Foundation-level questions

You'll find answers to these questions, and some explanation, at the end of the chapter. Set your timer for eight minutes then go for it.

1. Two management products are given to the Project Board after the end of the process Starting Up a Project. The first is the Project Brief. What is the second?

❑ a) The Benefits Review Plan

❑ b) The Risk Register

❑ c) A Stage Plan

❑ d) The Project Product Description (PPD)

2. The Lessons Log is used during the process Starting Up a Project to:

❑ a) Record details of things learned in the past that need to be taken account of in this project.

❑ b) Record what will need to be recorded in this project to pass on to future projects.

❑ c) Record who will be responsible in this project for recording any lessons learned, and who will be responsible for passing that information on.

❑ d) All of the above.

3. Which of these logs and registers is created in Starting Up a Project?

❑ a) Issue Register

❑ b) Project Log

❑ c) Quality Register

❑ d) Daily Log

4. Which two roles are appointed first in Starting Up a Project?

❑ a) Senior User and Project Manager

❑ b) Senior Supplier and Senior User

❑ c) Executive and Senior User

❑ d) Executive and Project Manager

5. Which of these questions is answered by the process Starting Up a Project?

❏ a) Do the benefits outweigh the costs of the project?

❏ b) Do we have a viable and worthwhile project?

❏ c) Does the Product Breakdown Structure reflect the full extent of the project?

❏ d) Have all the risks been documented and the associated risk actions approved?

6. Which of these is NOT covered in the process Starting Up a Project?

❏ a) Appointing the Project Board

❏ b) Appointing Project Support

❏ c) Appointing Programme Management

❏ d) Appointing Project Assurance

7. What's the difference between the Business Case included in the Project Brief and the one included later on in the Project Initiation Documentation (PID)?

❏ a) The Business Case isn't included in the Project Brief at all.

❏ b) It's less detailed than the version in the PID.

❏ c) It's more detailed than the PID version, to support initial decision making.

❏ d) There's no difference: the Project Brief version is carried forward into the PID.

8. Which of the following statements accurately reflects an important aim of the process Starting Up a Project?

❏ a) To do the minimum necessary in order to decide whether it's worthwhile initiating the project

❏ b) To document all aspects of a project in detail to allow Initiation, if approved, to proceed on a sound basis

❏ c) To build in a delay to the start of Initiation and so provide a cooling off period where managers can consider whether the project really is justified

❏ d) To carry out thorough risk analysis to prevent a high risk project ever being taken forward into Initiation

9. Which of the following is a true statement?

❑ a) Starting Up a Project is the first stage in any PRINCE2 project.

❑ b) Starting Up a Project is an optional theme in PRINCE2.

❑ c) Starting Up a Project includes consideration of the way in which work will be conducted – the project approach.

❑ d) Starting Up a Project ends with the production of the Project Initiation Documentation (PID).

10. After Initiation and the production of the Project Initiation Documentation (PID), the Project Brief is:

❑ a) No longer maintained

❑ b) Maintained as a section of the PID

❑ c) Held in the Daily Log and kept up to date to serve as the Project Manager's overview

❑ d) Used as a baseline for checks at the end to see whether the project satisfied its original objectives

Practitioner-level questions

There's some additional project scenario information for this section which you'll need for answering some of the questions. However, don't forget the original scenario information, which you'll find at the end of Chapter 2.

For advice on dealing with the different styles of Practitioner question, please see Chapter 2.

In the Practitioner exam you'll get 10 questions in a section and about 15 minutes to answer them. Also in the exam, you won't get a whole section on a single process; Starting Up a Project will always be combined with Initiating a Project. With typical *For Dummies* generosity though, you've got 12 questions here, and all on Start Up.

Read the extra project scenario, then set your timer for 18 minutes, but if you can answer the questions accurately in slightly less time, then that's good.

Additional scenario – the project approach

1. The Accommodation Manager, who left last month, won't be replaced until after the end of this project. Consequently we don't have a member of staff with qualified health and safety expertise at the moment. An outside agency must be used to check the proposed floor plan for the new business unit to ensure it'll provide a safe working environment.

2. Because the headquarters building is 200 years old, problems may occur when work is carried out to make the new doorways. Unforeseen difficulties have caused significant delay in other projects involving structural alterations at the headquarters.

3. Financial constraints mean that the project work, apart from phone line installation, must all be done by our own Headquarters Building Works Team. It's accepted that this limitation may extend the time needed for the project, because the Works Team is small and has some existing commitments.

4. The floor plan for the layout of the offices making up the new business unit must clearly show the position of electrical sockets, both new and existing.

5. The cost of the refurbishment project is expected to be between £25,000 and £27,000 depending on the exact nature of the new furniture needed.

6. Any new furniture purchased must be robust. It must also be of similar style to existing furniture in the headquarters building so as to be usable elsewhere, should that be necessary, in the future.

Warning: There may be errors in this information

Classic-style questions

		Answer the following questions about the project approach.
		Remember to limit your answers to the number of selections requested in each section.
1		Paragraph 1 is about the current lack of health and safety expertise. Which **1** action should be taken with this paragraph?
	A	Leave the paragraph in place, but specify which external agency is to be used.
	B	Remove the paragraph and put the information into the Risk Register.
	C	Remove the paragraph and escalate the problem to the Project Board instead.
	D	Remove the paragraph and put the information into the resource plans.
	E	The entry's correct, so leave it as it is.
2		Paragraph 2 is about the structural alterations for doorways. Which **1** action should be taken with this paragraph?
	A	Leave the paragraph in place, but put in more detail about possible problems.
	B	Remove the entry and put the information into the Issue Register.
	C	Remove the entry and put the information into the Daily Log.
	D	Remove the entry and put the information into the Risk Register.
	E	The entry's correct, so leave it as it is.
3		Paragraph 4 is about the need to show the position of electrical sockets on the floor plan. Which **1** action should be taken with this paragraph?
	A	Include more detail to say how the sockets should be marked (for example, in colour).
	B	Remove the entry and put the information into the Quality Register.
	C	Remove the entry and include it in the Customer Quality Expectations.
	D	Remove the entry and include it later in the Product Description for the floor plan.
	E	The entry's correct, so leave it as it is.
4		Paragraph 5 is about the cost of the project. Which **1** action should be taken with this paragraph?
	A	During the work of Starting Up a Project, transfer this information into the Project Plan.
	B	Change it to read 'Costs for a project are never certain, so it's not possible to include meaningful cost estimates until full planning has been done in Initiation.'
	C	Change it to read 'Costs will be £26,000 with a tolerance of plus or minus £1,000.'
	D	Remove the entry and put the information into the Business Case.
	E	The entry's correct, so leave it as it is.

Matching-style questions – true/false

Answer the following questions about starting up the New Business Suite project. For each statement in column 1, select the correct option of true or false in column 2. An option in column 2 may be used once, more than once or not at all.

	Column 1	Column 2
5	The three Project Board roles should be the first to be filled for the New Business Suite project as the board is responsible to Princess Projects Plc for the project.	A True B False
6	The estimated project length of five weeks should be included in the Business Case.	
7	No plans are produced in Starting Up a Project as the detailed work to find out what is involved in the project will not happen until Initiation.	
8	The board must consider the project Acceptance Criteria very carefully for the Project Brief, such as the furniture being of similar style to other headquarters furniture. This is because – to prevent confusion later in the project with 'moving goalposts' – once the criteria are agreed, they cannot be changed.	
9	There are likely to be risks connected with the structural work for the offices, because the headquarters building is 200 years old. However, these risks will not be considered during Starting Up a Project, because the Risk Management Strategy won't be produced until the Initiation Stage of the project.	
10	The Executive should be the first role to be appointed, and that appointment will be done by corporate management within Princess Projects Plc.	

More classic-style questions

	Answer the following questions about the process Starting Up a Project.
	Remember to limit your answers to the number of selections requested in each section.
11	Which **2** items of information should be included in the Project Brief for the project, or in one of its components?

	A	The Outline Risk Register containing brief information about the risk of structural difficulties in making the new doorways.
	B	The project will cover all of the work from after the offices have been vacated to being completely ready for new staff to move in to form the new business unit.
	C	The completed offices will be accepted by the manager of the new business unit by signing the standard company Project Completion Form (PM43).
	D	The Stage Plan for the Initiation Stage of the New Business Unit project.
	E	The doors on the offices must all be three hours fire-resisting, have three hinges, a matt plain wood finish and aluminium lever handles.

12	Which **1** role is responsible for creating the Outline Business Case for the project?

	A	Executive
	B	Project Manager
	C	Project Support
	D	Team Manager(s)
	E	None of the options above

Answers to the Foundation-level questions

1   **c.** A Stage Plan – for the Initiation Stage. The Project Product Description (PPD) is included in the Project Brief. Think of the brief as a folder, containing other things. [**Manual** A19 and Figure 13.2 Inputs to the 'Authorise Initiation' activity, **P2FD** Ch4 *Getting it together with the brief* and also *Planning the Planning: Initiation*]. The Benefits Review Plan and Risk Register aren't created until Initiation.

2   **a.** Record details of things learned in the past. In Start Up, the log is retrospective, looking back at past experience. The name of the activity in Start Up is 'Capture *previous* lessons'. The forward-looking information is recorded as the project progresses, and the log doesn't include in advance what should be recorded. Neither does it record responsibilities. [**Manual** A.14, **P2FD** Ch4 Learning Lessons from the Past]. You may think that this is a tough question, and so it is. It's here to reinforce the point that you need to understand what a product is, and that includes appreciating what information it contains.

3   **d.** Daily Log. Both logs (Daily and Lessons) are created in Start Up, while all three registers (Risk, Quality and Issue) are created in Initiation. There's no such thing as a Project Log in PRINCE2. Remember, logs are for informal control and registers are for formal control.

4   **d**. Executive and Project Manager. The Executive brings immediate decision-making authority, and the Project Manager brings project skills. The other board roles are appointed in the activity 'Design and appoint the project management team'. [**Manual** 12.4.1, **P2FD** Ch4 Appointing the first two key people]

5   **b.** Checking for a viable and worthwhile project, as set down in the purpose statement. [**Manual** 12.1 purpose statement and following paragraphs, **P2FD** Ch4 Seeing Why You Really Need Start Up]. On the first answer, remember that the benefits don't have to outweigh the costs. The project may be mandatory and have to be done anyway, even if there are no benefits at all, such as in response to a head office instruction. The third and fourth answers both relate to detailed things done later, during Initiation; they're not done in Start Up.

6   **c.** Programme management is not appointed in Start Up, or indeed in any other part of PRINCE2. It's not down to a project to decide on programme management which is at the management level 'corporate or programme management' and so above the PRINCE2 project. That's like a junior manager in an organisation choosing and appointing senior managers. A nice thought perhaps, but the reality is the other way around.

7   **b.** It's less detailed. At this point in its life, the Business Case is known as the *Outline* Business Case because it's sketchy. It's just enough to decide whether to go on to full planning and the Initiation Stage. It's only during Initiation that the full Business Case will be developed. If you think that question was a bit hard because you're doing this test before you've studied Initiation in detail, then there's no harm done because you need to be clear on the point. [**P2FD** Ch4 Writing the Outline Business Case]

8   **a.** To do the minimum necessary to check it's sensible to initiate the project. Start Up should happen fast; it's not a delaying tactic. It's like producing a quick sketch of the project to decide whether to go forward and, to use the words of the manual, for 'preventing poorly conceived projects from ever being initiated'. [**Manual** 12.1, **P2FD** Ch4 Getting Start Up Done Fast]

9 **c.** Work is done for the project approach. The work for the project approach is covered in the Start Up activity 'Select the project approach and assemble the Project Brief'. If you've forgotten all about the project approach, that's quite common, but go back over it to make sure that you're clear. [**Manual** 12.4.5, **P2FD** Ch4 Thinking Through the Project Approach]. Remember that Start Up isn't a stage. It comes before the project (which starts with Initiation) so it predates the project stages. And Starting Up a Project is obviously a process and not a theme as suggested in an incorrect answer, b. So, yes, you do have to watch every word.

10 **a.** The brief is not maintained after the production of the PID. The brief is like a sketch plan, and as such is a stepping stone on the way to the PID. Once the full plans of the PID are in place, the sketch isn't needed any more. The Project Brief is not maintained through the project. [**Manual** A.19.1]. It's also the PID, not the brief, that's used at the end to check on fulfilment of objectives.

Answers to the Practitioner-level questions

Classic-style questions

1 **E.** Leave the entry alone. It's forewarning a resourcing matter, and that's appropriate for the project approach. Don't expect every entry in a sample document, in this case the project approach, to be incorrect. Some of it will be right.

2 **C.** Transfer the information to the Daily Log. You need to be careful here and remember the detail of the method and keep in mind where you are at the moment. This section is about Starting Up a Project, so although the possible problem with the doorways represents a risk, the Risk Register won't have been created yet; that's done in Initiation. Any risks spotted during Start Up are noted in the Daily Log. If the project goes ahead and the risk is to be formally managed, it will be transferred to the Risk Register when the register is set up.

3 **D.** Put the information into the Product Description. It doesn't relate to the approach to the project. This sort of information is describing the nature of the product and belongs in the Composition section of a Product Description. You'll have found that question tough if you're doing these questions as you learn PRINCE2 rather than at the end, because you almost certainly won't have covered Product Descriptions yet, although you should be clear on the project approach. But if you're using this for revision having covered the whole method, then the question is significant because it's testing whether you know which information goes in which management product.

4 **D.** Cost estimates for the project appear in the Project Plan and also in the Business Case. Because no plans for the project will have been done in Start Up, the only possible place for cost estimates is in the Business Case, and in Start Up that's the Outline Business Case. Beware of seeing something that you have learned in PRINCE2, such as tolerances or the Project Plan, and wrongly jumping on that as the correct answer because it sounds familiar.

Matching-style questions – true/false

5 **B.** False. The Executive and Project Manager are the first to be appointed. See the first activity in the Start Up process model dealing with appointments, which is 'Appoint the Executive and the Project Manager'.

6 **A.** True. 'Timescale' is a heading in the Business Case, and that includes the Outline Business Case. [**Manual** A2.2, **P2FD** Ch11 Writing a Business Case]

7 **B.** False. The Stage Plan for the Initiation Stage is produced as part of Starting Up a Project. It's the final activity: 'Plan the initiation stage'. Having the plan means that if the Project Board approves the brief, it can check the plan for the Initiation Stage and, once approved, the Initiation Stage can start without delay. That approach follows the normal pattern of 'just before' for stage planning in the method. [**P2FD** Ch14 Figure 14-9 Planning points in a PRINCE2 project]. Even if the full details of the project are not known, as suggested in the question, the work involved in finding them out and creating the PID and the plan for the first delivery stage can and should be planned out using the Initiation Stage Plan.

8 **B.** False. The Acceptance Criteria are not carved in stone and may well be modified later – if that's appropriate. That can happen with more detailed thinking while writing the PID or even later on in the project on a stage boundary where checks are made on the Project Product Description (which includes the Acceptance Criteria) to see whether it needs revision. That work in the process Managing a Stage Boundary is covered by the activity with the understated title of 'Update the Project Plan'.

9 **B.** Risk is an important consideration during Starting Up a Project, although it's done at a high level in the process. The Project Brief includes a section on risk. It is, however, correct to say that the detailed work is done in Initiation, and actually that's at the same time as the Risk Management Strategy is produced.

10 **A.** True. The Executive is the first role to be appointed. Even if you didn't know that the Executive is appointed by corporate or programme management, you should have been able to work it out by logic, since there would be nobody else in the project management team to do it at that point. Equally you could have looked it up in the manual where the information appears as a rather awkward 'product' on the responsibilities table for the activity, and also in the section in the Organization chapter describing the Executive role, although a long way down a very long section. [**Manual** Table 12-1 and Section 5.3.2.1 Executive]

More classic-style questions

11 **B and C.** The project definition has its own section in the Project Brief, and the acceptance method is part of the Project Product Definition which forms part of the brief. There's a mention of risk in the Project Brief, but there's no Risk Register yet in PRINCE2 and there's no such thing as an Outline Risk Register. The Stage Plan for the Initiation Stage is sent to the Project Board at the same time as the Project Brief, but it's a separate document and not part of the brief. The Project Product Description (PPD) does contain quality information but it isn't in the form of quality criteria. Instead the PPD has the Customer Quality Expectations, the project Acceptance Criteria and project-level quality tolerances. The description of individual products and the detail of their quality criteria will go in the relevant Product Descriptions, which are done later – not in the PPD, which is at a much higher whole-project level. [**Manual** A.21.2, **P2FD** Ch4 Producing the Project Product Description]

12 **A.** The Executive. Others may contribute to the Outline Business Case, but it remains the responsibility of the Executive to produce it. [**Manual** Table 12-4]. Please note that you were being asked for just one answer here, unlike Question 11 where you were asked for two. In the Practitioner exam, all the questions in a block will require the same number of answers – or at least they have so far to the time of writing this. But as part of the objective of this book is to make you vigilant, the number of required answers changed for this second question in the panel. Sneaky, huh? Do watch out in the exam that you're absolutely clear on the number of answers required. Don't lose a mark simply because you didn't take on board the number of answers you were being asked for. There's more on exam technique for classic questions in Chapter 2.

Chapter 5

Directing a Project

. . . .

In This Chapter

▶ Understanding where the authority lies

▶ Knowing the key Project Board decision points

▶ Being clear on the boundary between the Project Manager and the board

▶ Practising with some questions

. . . .

*I*n terms of the number and nature of the activities involved, Directing a Project is one of the smaller processes. But you need to be very clear that in PRINCE2 this process is where the main authority resides. Yes, the organisation has an overall interest in the project, and the Project Manager has (perhaps substantial) delegated authority for day-to-day management. However, the Project Board is the body charged with making sure that the project runs properly and delivers what it's supposed to, and it's the Project Board to whom the Project Manager is primarily accountable. It's the Project Board's project.

In terms of the structure of the method, this process is particularly significant, because it covers decisions at key points in the project, punctuating the running of the other processes. Chapter 19 has more on key points for Project Board decision making.

This chapter covers some key revision points for the Project Board work covered in the process Directing a Project and provides some questions at both Foundation and Practitioner levels to help you practise for questions in the exams.

In this book, cross references to a section in the PRINCE2 manual are shown like this: [**Manual** 3.2.1]. Cross references to a section in *PRINCE2 For Dummies* are shown like this: [**P2FD** Ch11 Justifying the Project].

Revising the Directing a Project Process

As you revise the process, make sure that you're clear on how the activities are triggered. Most activities happen in response to something from the Project Manager. For example, the first activity, 'Authorize Initiation', is triggered when the Project Manager finalises the Project Brief and submits it to the board together with a 'Request to initiate a project'.

To help plan your revision, have a look at the following checklists – one for each exam – and make sure that you're clear on every point. If you can't tick off an item with confidence, that will warn you that you need to go and have another look at that area. If you've already passed the Foundation and are focusing on the Practitioner, still have a look at the Foundation checklist to be sure you're still clear on that information.

Revision checklist – Foundation

Check out the items on the following list. If you're not confident on any of them, don't tick them off until you've revised them again.

❑ The purpose statement, to the point that you can quickly recognise it and associate it with this process, and so that you can identify phrases belonging to it for 'missing words' Foundation questions.

❑ The fact that this process is overwhelmingly about making decisions – four of the five activities are entirely that, and the fifth is largely that.

❑ What each of the five activities are.

❑ The nature of the decisions being made in each of the four activities, other than 'Giving ad hoc direction'.

❑ The nature of the ad hoc direction in responding to the Project Manager's referral of something to the Project Board, or to receive reports, or to 'push' something into the project that has been received from outside it (such organisational instructions or a change in the business environment).

❑ The use of ad hoc direction to trigger a premature close of the project if, for example, circumstances change and the project isn't needed any more.

❑ The function of the Project Board to 'manage' the project and not 'do' it.

❑ How the board roles lock on to the 'BUS' viewpoints: business, user, supplier.

❑ Clarity on each of the board roles and its main responsibilities.

❑ How board responsibilities fit with Project Assurance and a Change Authority – that board members can do this work themselves or delegate some of it to others.

❑ Board meetings at end stage and also if something goes off track to the point where a stage must be re-planned.

Revision checklist – Practitioner

For the Practitioner exam, make sure you're still up to speed on the Foundation topics by looking at the Foundation checklist in the previous section, then check out these further points:

❑ How the process will be used in the context of a project. Make sure you're clear on the time-based things such as authorising the brief and, later, the Project Initiation Documentation (PID), as opposed to the ad hoc things that can come at any time during the delivery stages.

❑ The responsibility of the board, the responsibility of the Project Manager, and when the Project Manager needs to refer something.

❑ The use of the 'Give ad hoc direction' activity for inbound information coming in from the organisation and outbound information such as telling organisational management about project progress.

❑ The working of the exception mechanism, to the point of re-planning a stage or even the whole project if necessary. If you're reading this while you're learning PRINCE2 and haven't got as far as exception management yet, don't worry but mark this point to check up on later.

Clarifying Some Key Points

The process Directing a Project is quite small, with just five activities, so it's quite easy for it to pass you by in a blur without you grasping its significance. The Project Board is a pivotal part of PRINCE2 and in live projects it's actually a common point of failure in using the method. For the exams, you must make sure that you understand how the process functions and, if you covered the process quite quickly when learning it, that you haven't missed something important.

The process acts as a series of checks running through the project. These checks align with the management stage boundaries. PRINCE2 still insists on using the unwieldy name of *End Stage Assessments* for the end stage meetings of the Project Board to check the project, but pretty much the rest of the world calls them stage gates. The word 'gate' is actually a very good one in this context. It's a barrier you stop at, but one which can then open to allow you through to the next area.

There's a bit more to the process in the activity 'Give ad hoc direction'. That ad hoc direction activity can be fired off by a number of different things and includes giving general advice to the Project Manager, not just making decisions.

Understanding that boards manage, not do

It's easy to lose the focus on roles when thinking about particular people in the project. The word *role* is very significant because one person's job on a project may cover a single role, more than one role, or just part of a role. If you don't feel clear on this, have a look at the clarification of some key points in Chapter 12.

Project Board roles are all about managing the project, not about any aspect of doing it. Let's say that again for emphasis. The Project Board roles don't do anything on the project in terms of building or testing products. That doesn't mean that people on the board can't also do something in the project, but they don't do it in their role as Project Board members.

Focusing on decision making

The process Directing a Project is overwhelmingly about decision making. Where you encounter a situation in the exam where the board is involved with the Project Manager, then normally the Project Manager will be recommending something but the board be deciding it. That's like normal day-to-day management in an organisation. A staff member may well recommend something to the boss, but can't often insist on it. It's the boss who makes the decision, which may or may not align with the staff member's recommendation.

So, too, if the Project Manager needs to refer something to the board. The Project Manager will put the matter forward with a recommendation on a course of action. The board, as 'the boss', then makes the decision. The board may agree with the Project Manager, or may take a different view and instruct the Project Manager to take a different course of action. For example, as a solution to a problem, the Project Manager may recommend allocating an additional $50,000 to the project budget and carrying on. Having carefully considered the Project Manager's argument, the board may disagree and instruct the Project Manager to stop all work and shut the project down instead.

The activities and decisions are:

- **Authorize Initiation – decision:** Looking at the Project Brief and deciding whether it looks promising enough to justify starting the project and planning in detail (Initiation).

- **Authorize the project – decision:** Looking at the PID and deciding whether to commit to the delivery stages or to stop here. If the PID is okay, then looking at the Stage Plan for the first delivery stage and, if it's also okay, giving the Project Manager permission to start on that stage.

- **Authorize a Stage or Exception Plan – decision:** Checking the plan and authorising the Project Manager to tackle the next stage at the planned end stage (for authorising a stage) or where a stage boundary has been forced by an exception situation that requires the stage to be re-planned.

- **Give ad-hoc direction:** Giving advice, receiving reports and decision making. This activity is partly about making decisions on things that are beyond the Project Manager's delegated authority, such as changes that are beyond the limit of the Project Manager's change budget. It's partly about receiving Highlight Reports, though, and that part of the activity doesn't require any decision making. It's also about giving guidance to the Project Manager when asked, and passing on inbound information from programme or corporate management.

- **Authorize project closure – decision:** Checking that everything is complete and making the decision to close the project down.

So, of the five activities, four are solely decision making, and the fifth – Give ad hoc direction – includes a significant element of decision making.

Seeing where the process kicks in

Directing a Project is largely a responsive process. The activities are mostly triggered by the Project Manager, but could be triggered by programme or corporate management. Just occasionally, the trigger may come from within the board, and so within the process. In summary, the activity triggers are as follows:

- **Authorize Initiation** – Project Manager submits the Project Brief.

- **Authorize the project** – Project Manager submits the PID and the stage plan for the first delivery stage.

- **Authorize a Stage or Exception Plan** – Project Manager submits an End Stage Report for the work just completed together with a Stage Plan for the next stage or an Exception Plan for the rest of the current stage.

- **Give ad hoc direction** – Project Manager escalates an issue, or asks for advice or submits a Highlight Report, or programme or corporate management information arrives, or the Project Board itself triggers the process to give instructions to the Project Manager on some aspect of the project.

- **Authorize project closure** – Project Manager submits the End Project Report with a closure recommendation and related documents.

Wondering what an Exception Assessment is

One of the weaknesses of the 2009 PRINCE2 manual is the very limited reference to the term *Exception Assessment*. This assessment is an important control in PRINCE2, but it's hardly mentioned by name, and not at all in the 'Authorize a Stage or Exception Plan' activity within Directing a Project, which covers it. If you're vigilant – or it's been pointed out to you – you may have seen one passing reference in a paragraph. [**Manual** 10.3.4 Stage-level exceptions]. The only other reference is in, of all places, the glossary. Someone with long experience of PRINCE2 suggested to me that this may simply be a mistake, and that it was intended to remove the term from the 2009 edition but two bits got left behind. That sounds plausible, but either way it can be rather confusing to those learning the method, and that may include you.

You need to be clear on what the assessments are and what an Exception Assessment is in the context of the activity 'Authorize a Stage or Exception Plan'. The two triggers to this activity reflect the two plans mentioned in the activity name. At the planned end of stage, the Project Manager will produce a Stage Plan for the following stage. Together with an End Stage Report, this is given to the Project Board for the members to check the plan and approve it to authorise work to start on the following stage; that's the first trigger.

The second trigger can happen during the stage and occurs if something goes significantly wrong (usually) to the point that in order to recover from the problem, the rest of the present stage must now be run differently. Clearly, if the stage is now going to be run differently, the existing stage plan won't be of any use. So the Project Board tells the Project Manager to force a stage boundary that wasn't originally planned. The Project Manager produces a replacement plan – the Exception Plan – which, like any plan at project or stage level, must be approved by the board. Because an end stage was forced, there must be an assessment, but because it's not at the planned end stage, the meeting is called an Exception Assessment rather than an End Stage Assessment.

The two assessments – for a planned end stage, and a forced end stage because of the need for an Exception Plan – now clarify the title of the activity 'Approve a Stage or Exception Plan'.

Seeing the integration of exception management

Chapter 19 covers revision on how the method fits together, including how the seven PRINCE2 principles are supported through the method. However, it's important to spotlight one of the principles here in the process Directing a Project, because it's so fundamental. The important principle is that of 'manage by exception'. In the context of the Project Board, that basically means letting the Project Manager get on with things and standing back. Unless, that is, something goes significantly off track. If it does, the Project Manager must go back to the board, which will then step in to decide what to do.

The 'standing back' means that, in a PRINCE2 project, the Project Board does not have any regular progress meetings. The traditional monthly progress meeting is a no-no; it doesn't exist. More than that, regular progress meetings are anathema in the method. The Project Board won't meet until the end of the stage, unless something goes significantly off track. 'Significantly' means by more than the amount of leeway that the board members specified.

You'll find more on exception management in Chapter 17, which covers the Progress theme, and also in PRINCE2 for Dummies. [**P2FD** Ch17]

In the Practitioner exam, if the scenario mentions a monthly meeting of the Project Board, you should instantly be alerted, because this isn't the PRINCE2 way of doing things. In questions on how the project should be corrected, you should then be selecting options that say the meetings should be stopped and that if the project is to continue, then it should be using exception management.

Practising With Some Questions

Have a go with the following questions, which are in the exam styles. It helps if you can do them to time, but don't be too tough on yourself if you're still learning PRINCE2 and aren't quite up to speed yet. Remember that while learning later parts of the method, you'll be reinforcing the earlier parts – so your fluency should increase as the learning continues, and with that your speed of answering questions accurately.

Foundation-level questions

Set your timer for eight minutes and try these questions to check your knowledge and understanding of the process Directing a Project. Answers are at the end of the chapter.

Some of the answer options in this section include a short explanation, which, unfortunately perhaps, you won't get in the exam. The explanations don't give the answers away, but they should help if you're practising with these questions while learning PRINCE2 and aren't yet fully familiar with the whole method.

1. Which role is ultimately in charge of the project?

❑ a) Corporate or programme management

❑ b) The Executive

❑ c) The Senior User

❑ d) The Sponsor

2. What is the recommended frequency for Project Board meetings during a delivery stage to check progress?

❑ a) Monthly

❑ b) Weekly

❑ c) At the frequency set down in the 'Controls' section of the Project Initiation Documentation (PID)

❑ d) There are no regular meetings of the Project Board during the stages

3. In the event of the Project Manager being given conflicting instructions, whose instructions should he or she follow?

❑ a) The Executive's, as chair of the Project Board

❑ b) The Senior User's, as the role responsible for delivering the benefits

❑ c) The Senior Supplier's, as the role responsible for ensuring that the project is achievable

❑ d) Project Assurance's, as the role responsible for checking the running of the project

4. In the activity 'Authorize Initiation', which of the following would the Project Board use to support its decision on whether to go ahead and start the project?

❑ a) Mandate

❑ b) Project Brief

❑ c) Project Initiation Documentation (PID)

❑ d) Stage Plan for the first delivery stage

5. In which activity would the Project Board instruct the Project Manager to shut down the project prematurely, should that be necessary?

❑ a) Authorize Initiation

❑ b) Authorize emergency action

❑ c) Give ad hoc direction

❑ d) Authorize project closure

6. Which role is responsible for approving the Project Brief?

❑ a) Executive

❑ b) Senior User

❑ c) Senior Supplier

❑ d) All of the above roles working together

7. In which PRINCE2 process are the members of the Project Board appointed?

❏ a) Starting Up a Project

❏ b) Initiating a Project

❏ c) Managing a Stage Boundary

❏ d) Controlling a Stage

8. Which of the following is NOT an objective of the process Directing a Project? To ensure that:

❏ a) There's authority to initiate the project.

❏ b) There's authority to deliver the project's products.

❏ c) Corporate or programme management has an interface to the project.

❏ d) The products being produced by teams are delivered to expectations.

9. What is the final phrase in the following purpose statement. To enable the Project Board to be accountable for the project's success by making key decisions and exercising overall control while:

❏ a) Maintaining a low degree of risk exposure

❏ b) Ensuring that the benefits specified in the Business Case can be delivered

❏ c) Authorising spending only within the agreed financial tolerances (limits)

❏ d) Delegating day-to-day management of the project to the Project Manager

10. Which of the following is NOT an input into the activity 'Give ad hoc direction'?

❏ a) Highlight Report (the progress report from the Project Manager to the board)

❏ b) Exception Report (referral of something projected to go beyond the Project Manager's authority)

❏ c) Issue Report (a report setting down the detail of an issue being referred to the board)

❏ d) End Stage Report (a report giving the board details such as the final cost of a stage just finishing)

Practitioner-level questions

Have a go with these questions, preferably against the clock. In the Practitioner exam you'll get 10 questions in a section and about 15 minutes to answer them. Here we've given you 12 questions to practise with so you can have 18 minutes. Generous to a fault huh? The questions in this chapter are all about the process 'Directing a Project' because they're to help you revise this subject area. In the exam, however, you won't ever get a whole section on a single process. Directing a Project will always be bundled with the two other processes Managing a Stage Boundary and Closing a Project.

Read the extra project scenario, then set your timer to 18 minutes and try to answer the questions within that time. If you're near the start of your exam practice, don't worry if you go a bit over time on the first few sets of questions that you tackle in these chapters. You will pick up speed as you get the idea of the question formats, which is why the book has lots to practice on.

There's some extra project scenario information which you'll need to refer to for some of these questions.

Additional scenario

The offices have now been cleared of staff and unwanted furniture, and work is about to begin on making the openings for the new doorways. However, on looking more closely at the plans, the manager of the new business unit has realised that one new doorway isn't really needed. In fact, it would reduce wall space significantly, not just because of the doorway itself, but because of the space that would be needed to allow the door to open. Because the staff in that particular office can get to the other offices easily enough using adjacent doors in the corridor and the other new doorways, the wall space is more valuable than this particular new doorway.

The unit manager has asked the Project Manager to change the plan to have only three new doorways instead of the originally planned four. The Project Manager has put the details of this request onto an Issue Report and made an entry in the Issue Register.

Assertion–reason style questions

Each row in the table below consists of an assertion statement and a reason statement. For each row, identify the appropriate selection from options A–E that applies. Each option can be used once, more than once or not at all.

Selection	Assertion	Reason	
A	True	True	AND the reason explains the assertion
B	True	True	BUT the reason does not explain the assertion
C	True	False	
D	False	True	
E	False	False	

	Assertion		Reason
1	The Project Board members only need to see a high level management overview of the Project Initiation Documentation (PID)	BECAUSE	the detailed PID information isn't relevant to Project Board roles.
2	In the first delivery stage, the Project Manager has found that the cabling work can be done in parallel with the doorways work, and must now get the Project Board's permission to change the plan	BECAUSE	the Project Board has already agreed and approved the Stage Plan.
3	The Project Manager is reporting rapidly increasing cost forecasts because of unforeseen problems with the walls and flooring. The board may consider stopping the project, even before the stage end	BECAUSE	early closure is sometimes the most appropriate and responsible action if something has gone badly off track.
4	After the furniture has been ordered, the project costs are more clear. The Project Brief will be updated with this information	BECAUSE	the Project Brief forms an important part of the PID and will be needed at the end of the project to check that the business unit costs align with original estimates.
5	If the reduction in the number of doorways would have wider impacts and so actually be more expensive, the Project Manager must refuse the change	BECAUSE	in PRINCE2, project spending must always be contained within the original limits as part of effective project control.
6	At the end of the first delivery stage, when exact structural work costs are clear, the Executive will check the Business Case	BECAUSE	to remain viable, all projects must have financial benefits which are greater than project costs.

Classic-style questions

Answer the following questions about the issue concerning changing the plans to have only three new doorways and other changes, or possible changes, which might be considered in the project.

Remember to limit your answers to the number of selections requested in each section.

7	If the number of doorways is to be reduced, it will obviously need a change to the floor plan and affect the project time, cost and resource estimates. Having recorded the details of the requested change, which **1** action should the Project Manager take next?	
	A	Go ahead with the changes without informing anyone else.
	B	Determine the implications of such a change for the project and then put the matter to the Project Board for a decision.
	C	Refuse the change and close down the issue in the Issue Register, as it would be chaotic to alter products (in this case, the floor plan) that have already been agreed and signed off.
	D	Agree to the change, since it would save money and time rather than cost any extra, and tell the Project Board afterwards in the next Highlight Report (progress report).
	E	Ask the Project Board for its views (ad hoc direction) before making a decision.
8	At the monthly management board meeting, corporate management decided to increase the budget for the project by up to 25 per cent, if the extra money would be helpful. The e-commerce side of the business is growing strongly, and the new business unit will be even more important than previously thought. Which **1** action should the Executive take on being told this by the Managing Director of the company?	
	A	Nothing, but keep the offer of extra money in mind in case it's needed.
	B	Thank the Managing Director, but refuse the funds as the Project Plans have already been agreed as part of the Project Initiation Documentation (PID).
	C	Instruct Project Assurance to ignore any cost overruns in the project, up to 25%, because the extra funds will cover them.
	D	Send an issue to the Project Manager to put the extra funding offer on record.
	E	Send a memo to each of the staff members of the new business unit to tell them about the offer of additional funding, and ask them to send any requests for improved facilities to the Project Manager.
9	The reduction in the number of new doorways from four to three has been implemented, and the floor plan has been changed. As part of the checking of the adjusted Stage Plan, the Project Manager has realised that because of this change, the stage could be run in a slightly different way with more work being done in parallel. This would reduce the stage costs and bring the whole project forward by four days, giving earlier delivery. It would increase the risk, but only very slightly. Which **1** action should the Project Manager take?	
	A	Leave things alone, because the final delivery date has already been agreed.
	B	Ask the Project Board members, and particularly the Executive, for their views.
	C	Ignore the matter until the next end stage, and discuss it with the board then.
	D	Consult Project Assurance and if assurance is happy, then go ahead.
	E	Wait until the next Highlight Report (progress report) is due in three weeks' time and ask for Project Board members to notify their views then.

More classic-style questions

	Answer the following questions about the activities in the process Directing a Project.
	Remember to limit your answers to the number of selections requested in each section.

10		Before making a decision to start the New Business Unit project in the Project Board's activity 'Authorize Initiation', which **2** products (documents) should the Project Board check?
	A	Outline Business Case
	B	Risk Management Strategy
	C	Communications Management Strategy
	D	Highlight Report
	E	Stage Plan

11		If the structural work hits a lot of problems and costs rise significantly, the Project Board may want to abandon the project and close it down prematurely. Which **2** of the following are times when the board can order an immediate close because the structural work is exceeding its budget, and instruct the Project Manager to do the work in the process Closing Down a Project?
	A	During the work of Starting Up a Project
	B	After the project has finished but before all the benefits have been measured
	C	At the end of a delivery stage, during an End Stage Assessment (stage gate)
	D	At any point during a delivery stage
	E	None of the above. Once the project has been started, it must not be stopped before delivering its benefits. Consequently, in PRINCE2, the Project Board must ensure that the project goes through to its planned end as agreed and set down in the Project Initiation Documentation.

12		Which **2** of the following matters in the New Business Unit project would require Project Board involvement covered by the board's PRINCE2 activity 'Give ad hoc direction'?
	A	The Senior Supplier has insufficient current technical building knowledge to do project assurance work on the structural work, and so the Project Board appoints a dedicated person to do the checks for supplier-related Project Assurance.
	B	The corporate management board of Princess Projects Plc has said that it wants regular progress reports on the project to co-ordinate other plans connected with the launch date of the new e-commerce business unit.
	C	After consulting with corporate management, the Project Board has approved the Project Brief and now instructs the Project Manager to start the New Business Unit project and produce the Project Initiation Documentation (PID).
	D	Towards the end of the first delivery stage, the Project Manager updates the Business Case, including adjustment of the investment appraisal to use the latest cost estimates.
	E	Towards the end of the first delivery stage, the Project Manager prepares the Stage Plan for the second delivery stage and submits it to the Project Board for approval.

Answers to the Foundation-level questions

1   **b.** The Project Board isn't a 'voting democracy' and the Executive is ultimately in charge of both the board and the project. It's a common misconception, particularly by Project Board members anxious to avoid both responsibility and blame, that it's the Project Manager's project. Project Board members, including the Executive, often think that they're somehow an independent body who will attend meetings if it's convenient, eat the free lunches and ask the Project Manager some awkward questions. Wrong! If you're not clear on this, have a look at *PRINCE2 For Dummies*. [**P2FD** Chapter 12]

2   **d.** PRINCE2 uses 'exception management'. If you haven't learned about this yet, you may have got a clue having not seen any regular meetings covered in any of the activities of the Directing a Project process – or having read the earlier part of this chapter. Even stage end meetings are not regular in the sense that they're not at set time-based intervals; management stages will be different lengths.

3   **a.** In a live project, the Project Manager should also usually tell the Executive about conflicting instructions, not merely ignore instructions which may be from managers who are very senior in the organisation. The answer here reflects a specific section of the manual which is to emphasise the Executive's ultimate authority within the project, but remember that the manual is not intended to limit additional actions which may be sensible in the circumstances. [**Manual** 13.3 para 4]

4   **b.** The activity is to authorise initiation, so it's before initiation. Therefore you should have been able to determine that the answer was the Project Brief. The mandate is left behind once the brief is created, and it's the submission of the brief that comes immediately before the activity to 'Authorize Initiation' takes place.

5   **c.** The board would decide to close the project down prematurely in the activity 'Give ad hoc direction' and give the instruction to the Project Manager. The activity 'Authorize project closure' happens later, after the Project Manager has done the closure work covered in the process Closing a Project.

6   **d.** All of the Project Board roles approve the brief. Responsibilities in each of the activities are shown in the matrix at the end of each activity section in the PRINCE2 manual. [**Manual** Table 13-1]

7   **a.** The default in the manual is Starting Up a Project. The Executive and Project Manager are put in place in the first activity of Start Up, with the other board member appointments being made in the Start Up activity 'Design and appoint the project management team'. You may feel that this isn't a question about the process Directing a Project, but it's to make sure that you realise that the board is in place before the process starts.

8   **d.** The objectives are listed at the start of the Directing a Project chapter of the PRINCE2 manual. [**Manual** 13.2]. Option d is actually from a later process, Managing Product Delivery, which covers the work of Team Managers.

9   **d.** The purpose statement for each process and theme is at the start of its respective chapter in the manual.

10   **d.** The End Stage Report isn't 'ad hoc' but rather at the fixed points of the stage boundaries.

You may have noticed that the final three questions all had an answer of 'd'. Remember that there's no connection between the questions and that you may sometimes get a run of the same letter or a disproportionate number of answers over the whole paper with a particular answer letter. Always ignore previous answers and go with the letter that you think is correct, no matter how often it's come up before.

Answers to the Practitioner-level questions

Assertion–reason style questions

1 **E.** The board is responsible for approving the whole Project Initiation Documentation (PID) and have no business asking for a 'management overview' to be put at the front of it or reading selected parts! The board is responsible for making sure that the project will run properly, and members coming up with excuses such as that they haven't got time to read the PID are not acceptable. Imagine senior managers in a department claiming that they didn't have time to read the departmental strategy and objectives document for the coming year. Even if Project Assurance checks some of the technicalities, such as that the benefits calculations are correct, the board must still approve the whole PID and must read all of it. The responsibilities information in the method quite rightly makes no provision for this being delegated.

2 **D.** It's a common reaction to think that all issues must always go to the board. Remember though that the Project Manager has been appointed to manage the project on a day-to-day basis. If the Project Manager can deal with something and has the authority to do so, then he or she should get on with it without involving the board. Imagine what would happen in an organisation if every time staff members hit a problem or needed to make a decision they went to their boss! The senior managers of a department in an organisation can be responsible for that department without being involved in every single matter. They expect their staff to get on and manage most things and only involve the senior managers when it's really necessary or for things where those senior managers have instructed that they should be informed and involved. So too with the project. The day-to-day work of the PRINCE2 Project Manager is covered by the process Controlling a Stage, and the activity 'Take corrective action' within that process covers the work of the Project Manager adjusting the stage within his or her delegated authority to do so. The nature and extent of that delegated authority will have been recorded in the PID.

3 **A.** The project can be closed at any time using the activity 'Give ad hoc direction'. And the second statement is indeed the reason why the first is true. If a project is badly off track, then sometimes the responsible action is to close it down without throwing good money after bad on a failed project.

4 **E.** The Project Brief stops at the end of Start Up. Any new information is reflected in the PID, and the brief isn't kept up to date. A check of Appendix A in the manual will confirm that the brief does not become part of the PID. Have a look at *PRINCE2 For Dummies* for more help on the nature of the brief and the PID. [**P2FD** Ch5]

5 **E.** The Project Manager can always refer a worthwhile change to the Project Board where it's beyond his or her authority (because of budget or any other limit) to approve it. Neither is it the case that all projects must be contained within the original budget. If someone comes up with a great idea that will make huge savings in the organisation for a small increase in the project budget, then it's highly likely to be agreed provided there are no constraints involved, such

as time. Depending on the spending authority given to the board by programme or corporate management, the Executive may need to seek further authority above the level of the project. It's important to take on board that PRINCE2 doesn't prohibit change – even large scale change – but it does control it.

6   **C.** The Executive is responsible for the Business Case, so must check it at the end of the stage after working with the Project Manager to make any changes. However, it's not true that all projects must show financial benefits. A project may be justified by being a compliance project, for example, where it's being done because of an instruction from head office or perhaps to comply with a change in the law.

Classic-style questions

7   **E.** It would be sensible to check things out with the Project Board, and especially the Senior User, as the floor plan is a fundamental product in a project of this type. Note in this explanation the use of the word 'sensible'. This is my judgement as the author of this book and the person who wrote the question. If you agree with me, then you're right; you get the mark and your name goes up in lights. If you disagree with me, then you're wrong; you're the weakest link and you must take the walk of shame. Despite what you may think, I'm not on a power trip here but giving an example of a question which is a judgement call. In such cases, you hope that your view is the same as that of the person who set the question. Some of the possible answers are clearly wrong, but with the remainder it comes down to your judgement.

8   **D.** The possibility of a 25 per cent increase in funding is an important matter and should be put on record within the project. The point of this question is to reinforce that issues don't just get referred 'up' to the Project Board but can be sent 'down' from the board to the Project Manager. In this example, it's the result of inbound information coming to the board, and specifically the Executive, from outside the project. Anyone can submit an issue, and that includes Project Board members. The other answers are wrong, and some dangerously so. It would be an undermining of assurance, for example, to tell assurance staff to ignore cost overruns. That would be to abandon financial control. If extra things are added to the project to take advantage of the 25 per cent increase, then fine – but the financial management should still be there for that additional authorised work.

9   **B.** Of the options, B is the only correct answer. It could be that the Project Manager has sufficient delegated authority to make the decision, but that wasn't one of the answer options. Of the others, A is incorrect because that would mean that useful change would be excluded when actually the project might benefit from it considerably. C and E would both introduce unnecessary delay. D represents a misunderstanding of the function of Project Assurance. Assurance is primarily an audit function to check things, not an active function responsible for making control decisions.

More classic-style questions

10   **A and E.** The Outline Business Case is part of the Project Brief. Accompanying the Project Brief when it's submitted to the Project Board will be the Stage Plan for the Initiation Stage, produced in the last activity of the process 'Starting Up a Project'. The strategies are produced in Initiation, which comes later, and Highlight Reports (progress reports) are generated during stages, not at the end of Start Up (the case here) or at the end of project stages. The point of this question is two-fold. First to make you think about where you are in the method, what has come before this point (Start Up) and what comes after (Initiation). Second, to make sure that you've taken on board the fact that the Initiation Stage has a Stage Plan, like any other project stage. That Stage Plan must be agreed before the stage starts.

Where a Practitioner question is about a particular activity, stop for a moment and 'locate yourself' in the method. Think where the activity is within the processes, who is doing it and when it's happening. When you're clear on that, it often makes it easier to sort out which are the right answers and which are the wrong ones, or at least to rule some of them out and so narrow your field of focus.

11 **C and D.** The board could decide not to 'Authorize a Stage or Exception Plan' and instruct the Project Manager to shut the project down instead. Also, at any time by using the activity 'Give ad hoc direction' the board could order the project to be closed down. In either case, the Project Manager would do an orderly shut down using the process 'Closing a Project' and then come back to the Project Board to 'Authorize project closure'. An example of this 'crash stop' instruction is if Princess Projects Plc suddenly decided to outsource its e-commerce work and so didn't need the new business unit accommodation prepared after all. The refurbishment work might then be put on hold until a new use was found for the office accommodation, which might then need a different layout. Option A is a wrong answer and is making the point that the project hasn't started yet. The project starts with the Initiation Stage, not Start Up. B is incorrect because the project is already closed even though there are one or more post-project Benefits Reviews still to come. Option E is nonsensical when you stop to think about it. If the project is no longer justified, it doesn't make sense to continue it.

12 **B and D.** The board (often the Executive) communications with corporate or programme management are covered by the ad hoc direction activity. D is the other correct answer because the Executive owns the Business Case. It follows that the Project Manager would consult the Executive when adjusting the Business Case. The need for this consultation is described in the manual in the context of the process Managing a Stage Boundary. If you haven't learned the content that far yet, you may still have realised that the ownership element indicates Executive involvement before the formal step of approving the next Stage Plan. Option A is part of the work of the process Starting Up a Project. Option C is part of the work of Directing a Project but is covered by the earlier activity of 'Authorize Initiation'. Option E involves Project Board work but with the activity 'Authorize a Stage or Exception Plan', not 'Giving ad-hoc direction'.

So, how did you get on? If you got questions wrong but can now see why, then that's great and a useful part of your revision. If you got questions wrong, and when you looked at the answers you said to yourself 'Oh yes, of course,' then you may be misreading the questions. In the exam, read the questions very carefully to be sure you're clear on what they're asking.

Chapter 6

Initiating a Project

· ·

In This Chapter

▶ Seeing what Initiation is all about

▶ Understanding the difference from the Initiation process and the Initiation Stage

▶ Focusing on areas that could cause you a problem

▶ Practising with questions in the exam styles

· ·

*I*nitiating a Project is a very significant process in PRINCE2, because it marks the start of the project. Unlike the process Starting Up a Project which is pre-project preparation, the work of the Initiation process falls into the first project stage.

The process is all about getting the Project Initiation Documentation (PID) ready. It's the PID that the Project Board uses as an information base to decide whether to commit to running the delivery stages of the project. Initiating a Project also kicks off another PRINCE2 process: Managing a Stage Boundary, to produce a Stage Plan for the first delivery stage. That way, if the Project Board does decide to continue with the project, the first delivery stage can start immediately, because the plan is in place.

Revising the Initiation Process

Have a look at the following checklists to make sure you feel confident about all the different aspects of Initiation, both the content and the way that the process works. If you can't tick an item confidently, target that area for revision.

At Foundation level, you're not required to know all of the activities in all of the processes in detail, but Initiation is one where you are. Be sure then that you know the activities, the overall suggested sequence of those activities, what's happening in each and who's doing what. If that sounds daunting, don't worry too much, because the latest version of PRINCE2 continues an underlying logic from earlier versions that makes a lot of the method easy to predict. You'll find that although the detail of the activities isn't exactly self-evident, it's generally sensible, and that makes it easier to get to grips with it all.

Revision checklist – Foundation

❏ The purpose statement for the process – make sure you can recognise it to be able to identify missing words and know which process the statement belongs to.

❏ An awareness of the contents of the PID, although you don't need to memorise the list of contents.

❏ The use of the PID in a PRINCE2 project.

❏ The difference between the PID and the Project Brief: the PID extends and refines the brief, fleshing out some things that were in the brief but which now need more detail, and then adding new content that the brief didn't cover.

❏ The fact that the process Managing a Stage Boundary, not the process Initiating a Project, is used to create the Stage Plan for the first delivery stage. (There's an explanation on this in the section 'Clarifying Some Key Points' later in this chapter.)

❏ The activities within the process, so that you can recognise their names if you see them in a Foundation question, what's happening in each one, and the suggested sequence in which they should be done.

❏ Responsibilities for the work in Initiation – primarily for the Project Manager, but others are involved too. If you're unsure, you can check this out in the PRINCE2 manual by referring to the responsibilities matrix for each activity.

❏ Which PRINCE2 management products are feeding in from Start Up, and why they are used – the Project Brief, of course, but also the Project Product Description (PPD) and Outline Business Case within the brief, then the Daily Log and the Lessons Log.

❏ The PRINCE2 management products created or modified by the process. Notably the PID and the full Business Case within it. But then also the three registers and the four strategies.

❏ The difference between a register and a log – the formal/informal divide.

Revision checklist – Practitioner

❏ The contents of the management products created during Initiation and how those products are used. The products are the PID and, within it, the four strategies, the Business Case, the Benefits Review Plan and the Project Plan. Then the three registers, ongoing use of the logs and the Configuration Item Record (for both management and specialist products). Your understanding of these products should be detailed enough to quickly spot what's wrong if you're given a product with mistakes in it or you're asked in which product a particular piece of information should be recorded.

❏ The flexibility in applying activities so that they're suitable for a particular project.

Clarifying Some Key Points

Here are some notes on a few aspects of the process to help you revise. This section picks up on areas where you may be having a bit of difficulty, or where you may think your understanding is insufficiently clear. Have a look at each heading and perhaps the first sentence of each point. If you think you're not having problems, that's great: you can skip that section. If you think the heading pinpoints something where you're not clear or you want to be absolutely sure you've got it right, then read on in that section.

Getting an overview of Initiating a Project

In a nutshell, this process:

✔ Marks the start of the project. The project begins as the process Initiating a Project begins.

✔ Covers the production of the Project Initiation Documentation (PID).

✔ Covers the production of the Project Plan, which forms a section of the PID.

✔ Is primarily the responsibility of the Project Manager, although the Project Manager also consults other people, including Project Board members (something that isn't conveyed by the main process model for PRINCE2).

✔ Calls the process Managing a Stage Boundary to produce a Stage Plan for the first delivery stage.

Understanding the process and the stage

As you've probably already realised, some of the language in PRINCE2 can be a bit confusing, particularly when you're learning PRINCE2, and the large array of different expressions start to fly round your head. It's worse if you work in a business rather than a specialist project environment, or if the language conflicts with terms that your organisation or industry already uses in a different sense.

The particular problem here is that the Initiation Stage and the process both include the word 'initiation'. The word isn't perhaps the best one, but that doesn't present much difficulty once you know PRINCE2. What does cause confusion when people are learning the method is the use of the word 'initiation' in both the process and the stage.

The first stage of any PRINCE2 project is the Initiation Stage. The Initiation Stage is a block of time at the front end of the project when planning work – and only planning work – is done. The stage is basically to cover the work necessary to plan the whole project and produce the Project Initiation Documentation (PID), and then to plan the first delivery stage at a lower level of detail and in line with the PID. The Initiation Stage is *driven* by the process 'Initiating a Project', but that's not the only process used. Towards the end of the Initiation Stage, the process Managing a Stage Boundary is called in order to create the more detailed Stage Plan for the following stage, the first delivery stage.

Knowing why feasibility isn't Initiation

If you were involved in projects before you started learning PRINCE2, which you probably were, you may be confused between Initiation and feasibility. Actually, they're completely different. The Initiation Stage and the process Initiating a Project are all about project planning. 'Technical' is a dirty word in PRINCE2 for historical reasons, but it helps to make things clear on this point. Initiation is not about the technical work; it's about the project management work.

An example of feasibility work is to look at different possibilities for the new entrance and reception facilities at Princess Projects Plc headquarters. One option is to build a completely new extension to the building as a purpose-built entrance area. Another is to modify a large office by the car park and turn that into a smart entrance and reception area. A third possibility is to renovate the existing entrance area to make it more modern and provide a reception area with visitor chairs and magazine racks. None of these options are anything to do with planning and project control. Instead the options are technical things – or, to use the PRINCE2 word, 'specialist' things. All of the different feasibility options have different Business Cases (costs, risk, timescale, and so on) and need very different project plans.

In cases where it's not clear which way to go, or even what the possibilities are, the answer isn't to do feasibility work as part of Initiation or even Start Up. The most common solution to the problem is to run a feasibility project which can be controlled under PRINCE2 like any other project. That feasibility project delivers a feasibility study report which sets out the different options, each with its own Business Case and each with its own outline plan. The organisation selects an option or a hybrid of different options, and a new project can be started up and initiated to implement that option.

In short, then, doing a feasibility study is specialist work which itself needs to be project managed. The research of the options, the costing and sizing of the candidate projects, and the production of the feasibility report are all part of the work being carried out in delivery stages, not in the planning stage of Initiation.

Seeing how the PID fits with other products

Many people think of the Project Initiation Documentation (PID) as a single document. The reason for that is that it's often presented as a single document. However, when learning the PRINCE2 method, it's easy to get confused about the many products, and sometimes you just can't see why you're getting questions on them wrong. In the Initiation Stage, you produce the PID, the Business Case, the Risk Register, the Project Plan, and the Stage Plan for the first delivery stage. So, to take just two of them, why is it unusual to mention the PID and the Business Case in the same breath, and why do some products seem to disappear at the end of the stage? Surely the Project Board needs to see the Business Case at the end of Initiation, but it's no longer mentioned.

The answer is that the PID is like a folder; the clue is in the name Project Initiation 'Documentation'. It's absolutely true that the board needs to see the Business Case after Initiation. But if the board has got the PID, then it's got the Business Case, because the Business Case is contained in the 'folder' which is the PID. The same is true of the Project Plan.

If you're still a bit unclear about products (and it's a new concept to most people, since they're more familiar with thinking about projects in terms of activities) have a look at *PRINCE2 For Dummies*. [**P2FD** Ch14 Planning with Products]. In the context of this chapter and Initiation, the products under discussion are 'management products' – the ones used to project manage the project.

As part of your revision, you need to make sure you're clear about which management products are included in the PID 'folder' and what other management products are created or updated during Initiation and which then accompany the PID.

Appreciating the full use of the PID

When learning all about the process Initiating a Project, you can become focused on the need to have the Project Initiation Documentation (PID) to pass on to the Project Board for its decision on whether to authorise the start of work on the first delivery stage. The PID has several functions, though:

- ✔ **To define the project.** The PID sets down exactly what the project is (the scope) and how it's to be controlled.

- ✔ **For decision support.** The PID gives the Project Board the information it needs at the end of the Initiation Stage in order to reach a decision on whether to commit to the whole project and, specifically, to authorise the first delivery stage (the stage after the Initiation Stage).

- ✔ **As an ongoing reference.** The PID is kept up to date throughout the project as an ongoing, definitive statement of what the project is and how it's being controlled. It's useful, for example, to Team Managers coming into a project part-way through as a reference to understand how the project is being run.

Getting clear on the Benefits Review Plan

Make sure that you're clear on the contents and function of the Business Case and the contents and function of the Benefits Review Plan. Sometimes the review plan becomes a little fuzzy as you work through the other detail of the method.

The *Business Case* is all about justifying the project. It details that justification and provides associated information, such as the estimated cost and time of the project and the degree of risk. If the project is justified, or part justified, by benefits – which is most projects – then the Business Case includes the details of the benefits and the likely value of them.

In contrast, the *Benefits Review Plan* is all about the actual measurement of benefits. Benefits Reviews are the checks to see that the benefits are actually there. So the plan is simply to set out when each review will take place and what benefits will be checked in each one. It also includes associated detail such as who's responsible for carrying out each review.

There's a tendency to think that benefits are only checked after the end of the project. If you've never encountered PRINCE2 before studying for the exams, then you're unlikely to make this wrong assumption. But if you work with colleagues who learned earlier versions of PRINCE2, then you may have picked this up from them, because before the 2009 edition it was emphasised. The 2009 edition is an improvement over earlier versions when it comes to benefits reviews, because the Benefits Review Plan specifically addresses the point that benefits can come on stream at different times:

- ✔ **During the life of the project.** If products are being taken into operational use during the project, not just in one 'big bang' at the end, then benefits are likely to come on stream during the life of the project as well. It's a real comfort factor for the Project Board and other stakeholders to get some early feedback on whether the project is leading to the benefits that were anticipated, even if it's just one or two of the benefits.

- ✔ **At the end of the project.** Some benefits are likely to be realised as soon as the project completes delivery of products, so benefits can be measured then and reported then in the End Project Report (as part of the review of the Business Case in that report). [**Manual** A.8.2, **P2FD** Ch9 Looking at business benefits]

- ✔ **After the end of the project.** In other words, post project. And this is where earlier versions of PRINCE2 laid the emphasis with the Post Project Review (PPR). In the 2009 edition of the method, PPR is now gone, but if your organisation still uses that term, be careful that you don't carry that earlier emphasis into the exam. That's not to say that you won't have one or more reviews after the end of the project; it's very common to need them. It's just that PRINCE2 is now much more specific about having reviews earlier as well.

Practising With Some Questions

On the following pages, you'll find some questions based on the Initiating a Project process. The answers are on the grey-edged pages at the end of the chapter.

The questions in this chapter are examples for you to practise with, preferably to time. They don't cover everything that you're likely to be asked. To prepare for the exam, you need to be confident in all areas of the subject, not just to learn the answers to these particular questions.

Foundation-level questions

You'll find answers to these questions, and some explanation, at the end of the chapter. Set your timer for eight minutes then go for it.

1. Which of the following does NOT form part of the Project Initiation Documentation (PID)?

❑ a) Business Case

❑ b) Project Plan

❑ c) Risk Management Strategy

❑ d) Stage Plan for the first delivery stage (the stage after the Initiation Stage)

2. Which of the following strategies defines how change control will be carried out?

❑ a) Risk Management Strategy

❑ b) Quality Management Strategy

❑ c) Configuration Management Strategy

❑ d) Communication Management Strategy

3. Which of the following is an accurate definition of a stakeholder in PRINCE2?

❑ a) Someone who's a member of the project's Project Board

❑ b) Someone who can affect, or be affected by, the project

❑ c) Someone with financial responsibility for the project

❑ d) Someone who's responsible for the delivery of business benefits

4. Which of the following is used in PRINCE2 to record when business benefits will be measured?

❑ a) Benefits Register

❑ b) Business Case

❑ c) Benefits Review Plan

❑ d) Project Cashflow

5. Which of the following options names plans which are created in the process Initiating a Project?

❑ a) Project Plan and Benefits Review Plan

❑ b) Project Plan together with all Stage Plans

❑ c) Project Plan and Business Plan

❑ d) Benefits Review Plan and Team Plan

6. Which of the following does PRINCE2 include as a section in the full Business Case?

❑ a) Benefits Review Plan

❑ b) Benefits Realization Schedule

❑ c) Investment appraisal

❑ d) Cost–benefit analysis

7. Which role is responsible for producing the Project Initiation Documentation (PID)?

❑ a) Executive

❑ b) Senior User

❑ c) Sponsor

❑ d) Project Manager

8. Which of the following phrases is part of the purpose statement for the process Initiating a Project?

❑ a) To establish a clear organisation structure for the project

❑ b) To produce a Stage Plan for each delivery stage to determine total costs

❑ c) To ensure that all risks in the project have been identified and their management planned

❑ d) To establish solid foundations for the project

9. Which of the following is NOT used as an input to the activity Prepare the Risk Management Strategy?

❑ a) Project Mandate

❑ b) Project Brief

❑ c) Lessons Log

❑ d) Daily Log

10. Which of the following products are created in the process Initiating a Project?

A. Risk Register

B. Issue Register

C. Project Plan

D. Project Product Description

❑ a) A, B and C

❑ b) A, B and D

❑ c) A, C and D

❑ d) B, C and D

Practitioner-level questions

There's no additional scenario information for these questions. However, don't forget to keep in mind, where you need it, the original scenario information, which you'll find at the end of Chapter 2.

To read some advice on dealing with the different styles of Practitioner question, please also see Chapter 2.

Set your timer to 18 minutes, but if you can answer accurately in slightly less time, then that's good. In the exam you'll have 10 questions in a section, about 15 minutes to answer them and the section will cover Start Up as well as Initiation. This part of the chapter gives you a generous 12 questions – hence the 18 minutes – and just on the process Initiating a Project, so you've got lots to practise with.

Classic-style questions

Answer the following questions about the Project Initiation Documentation (PID) for the New Business Unit project.

Remember to limit your answers to the number of selections requested in each section.

1		Which **2** statements should be included in the Business Case?
	A	The new business unit will be located in a suite of three offices at headquarters.
	B	The cost of structural alterations is high because the building is very old.
	C	The project is expected to take five weeks.
	D	The Executive will be responsible for the Business Case throughout the project.
	E	A major risk facing the project is problems with the new doorways causing delay.
2		Which **2** statements should be included in the Communications Management Strategy?
	A	Project Support will assist the Project Manager in keeping track of progress.
	B	There will be one Senior Supplier and one Senior User on the Project Board.
	C	The members of the management board are stakeholders and are to be kept informed of project progress by being included in Highlight Report (progress report) distribution.
	D	Communications asking for change will be prioritised on a five-point scale, where 1 is top priority and considered essential, and 5 is a low priority, cosmetic change.
	E	A Highlight Report (progress report) is to be produced every two weeks.
3		Of the following statements, which **2** should be included in the Configuration Management Strategy?
	A	Issues will be sent direct to the Project Manager, not to Project Support.
	B	The Project Manager is responsible for maintaining this strategy during the project.
	C	The Issue Register will have the standard PRINCE2 headings but with the additional section of 'contact'. This will be used to record the name of the person who knows most about the matter covered by the issue, who may or may not be the issue author.
	D	The Project Initiation Documentation will be formally approved by the Project Board, and a copy of the Business Case will be sent to the Director of Finance.
	E	The Project Plan will go through formal Quality Review before being approved.
4		Identify **2** decisions that are made in the process Initiating a Project.
	A	The frequency at which the Project Manager will report progress to the Project Board.
	B	The quality activities to be carried out in each stage.
	C	Whether the project should continue beyond Initiation into the first delivery stage.
	D	How stage-level products will be allocated to teams to create and check.
	E	The number of management stages in the project.

Matching-style questions

	For each item of information in column 1, please select the correct product from column 2 in which the item should be recorded as part of the work involved in Initiating a Project. An option in column 2 may be used once, more than once or not at all.	
	Column 1	Column 2
5	New risks identified by those working in the project will be notified to the Project Manager by submitting an issue.	A Risk Register
6	The scale to be used for priorities is MoSCoW: Must have, Should have, Could have, Won't have.	B Risk Management Strategy
7	The resourcing schedule assumes that the project won't be delayed by more than two weeks, and so there won't be a resource conflict on the electrical work. (The electrician is already committed for the company's stand at the annual trade exhibition.)	C Quality Register D Quality Management Strategy E Project Plan
8	Audits will be performed at least twice in each stage to be sure that tests have been carried out and that they've been done by the right people.	F Issue Register
9	There may be a delay in staff vacating the last office, leading to delay on starting structural work for the new doorways and so to the whole project.	G Configuration Management Strategy
10	Electrical safety standards will be met on all installations, and health and safety standards will be met for the final design and also in carrying out work.	H Change Register
11	A risk workshop will be run towards the end of the Initiation Stage, and this will be the main technique used to identify risk affecting this project.	

Sequence question

	Answer the following question about the sequence in which the following management products will be produced for the New Business Unit project.	
12	Which sequence shows the correct order in which these items will be created if the Business Unit project is following the default sequence of activities shown in the PRINCE2 manual?	
	1. The Benefits Review Plan	
	2. The Risk Register	
	3. A statement on the tailoring of PRINCE2 to meet the specific needs of the project	
	4. The Communication Management Strategy	
	5. A project-level Product Flow Diagram	
	A	1, 2, 3, 4, 5
	B	2, 5, 1, 3, 4
	C	1, 2, 5, 3, 4
	D	2, 4, 5, 1, 3
	E	4, 2, 1, 5, 3
	F	3, 1, 2, 4, 5

Answers to the Foundation-level questions

1 **d.** Stage Plan for the first delivery stage. The Business Case, Project Plan and Risk Management Strategy are included in the PID. [**Manual** A.20.2]. The Stage Plan is separate, because it's not 'whole project' – there are usually a series of Stage Plans, because most projects are multi-stage – and the Project Initiation Documentation (PID) covers the whole project.

2 **c.** The Configuration Management Strategy is badly named, because the name leads you to think it covers just Configuration Management. In fact, the strategy also covers issue handling and change control. Configuration management is, of course, closely coupled with change control, but they're not the same thing.

3 **b.** You'll find some definitions in the glossary of the manual, and this is worth a look through when you're revising. In this case, the glossary helps because the main body of the manual introduces confusion where it talks of stakeholder engagement but doesn't first make a clear distinction between stakeholders within the project and those outside it. As with much of the 2009 manual, if you already understand the method you can make sense of the text, but if you don't know the method you can become very confused.

4 **c.** Some questions are easier to answer if you look carefully at the exact words. Here the word 'plan' within the name 'Benefits Review Plan' hints at the answer, even if you didn't already know.

5 **a.** A Stage Plan is created on the stage boundary, just before that stage begins. Stage Plans are not created *en bloc* for the whole project during Initiation. There's no such thing as a Business Plan in PRINCE2. When needed, a Team Plan is created when a Work Package (assignment) is received by a Team Manager during a delivery stage, not during Initiation.

6 **c.** The Benefits Review Plan is a separate product. There's no such thing as a Benefits Realization Schedule in PRINCE2, and cost–benefit analysis is a technique, not a heading in the Business Case. 'Investment appraisal' is a heading in the PRINCE2 Business Case. [**Manual** A.2.2, **P2FD** Ch11 Writing a Business Case]

7 **d.** The Project Manager consults others while producing the PID, but is responsible for it.

8 **d.** Sadly, there's no short cut here. You need to be familiar enough with the purpose statements to be able to recognise what is a part of a statement and what isn't. The trouble is that the statements are generally worded in a strange and contorted way, so it's not immediately apparent what process or theme a particular phrase belongs to. [**Manual** 14.1]

9 **a.** Unless you're blessed with a photographic memory, you're not going to remember all of the 'activity summary' diagrams in the manual. However, they do form a useful reference to help you be clear on things when revising. Each activity has an activity summary diagram, and the relevant one here makes the inputs clear. [**Manual** Figure 14.2]. For this question, you should have picked up on the mandate being the answer, anyway, because it's left behind once the Project Brief is prepared back in Starting Up a Project.

10 **a.** The Project Product Description (PPD) is created in Starting Up a Project. It may be updated during Initiation, but the question specified 'created'. Again, a warning to take note of every word in the questions, especially when you're under time pressure.

Answers to the Practitioner-level questions

Classic-style questions

1 **C and E.** 'Timescale' and 'Major risks' are both headings in the Business Case. [**Manual** A.2.2]. The Practitioner is an open-book exam in that you can refer to your copy of the manual. As advised in Chapter 2, if you get questions of detail on any PRINCE2 product, then it's sensible to flip the manual open. You can then glance at the composition of the product while you're dealing with the question. This question becomes relatively easy to answer with the manual open at the composition section of the Business Case, and that's the exam strategy point I'm making in this question.

2 **C and E.** Stakeholders are described in the strategy, as is the timing of communications, which includes the Highlight Report. In the context of this book, there's an exam strategy point behind this question too. The answer letters are exactly the same as in Question 1: C and E. Be careful not to try and replace your PRINCE2 knowledge with second-guessing what the person setting the question would or wouldn't have done in terms of the structure of the paper.

3 **A and C.** It's an option in PRINCE2 for issues to go to Project Support first, so the clarification on this point for the project is appropriate to the 'Issue and change control procedure' section of the strategy. The content of the Issue Register is appropriate to the 'Records' section. [**Manual** A.6.2 Records]

Answer B, that the Project Manager maintains the strategy, is arguably something that could go in the 'Roles and responsibilities' section of the strategy, but it would not be a very good answer. The default for any PRINCE2 project is that the maintenance responsibility lies with the Project Manager, so there's little point saying it. The main focus of the 'Roles and responsibilities' section is to say who's responsible for actually doing the configuration management. This answer is included to give an example of where you might find more answers than you need, in which case go for the 'most right'. For more on exam strategy if you find more than one correct answer, have a look at Chapter 2.

Answers D and E are not strategic matters, and E especially is more suited to the Product Description. If you haven't learned as far as Product Descriptions yet, don't worry, but you should see nevertheless that these answers are matters of detail on specific documents, not something at a strategic level.

4 **A and E.** The frequency of progress reporting by the Project Manager is determined in Initiation, because it will apply for the whole project. The information is recorded in the Communication Management Strategy and may also be mentioned in the 'Controls' section of the Project Initiation Documentation (PID). The number of management stages is also decided and built into the Project Plan drawn up in Initiation. The exact quality activities to be carried out in the different stages is done as part of stage planning, just before that stage starts, not in Initiation. Similarly how stage-level products will be allocated is done either as part of stage planning or later in the stage as the work progresses. Even if you've not learned that far in the method yet, you should be aware that the process Initiating a Project is to do with project-level plans and controls, not stage level plans and controls. Whether the project should continue into the delivery stages is a decision made at the end of the Initiation Stage. However, it's covered by the process Directing a Project and is the first activity in that process; it's not covered by any of the activities in Initiating a Project.

Matching-style questions

5 **B.** The procedures for handling risks are included in the Risk Management Strategy. If you associate the word 'strategy' with the thought 'It's *how* we're going to do this,' it often becomes much easier to spot if something is likely to be in a strategy where you don't already know for sure.

6 **G.** The Configuration Management Strategy includes a scale for the priority of issues and changes. The Risk Management Strategy also has scales, but risks don't have priorities, so MoSCoW wouldn't be used. Risk scales are to do with things like severity and impact.

7 **E.** The Project Plan includes the 'planning assumptions' on which the plan is based. This note explains a planning assumption about the timing of the electrical work.

8 **D.** This is a 'how we're going to do this' relating to quality, so it belongs in the Quality Management Strategy. It belongs in the section 'Timing of quality management activities'. [**Manual** A.22.2, **P2FD** Ch13 Writing a Quality Management Strategy]

9 **A.** This is a risk, and quite a significant one, and so requires an entry in the Risk Register.

10 **D.** The Quality Management Strategy again, this time the 'Quality standards' section, which is listed as an example in the 'Quality control' part of the strategy. [**Manual** A.22.2]. If you're particularly aware of the products in Start Up and Initiation, your thoughts may have strayed to the Project Approach as a possibility. However, if they did, you should have got back on track pretty quickly, because the Project Approach isn't listed in column 2 as an option.

11 **B.** The Risk Management Strategy and the 'Tools and techniques' section within it.

Sequence question

12 **D.** The sequence is:

2 The Risk Register is created as part of the activity 'Prepare the Risk Management Strategy'.

4 The Communication Management Strategy has its own activity, so this is an element in the sequence which you should have found easy, simply by looking at the process model. [**Manual** Figure 14.1]

5 The project-level Product Flow Diagram is part of the Project Plan.

1 The Benefits Review Plan is produced during the activity 'Refine the Business Case'.

3 The statement about the tailoring of PRINCE2 is included in the final Project Initiation Documentation (PID). You may argue that it can be done earlier than this, and you're right. However, it isn't mentioned in the earlier activities of the process, and the question did specifically state that the answer should be according to the default sequence as shown in the manual. Be careful here not to confuse what's in the manual with what may be acceptable practice in live projects. An exam strategy point behind this question is to remind you that the exam is based on the manual.

Chapter 7

Controlling a Stage

The process of Controlling a Stage can seem a bit daunting when you see the number of activities. Indeed, it's a busy process, but it's very straightforward when you take on board that it's simply the day-to-day work of the Project Manager (not counting the end stage stuff that the process Managing a Stage Boundary covers).

Revising the Controlling a Stage Process

The Controlling a Stage process is basically so simple that if it didn't already exist, you could quickly design it yourself. When I'm delivering a training course, I often get those on the course to do pretty much that. Without them looking at the book or any other notes, and before we've done the course session on the process, I ask them to tell me exactly what the activities are going to be. 'And' I tell them, 'I do mean *exactly*!' And they do; often much to their surprise, but they do because they can put together things I've taught them earlier on the course. Because PRINCE2 is basically logical, it's also very predictable. Picking up my approach from the course, what is the Project Manager doing day to day then?

✔ Controlling the flow of work out to project teams

   • Giving out work assignments (Work Packages) to Team Managers

   • Checking progress on the Work Packages

   • Getting the work back when it's finished

✔ Dealing with any new issues and risks that are sent in

✔ Checking how the stage is going against its plan, and whether the risk situation has changed or whether anything is affecting the Business Case

✔ If the stage is going off track, taking action in one of two ways:

- Dealing with it if it's within the Project Manager's delegated authority; that may involve changing the plan a bit, and so affects how further Work Packages are given out to teams

- Referring the problem to the Project Board if it's beyond the Project Manager's authority to deal with – such as when a stage will go significantly over its planned time no matter what the Project Manager does

✔ Reporting progress to the Project Board with the information and at the frequency set down in the Communications Management Plan or the 'Controls' section of the Project Initiation Documentation (PID)

There's nothing difficult about that bullet-point list. When you see the activities in groups – such as the three activities dealing with the control of Work Packages – then the process actually becomes very easy to absorb. The underlying logic of the process can drive your memory and your understanding and make revising that much easier.

To help plan your revision, have a look at the following two checklists. If you can't confidently put a tick against any item, then highlight that point for extra revision and have a closer look at it. If you've already done Foundation and are revising for the Practitioner exam, do cast an eye over the Foundation checklist nonetheless, to be sure that you've retained an understanding of all those areas. Don't just focus on the additional areas needed for the Practitioner exam.

Revision checklist – Foundation

❑ Work Packages – an instruction pack asking a Team Manager to build a product, or more than one if it makes sense to do them together.

❑ Work Packages as a control – Team Managers don't just start work when they feel like it, but when they are instructed to do so with the issue of a Work Package.

❑ Each team involved in the stage will work through one or more Work Packages in that stage. A team may have a whole series of Work Packages or just one or two.

❑ The boundary between the process Controlling a Stage and Managing Product Delivery is usually the customer–supplier interface. If you have supplier teams, their Team Managers will be involved with the Managing Product Delivery process.

❑ The Controlling a Stage process repeats for as many stages as there are in the project.

❑ The activities in the process – look at the process model and check that you know what each activity is about and what management products it involves, either to update or create those products.

❑ Controlling a Stage drives the delivery stages but 'calls' other processes for parts of the work. For example, it calls the Managing a Stage Boundary process towards the end of the stage to prepare for the End Stage Assessment and to produce the Stage Plan for the following stage. That's with the exception of the final stage in the project, where the Closing a Project process is called instead.

❑ The Highlight Report – the progress report produced by the Project Manager on a regular, timed basis and sent to the Project Board and any others who need to see it, as set
down in the Communications Management Strategy.

❑ The two levels of action if a stage deviates from its plan. If Project Managers can
resolve the matters within their own authority limits, they will 'Take corrective action'.
If they cannot resolve matters within their delegated authority limits they must use the
activity 'Escalate issues and risks' to refer the matters to the Project Board.

❑ Not all issues go to the board. Project Managers deal with most issues within their
delegated authority. If issues are beyond Project Managers' authority, they must go to
the board or, if a matter is to do with a change and a Change Authority has been put in
place, by referring it to that Change Authority.

❑ Inbound issues can be dealt with formally or informally, and that makes a difference in
how they are captured in the activity 'Capture and examine risks and issues'. There's
more on risk handling and issue handling later in the chapter in the section 'Clarifying
Some Key Points'.

❑ The use of the Issue Report and the information it contains.

Revision checklist – Practitioner

Check out these additional areas for your Practitioner revision:

❑ The Work Package function to specify the interface between the Controlling a Stage
process and Managing Product Delivery. In other words, how it sets down the way in
which the Team Manager and Project Manager will work together while a particular
part of the work is being carried out, such as the requirements for progress reporting.

❑ The default in PRINCE2 is for the Project Manager to come from the customer side of
the customer/supplier environment, not the supplier side.

❑ The products of Controlling a Stage – are you sure that you understand all the headings in each product and how that product is used in the process?

- Configuration Item Record
- Exception Report
- Highlight Report
- Issue Register
- Issue Report
- Lessons Log
- Product Status Account
- Quality Register
- Risk Register
- Stage Plan
- Work Package

❑ The adjustment of products to fit the needs of the project.

Clarifying Some Key Points

This section gives a bit of help on some key points in case you're not quite sure of them. If, when you look at a heading, you feel confident that you know about the area, then simply skip it and move on to the next one.

Understanding Work Packages

If you've read this chapter from the beginning, then you've probably already picked up on what a *Work Package* is, even if you weren't absolutely clear before. It's simply a work assignment given to a Team Manager by the Project Manager.

You can think of the Work Package as being an instruction pack where the Project Manager tells the Team Manager:

- What is to be produced in the assignment
- How things are to be communicated to the project management level from the delivery level (such as team progress reporting – Checkpoint Reports)
- How the finished work is to be returned or reported as complete

The Work Package, then, is both an instruction and an authority to produce a single product or perhaps two or three products which it makes sense to work on together. For example, for the cabling in a new suite of offices, there's a need, say, for mains electrical cabling, lighting cabling and computer cabling. A decision has been made to give that work to a cabling company, and that company will send in a cabling team. But it makes sense for the team to do all the cabling at once and so 'build' the three products in parallel rather than do all of the mains cabling and finish it, then tackle the lighting and finally the computer cabling. The Work Package will specify that there are three products involved, and it will include copies of the three Product Descriptions.

Getting to grips with exception management

Exception management works at different levels in PRINCE2. Basically it allows everyone to get on with the job unless something is projected to go outside pre-specified limits such as a cost band. To revise exception management, have a look at the Progress theme chapter, Chapter 17. However, *PRINCE2 For Dummies* has much more detail, if you need clear explanation. [**P2FD** Ch17 Managing 'By Exception']

The Controlling a Stage process is the filling in the sandwich of the three levels where exception management is used in PRINCE2: project level, stage level and team level. The Project Manager is accountable to the Project Board for running the stage within the predetermined limits, but will also set limits (tolerances) on the Team Managers for their Work Packages. So, the Project Manager will receive information on the status of each Work Package relative to its tolerance limits, but will also report to the Project Board on the status of the stage within its tolerances.

Being clear on when to escalate and when not to

The Project Manager has delegated authority to manage the stage. The Project Board should not, then, be involved in the day-to-day work of management. Owing to the rather strange approach and wording of the 2009 edition of the manual in relation to issue handling, you may be forgiven for thinking that the board is very involved in day-to-day things. However, the reality of the underlying dynamic is still the same: the Project Board stands back and lets the Project Manager get on with it, but within limits.

Consequently, Project Managers need only escalate something to the Project Board when the action will exceed their delegated authority. That doesn't mean that the Project Manager can't ask for a view, though. Just as in normal organisational management someone can 'run it past the boss', so too the Project Manager can get a view from one or more members of the Project Board. Giving such advice is a function of the Project Board in its activity 'Give ad hoc direction' within the process Directing a Project.

Appreciating the extent of the stage status review

When you first look at the activity 'Review the stage status', you'll probably think about progress control. That's fair enough, because it's an important function of the activity. However, the activity has a wider scope, and you need to be aware of it. You'll probably appreciate that the Business Case is checked at the end of each stage. In most projects, and especially those in a dynamic business environment, it clearly makes sense to check the Business Case more often than that. If so, then this is the activity that covers it. Equally, in a project with any degree of risk, you're not going to leave risk monitoring until the end of the stage, although it's an important check at that point. More frequent monitoring of risk is also done during a stage, and again it's the 'Review the stage status' activity that covers it.

The review activity will normally be triggered at set time intervals, such as every week or every two weeks. However, there's a second important trigger that you should be aware of, which is the area of issue handling. In the process, model you'll see that the activity 'Capture and examine issues and risks' leads in to the review activity. The review comes before taking any necessary action on the issue to adjust the stage or escalate it to the Project Board. Have a look at Figure 7-1 to see the flow. For clarity in the figure, the flow is from left to right.

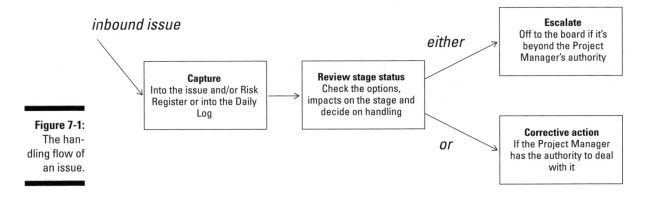

inbound issue

Capture
Into the issue and/or Risk Register or into the Daily Log

Review stage status
Check the options, impacts on the stage and decide on handling

either

Escalate
Off to the board if it's beyond the Project Manager's authority

or

Corrective action
If the Project Manager has the authority to deal with it

Figure 7-1:
The handling flow of an issue.

Handling issues and risks

An issue can be sent to the Project Manager from anyone 'with an interest in the project or its outcome', which could be someone completely outside the project. In a real project, you may have very good reason to question that, but remember that the exams are based on the manual.

Using more than one register

Remember than an issue can lead to entries in more than one register. For example, if someone sends in details of a problem, it may be significant enough to record in an Issue Report, with the control information duplicated in the Issue Register. However, examination of the issue may also reveal a significant risk that even the author of the issue was unaware of. This may justify an entry in the Risk Register.

It doesn't help that, unlike earlier editions, the 2009 edition of the PRINCE2 manual doesn't include information in Appendix A for an issue. There's a short explanation in the main text, repeated in the glossary, but that's both inaccurate and misleading, because it describes the issue as 'a relevant event that has happened', but the continuing explanation correctly lists examples, of which some are not events!

Appreciating the types of issue

There are three types of issue, and you need to understand all three. You'll find more on revising this area in Chapter 16, which covers the Change theme. Chapter 16 also has a quick quiz so you can quickly check your understanding of the three types. If you're struggling with the types, stick with it because the problem is in the wording of the 2009 edition of the PRINCE2 manual, which is particularly poor in the area of change and issues. The 2009 manual mostly makes sense if you already understand PRINCE2, but it's an uphill struggle if you're trying to get to grips with the method for the first time – so don't think it's just you having difficulty. You might find *PRINCE2 For Dummies* rather easier to follow for explanation, if you have a copy to hand.

Practising With Some Questions

On the following pages you'll find some questions based on the Controlling a Stage process. You'll find the answers, with a bit of explanation, on the grey-edged pages at the end of the chapter.

The questions in this chapter are examples, and some are aimed at bringing particular points of exam strategy to your attention. Before your exam, you should also have a go with the official practice papers available from your training provider or from the exam authority. For the Foundation, do the official sample paper after you've finished learning the method, or when you've nearly finished. That's because, unlike in this book, the questions are not grouped by subject but rather are in random order.

Foundation-level questions

Have a go with these questions to check your knowledge at Foundation level. Try to do the questions in eight minutes or less.

1. What's the name of the progress report produced by the Project Manager in the process Controlling a Stage?

❏ a) Stage Progress Report

❏ b) Highlight Report

❏ c) Checkpoint Report

❏ d) Stage Control Report

2. Progress reports, produced during each stage, are sent to Project Board members. What does the Project Manager check to see whether a copy should be sent to anyone else?

❏ a) Daily Log

❏ b) Communications Plan

❏ c) Issue Log

❏ d) Communications Management Strategy

3. Why does the Project Manager check the Benefits Review Plan from time to time during a delivery stage?

❏ a) To update it with benefits achieved to date

❏ b) To record who is responsible for specifying benefits

❏ c) To enter details of disbenefits identified in the Initiation Stage

❏ d) To see whether any benefits reviews are due and, if so, arrange them

4. If Project Managers notice that a stage is deviating from its plan, what should they do if control action is within the authority limits delegated by the Project Board?

❑ a) Take corrective action and continue with the stage, adjusting any Work Packages as necessary.

❑ b) Record a recommended action and, before taking it, confirm that the board is happy for the delegated allowance to be used in this way.

❑ c) Implement the control action but inform the board afterwards of the exact nature of the problem and the action implemented to correct it.

❑ d) Plan a preferred action and get approval from Project Assurance before taking it, to be quite sure that required standards and controls are complied with.

5. When Project Managers receive a progress report from a Team Manager, what should they do?

❑ a) Copy it to the Project Board members for information.

❑ b) Pass it to Project Assurance for checking that the data is accurate.

❑ c) Update the Stage Plan with the progress data.

❑ d) Update the Work Package with the progress data.

6. If a valid new risk is reported to the Project Manager by a team member, what first action should the Project Manager take?

❑ a) Make an entry in the Risk Register.

❑ b) Refer the risk to the Project Board, which has ultimate authority for risk.

❑ c) Write a Risk Report.

❑ d) Refer the risk to the team member's Team Manager.

7. If the stage is projected to go only very slightly outside stage cost tolerance (the plus and minus amounts set by the Project Board), but this will not affect project cost tolerance, what should the Project Manager do?

❑ a) Escalate the matter to the Project Board immediately.

❑ b) Keep the position under regular review, and escalate the matter to the Project Board if it does worsen and threaten the project cost tolerance.

❑ c) Inform the Project Board of the problem in the next Highlight Report (progress report) and include the new cost projection in that report.

❑ d) Ignore the matter until the end of the stage and report the minor cost overrun in the End Stage Report.

8. Which statements are a stated purpose of the process Controlling a Stage?

    A. Report progress to the Project Board

    B. Deal with issues

    C. Assign work to be done

    D. Create Exception Plan(s) if required

    ❏ a) A, B and C

    ❏ b) A, B and D

    ❏ c) A, C and D

    ❏ d) B, C and D

9. Which PRINCE2 activity does a Project Manager perform before taking action to correct a stage that's deviated from its plan, or before escalating details of that deviation to the Project Board?

    ❏ a) Give ad hoc direction

    ❏ b) Review the stage status

    ❏ c) Review Work Package status

    ❏ d) Report highlights

10. When performing the activity 'Review Work Package status', the Project Manager updates the Stage Plan. Why is this?

    ❏ a) To check whether the team has any further Work Packages to do in the stage, in order to start preparing the next Work Package, if there is one, for the team

    ❏ b) To update the plan with actuals (time actually taken and money spent) to date, forecasts and adjustments, using progress information from the Team Manager

    ❏ c) To monitor whether the project remains likely to finish within the tolerances (upper and lower limits) set by corporate or programme management

    ❏ d) To record details of Project Assurance checks carried out on the related Work Package, and the time and cost of performing those checks

Practitioner-level questions

Have a go with these Practitioner-level questions against the clock. There's no additional project scenario for these questions, but do keep in mind the original scenario information set down at the end of Chapter 2.

You should allow 18 minutes for answering these questions, which is because there are 12 to have a go with. In the exam, you'll have 10 questions in a section and about 15 minutes to answer them. You can look at your PRINCE2 manual to help answer, but try not to look up so much so that you time out. If you're unclear on how to tackle any of the styles of question, have a look at Chapter 2 where you'll find some help.

Matching-style questions

	Answer the following questions about the project to prepare the new e-business office suite. For each item in column 1, select the correct PRINCE2 product in column 2 where that information would be recorded first. An option in column 2 may be used more than once or not at all.	
	Column 1	Column 2
1	A team member has sent in a new risk about the effectiveness of quality checks. The Project Manager disagrees that it is a risk.	A Checkpoint Report
2	A Team Manager has texted the Project Manager to say that the furniture supplier just phoned to say that some items ordered are not in stock and while they can be obtained, they won't arrive until two weeks after the rest of the new furniture.	B Issue Report C Highlight Report D Exception Report
3	The Project Manager has just entered a low probability risk into the Risk Register related to project staff availability in the final stage of the project. Project Board members now need to be made aware of the risk, though it's not urgent and they don't need to take any action at the moment.	E Daily Log F Lessons Log G Risk Register
4	The new manager of the e-commerce unit has said that due to a major new product launch, which will promote ordering through the web site, the offices could be needed a week earlier than planned.	H None of the products A-G above
5	The Senior User has been checking the last Highlight Report and now wants to ask the Project Manager a question about the forecast stage timing.	
6	A Team Manager has assembled information on the progress of her current Work Package and it's time to pass this information on to the Project Manager.	

Classic-style questions

	Answer the following questions about the activities in the process 'Controlling a Stage' in relation to the project to refurbish the suite of offices for the new e-commerce unit.
	Remember to limit your answers to the number of selections requested in each section.
7	A team member has found a way of doing some of the cabling work more quickly and cheaply by using existing but disused cables running under the office floors. He has submitted an issue asking for permission to do this and for the cabling plan to be changed. What should the Project Manager do about this issue?
A	Accept the idea immediately as it is a benefit, and alter the cabling plan as requested.
B	Refer the issue to the Senior Supplier to make a decision.
C	Refer the issue to Project Assurance as it will change an agreed document.
D	Investigate the matter to find out if the team member is right and if the existing cabling is suitable for use in the way suggested.
E	Refuse the suggestion as the cabling plan has already been checked and signed off.
8	In a regular check of the stage status, the Project Manager has discovered that costs have risen because some essential electrical fittings were slightly more expensive than budgeted. Because of other small overspends on earlier items, this will take the stage over the cost tolerance (limit) set by the Project Board. The projected overspend is trivial at only £1.05 over tolerance, however at this point in the stage it's unlikely that any further purchases will be cheaper to offset this overspend. What should the Project Manager do?
A	Report the matter to the Project Board immediately as an exception - a projected breach of the financial limits on the stage – albeit a small one.
B	Monitor the spend and only report it if the overspend gets significantly worse on remaining things to be purchased in this stage.
C	Do nothing for the moment, but report the matter on the next Highlight Report.
D	Ignore the overspend and mention it in the report at the end of the stage.
E	Tell the team not to install the more expensive items and to return them for a refund.
9	Towards the end of the first delivery stage, the Executive attended a senior management briefing in the company where the new Managing Director expressed serious concerns about excessive email and paper communications throughout the organisation. The Executive has now instructed that Highlight Reports should not be produced at set intervals but only when requested by her. What should the Project Manager do?
A	Inform the Executive that the requested is refused because it doesn't comply with the chosen, PRINCE2, project method.
B	Refer the matter to Quality Assurance, which has responsibility for organisational standards, including project standards and put an entry in the Risk Register.
C	Accept the request and make a note of the instruction in the Daily Log.
D	Explain the functioning of the Highlight Report to the Executive in the context that there are no regular progress meetings in PRINCE2. If the Executive still insists, make a note in the Daily Log and also update the Communications Management Strategy.
E	Ignore the request as the PRINCE2 method is a published 'best practice' authority.

Sequence question

	Answer the following question about the sequence of actions for handling a stage level exception (projected breach of stage limits set by the Project Board).
10	A problem has been reported in the project to prepare the offices for the new e-business unit. It is likely that the problem will only lead to a breach of stage cost tolerance, not time tolerance, if some slight adjustment is made to the work being done by one of the teams. Which sequence gives the correct order for the handling of a stage level exception in the process Controlling a Stage where there is no identified need for exception planning.

1. Adjust the Work Package(s) as necessary

2. Record and examine the issue reporting the problem

3. Receive ad hoc direction from the Project Board

4. Adjust the Stage Plan to show the change in work to be done by the team involved

5. Escalate the issue

A	2, 5, 3, 4, 1
B	2, 4, 1, 3, 5
C	5, 3, 2, 1, 4
D	5, 3, 2, 4, 1
E	3, 1, 4, 5, 2
F	4, 5, 3, 2, 1

More classic style questions

	Answer the following questions about issue handling in the process 'Controlling a Stage'. Remember to limit your answers to the number of selections requested in each section.	
11	During the first delivery stage the team discovered damaged wood that will need repair first. What **1** option correctly reflects action, or lack of it, to update the Project Plan?	
	A	No modification is needed of the Project Plan since it only showed what was expected at high level at the start of the project
	B	The Project Plan should be updated at the end of the stage
	C	The Project Plan should be updated immediately
	D	The Project Board should be consulted on whether or not the Project Plan should be kept up to date with changing detail, or if Stage Plans will be enough on their own.
12	After the start of the first delivery stage, a team member has found a faster way of doing some preparation work on the walls and ceilings of the offices, without reducing quality, and has suggested this on an issue. What **1** action should the Project Manager take?	
	A	Ignore the issue as the work is the responsibility of the Team Manager
	B	Record the issue in the Issue Register or Daily Log and investigate it further
	C	Refer the matter on to the Senior Supplier for decision and any necessary action
	D	As it's minor matter, send the issue back to the team member without recording it and tell them to go ahead as suggested if they're sure it will work

Answers to the Foundation-level questions

1   **b.** The Highlight Report, produced in the activity 'Report highlights'.

2   **d.** In its 'Reporting' section, the Communications Management Strategy includes details of the recipients of communications, and such communications include the Highlight Report. The thinking in the manual around the area of communications management and the Project Controls section of the Product Initiation Documentation (PID) remains fuzzy, but in this question the PID wasn't listed as an option. Be careful: there's no such thing as a Communications Plan in PRINCE2. Some questions may include plausible-sounding answer options, and you need to be really sharp on what is PRINCE2 and what isn't, particularly if your organisation uses the non-PRINCE2 term.

3   **d.** Remember that benefits may come on stream during the project, not just at the end of it and after it. The Benefits Review Plan lists all benefits checks. It's a plan for checking benefits, as its name suggests, and it isn't used for recording benefits.

4   **a.** The whole point of giving delegated authority is that someone can get on with the job within those limits. The Project *Manager* should get on and manage. You'll find this reflected in the flow of the activities in the process, and it's the content of the activity 'Take corrective action'. The Project Manager may take advice before setting action in train, but that may not be necessary. The other answer options indicate mandatory involvement of others in the handling of every issue, and that just isn't true.

5   **c.** The progress information from a team will be fed into the Stage Plan.

6   **a.** It's important to 'capture' risks, and that's part of the function of the Risk Register. It's unlikely that the full information will be available yet – such as on how the risk will be handled – but that doesn't stop the Project Manager setting up the entry, which can be supplemented with further details as they become available.

7   **a.** The Project Manager has no discretion to do anything other than refer the matter to the board and to do so without delay. The tolerances represent a specific instruction from the Project Board – the Project Manager's 'boss'– that should the projections go outside the stated limits, then the board must be told immediately.

8   **a.** A no-brainer once you see the purpose statement for the process. [**Manual** 15.1]. This question is to reinforce the point that you need to be able to recognise the elements of purpose statements, although you don't need to learn them by heart. This question is kinder than it might first appear if you're familiar with the stage boundary work, because then you should have picked up on the point that exception planning falls into the Managing a Stage Boundary process, not this one, which is Controlling a Stage.

9   **b.** This is a check to see 'where we are now' before deciding whether action is within the Project Manager's delegated authority. If you're not clear on the point, have a look at Figure 7.1 earlier in this chapter.

10   **b.** The Stage Plan must be kept up to date to serve any useful function in controlling the stage, and so actuals are entered when this information arrives from Team Managers in, or accompanying, Checkpoint Reports. [**Manual** 15.4.2 last bullet point, **P2FD** Ch7 Controlling the flow of work to teams – Checking progress on Work Packages]

Answers to the Practitioner-level questions

Matching-style questions

1   **E or H.** Team members sometimes misunderstand things and can even get carried away in their enthusiasm for spotting risks. The Project Manager is responsible for the Risk Register and can't be dictated to by over-zealous team members who were watching disaster movies at home the previous evening and who now warn that asteroid collisions may damage the project. The matter may be recorded in the Daily Log together with the Project Manager's reasons for turning it down, or dealt with by talking to the team member involved and not using any of the documents. The answer E is usually better practice, so that there's a brief record of what happened if it's questioned later.

2   **B.** This looks serious enough for the issue to be formally handled. The first step is to record the detail of the issue, using the Issue Register and an Issue Report. There may or may not be associated risks requiring one or more entries in the Risk Register, but that would come when the issue is thoroughly examined and the question asked where that information would be recorded *first*.

3   **C.** The Project Manager can use the Highlight Report to bring things to board members' notice, including a new risk where the members don't need to take any action. [**Manual** A11.2, Key issues and risks, **P2FD** Ch7 Warning the board of issues and risks]

4   **B.** Another issue. You might argue that this is a risk, but it would almost certainly be handled as an issue of which one dimension is risk. This question involves some degree of personal judgement, and it's here to show that sometimes the answer is not always clear cut. The person who set the question probably thinks that the answer is very clear, but other practitioners may disagree – and do in the PRINCE2 trainer events when questions are discussed! In cases like this, choose the answer which seems the 'most right' and most in line with the manual.

5   **H.** There is – quite rightly – no product to cover a minor enquiry from a Senior User, and such an enquiry certainly wouldn't be an issue. Any board member can lift the phone to talk to the Project Manager about something on a Highlight Report without it being formally recorded. Imagine if every time your boss asked you something, it all had to be written down – completely unnecessary and very impractical.

6   **A.** The Checkpoint Report is the progress report from a Team Manager to the Project Manager. Don't confuse this with the Highlight Report, which is the progress report from the Project Manager to the Project Board (that's the next level up).

Classic-style questions

7   **D.** The process model shows that the first activity for an inbound issue is 'Capture and examine issues and risks', and this action falls into the 'examine' part.

8   **A.** If the Project Manager calculates that the stage will finish outside tolerance and cannot adjust it to bring it back within the limits, then the stage is in exception. The Project Manager has no discretion whatever and must report the exception immediately. It would be pointless to return the items, which are described as 'essential', and so not being able to complete the project.

9   **D.** The Project Manager is bound, ultimately, to do as the Executive instructs, but it makes sense to talk about it first to explain the function of the Highlight Report. Remember that the strategies are not carved in stone and can be modified during the project, although this would more normally happen at a stage boundary.

Sequence question

10   **A.** You can follow this sequence through by looking at the activities in the process model, but hopefully you answered the question without needing to look at your PRINCE2 manual. Although exception handling is covered in the Progress theme, you really need to be familiar with it to make sense of the Controlling a Stage process, even if you haven't tackled the Progress theme yet.

More classic-style questions

11   **B.** The 'official' and so correct exam answer is that the Project Plan will be updated on the stage boundary, not in the process Controlling a Stage, which is the subject of this section. In practice, that's likely to be different, but this question is partly to emphasise the point that the exams are based on PRINCE2 as set down in the manual.

12   **B.** The Project Manager should record the issue one way or the other (register or log) and then check it out. It shouldn't be ignored or passed to a Project Board member. Neither should a Project Manager send it straight back and tell the team member to get on with it. What if the team member was wrong? At the very least, the Project Manager would be likely to talk to the Team Manager about the issue, as part of the 'examine' function of the activity 'Capture and examine issues and risks'.

Chapter 8

Managing Product Delivery

*A*s you come to revise the process of Managing Product Delivery, you'll be pleased to know that there's some good news. In fact, there are two bits of good news. The first is that, because this process has the smallest number of activities, with just three, it will be fairly fast to revise. The second bit of good news is that the activities are particularly simple in concept. Don't think that because it's so straightforward you must have missed something!

Revising the Managing Product Delivery Process

The process covers the work to deliver the product or products involved in a particular Work Package. The Work Package is simply a work assignment from the Project Manager. It may be to build a single product, or perhaps two or even more, when it makes sense to build those products together.

As you revise, make sure you're clear on what a Work Package is. For the Practitioner exam in particular, check that you know what the individual headings in the Work Package are all about. If you think any explanations in the manual are unclear, make some short notes on the manual pages so you can look at your reminders during the exam.

You can't take any PRINCE2 reference material at all into the Foundation exam. For the Practitioner-level exam, you can take in your copy of the PRINCE2 manual complete with any notes you've written onto the manual pages. However, you can't take in separate notes in any form, even sticky notes stuck to the pages of the manual.

'Managing Product Delivery' is part of PRINCE2, of course, which in turn is all about project management. So, the activities in this process are not about doing the teamwork but about managing the teamwork. In fact the biggest part of the project is here because, in terms of PRINCE2, this is where all the team products are built and tested, but in management terms it's all very easy.

The three activities in the process can be summed up as 'get the Work Package, build and test the product(s), and then hand the product(s) back'.

Revision checklist – Foundation

For the Foundation exam, run through this list to make sure that you're familiar with each area. If you're unsure of anything, don't tick it off until you've revised it again.

- ❑ Appreciate that the activities cover the work of the Team Manager, not the Project Manager (unless the project doesn't have any Team Managers).

- ❑ Understand that each team may work, sequentially, on more than one Work Package in each stage, so each Team Manager may use the Managing Product Delivery process several times in a stage.

- ❑ Understand that the Work Package provides instructions to build the one or more products covered by the package, and includes a copy of the relevant Product Description(s).

- ❑ The use of the Work Package as an instruction pack, but also as the authority which is the trigger for the Team Manager to start the work. Team Managers don't just do project work when they feel like it. The Work Package is a Project Manager control mechanism.

- ❑ The purpose statement and objectives for the process.

- ❑ The three activities, and the fact that the middle one, 'Execute a Work Package', is not only where team products are built but also where all the testing is done. It's too late to start testing products in the third activity when they're being returned.

- ❑ Following on from the last point, that Quality Review is a type of test (typically of a printed product such as a technical specification or plan). If the technique is to be used for a specialist product in a Work Package, as required in the Stage Plan, it will be done in the 'Execute a Work Package' activity.

- ❑ That the results of a Quality Review go into the Quality Register, just like for any other test.

- ❑ Team Plans are optional. If the Work Package is straightforward, the Team Manager may be able to control it with the detail set down in the Stage Plan, and so won't need to produce a Team Plan.

- ❑ Checkpoint Reports, at the frequency set down in the Work Package, and with the content specified there too.

- ❑ Appreciate that the team doing the Work Package may be from outside the customer organisation, and its Team Manager may not even know that the project is running under PRINCE2, because the Work Package gives the information that the Team Manager needs to do the job.

Revision checklist – Practitioner

For the Practitioner exam, make sure that you're still familiar with the Foundation-exam areas in the previous section, then check these additional ones:

❑ Work Packages – when they are created, what they're all about and what each heading means.

❑ The Quality Register, and that you understand that it will be kept up to date with the results of tests. If something fails a test and needs to be re-worked and then re-tested, that new quality activity (the re-testing) will be entered into the Quality Register.

❑ The detail of the Checkpoint Report. Are you clear enough on the headings and the use of each one, so that you can pick out wrong entries in an example with errors?

❑ How the activities work and can be adjusted to fit the project. For example, adjusting the first activity 'Accept a Work Package', depending on whether a Team Plan is needed. That includes feeling confident to spot where the activities have not been used sensibly in the scenario project in the exam.

❑ The management products involved in the process – what they are, how they are used in the process and by whom:

   ❑ Checkpoint Report – to report progress on the Work Package

   ❑ Configuration Item Record – to record changing information such as 'draft' and 'final' states as the work progresses

   ❑ Issue Report – may be created by a knowledgeable PRINCE2 Team Manager rather than just sent as a free-form issue

   ❑ Product Description – one or more are included in the Work Package

   ❑ Quality Register – to keep track of quality actions and also to enter any new ones that become necessary (such as re-testing of products which initially failed a test)

   ❑ Work Package – the 'instruction pack' to build one or more products and, as a Project Manager control mechanism, to control the flow of work to teams

❑ The fit of the principles and themes with the process (there's more on this in Chapter 19).

Clarifying Some Key Points

Because the overall process is pretty simple, you may have understood everything the first time around. However, skim through the following section to check that you're really clear. If, as you start to read about a point, you know you're clear on it already, then skip ahead to the next one.

Understanding who runs the process

By default, the Managing Product Delivery process is run by a Team Manager, but remember that the Team Manager role is optional. In a small project with only one team, there may not be a Team Manager, so the Project Manager will run the process instead. In turn, that will make the interface between this process, Managing Product Delivery, and the main process being used by the Project Manager during the stage Controlling a Stage nominal. The divide will still be there, but it will be limited because a Project Manager is not going to sit in the office, alone, and formally discuss the Work Package and agree it with him or herself!

In a larger project with a number of teams working simultaneously on Work Packages, a similar number of Team Managers will use the process at the same time.

Seeing when to produce a Team Plan

In PRINCE2, Team Plans are optional. The default place to create a Team Plan, if one is needed, is in the first activity of the process, which is 'Accept a Work Package'. It's possible that Team Plans will be created at the same time as the Stage Plan in the process Managing a Stage Boundary, and the stage plan built up from the Team Plans, but that more unusual application doesn't usually figure in the exams.

The choice over whether to produce a Team Plan will lie primarily with the Team Manager, although the Team Manager may well discuss this with the Project Manager. The decision hinges on whether the Team Manager thinks that he or she can control the delivery of the Work Package using just the Stage Plan. If the project is a big one and the Stage Plan, therefore, is still relatively high level, there may not be enough detail in that plan for effective Work Package control. In that case, the Team Manager will develop a Team Plan. This will be checked out with the Project Manager to make sure it's consistent with the relevant part of the Stage Plan.

Understanding the exception cascade

If you haven't learned as far as *Exception Management* yet, then in brief it's where work is allocated with plus and minus limits within which the job must be accomplished. The most common limits are time and cost. While work is proceeding on track to end somewhere between the upper and lower limits, the manager in charge of the work can continue. However, if at any point the work is forecast to go above an upper limit or fall below a lower limit, then the matter must be reported immediately.

Exception Management is an important control in PRINCE2. When you first learn about it you will probably do so in the context of stage management, where the limits are set by the Project Board to define the Project Manager's delegated authority for that stage. However exception works at more than one level; in the context of this process, Managing Product Delivery, you need to appreciate that tolerance limits may have been set for the Team Manager by the Project Manager. Those tolerances will be recorded in the Work Package. If, at any time during the work, the Team Manager calculates that this assignment will finish outside one or more of the tolerance limits, then the Work Package is said to be *in exception* – hence the name of this control being Exception Management.

If you've learned about tolerances but are still a bit unclear, try looking at *PRINCE2 For Dummies*. [**P2FD** Ch17 Managing 'By Exception']

It's possible that an exception on a Work Package – where it's projected to exceed the tolerance limits – may send the whole stage into exception, and so the matter will need to be referred to the Project Board. It's important to appreciate, however, that if that is the case, then the matter is being referred to the Project Board because it's a stage exception, not because it's a Work Package exception. An exception is reported to the management level above – to the level that set the tolerances. It may well be that a Work Package exception sets off a cascade and even the project ends up in exception, in which case the Executive will need to report it to corporate or programme management.

Looping the loop with teamwork

Each team will receive one or more Work Packages in a stage, so the process is repeated, potentially many times, in each stage as each team works on a Work Package. Different iterations of the process can be running at the same time and be at different points. So, while one team is hard at work building and testing products, the Team Manager of another is just receiving the next Work Package for the team, while a third Team Manager is in the process of notifying the Project Manager that a Work Package is now complete.

Practising With Some Questions

This next section gives some questions to practise with in both Foundation and Practitioner formats. All the questions are to do with the Managing Product Delivery process, so you can have a go at them as you're learning about this particular part of the method.

For the Foundation exam, remember that the exam itself, and the practice papers supplied by the Exam Board, will have questions in random order, not grouped by subject. It's difficult to use the official Foundation sample papers until you've learned the whole method.

For the Practitioner exam, you won't get a whole section on Managing Product Delivery. The process will be grouped with one or two other processes to make up an exam section. Typically, and predictably, Managing Product Delivery is grouped with at least the process of Controlling a Stage.

Foundation-level questions

Test your knowledge of Managing Product Delivery with these Foundation-level questions. Set your timer for eight minutes and go for it. You'll find the answers and a bit of explanation at the end of the chapter.

1. Which of the following is a report produced in the process Managing Product Delivery?

❑ a) Lessons Report

❑ b) Checkpoint Report

❑ c) Highlight Report

❑ d) Work Package Report

2. Which of the answer options completes the following purpose statement?

The purpose of the Managing Product Delivery process is to control the link between the Project Manager and Team Manager(s), by placing formal requirements on:

❑ a) The successful delivery of products to the required level of quality

❑ b) The reporting of progress, spending, issues and new risks

❑ c) Accepting, executing and delivering project work

❑ d) The delivery of work within specified time and cost constraints

3. The activities of the process Managing Product Delivery cover the work of:

❑ a) Team members

❑ b) The Team Manager

❑ c) The Project Manager

❑ d) The Project Board

4. Which of the following activities of the process Managing Product Delivery covers the management of the required tests of specialist products?

❑ a) Accept a Work Package.

❑ b) Execute a Work Package.

❑ c) Deliver a Work Package.

❑ d) None of the above; it's covered by an activity in the process Controlling a Stage.

5. What plan may be created in the activity 'Accept a Work Package'?

❑ a) Project Plan

❑ b) Stage Plan

❑ c) Exception Plan

❑ d) Team Plan

6. If a Team Manager finds a better way of doing something and wants this reported as a lesson learned that will help future projects, what should the Team Manager do?

❑ a) Submit a Lessons Report.

❑ b) Make a note in the Lessons Log.

❑ c) Report the lesson to Project Assurance.

❑ d) Note the lesson on the next Checkpoint Report.

7. If a Team Manager calculates that the work of a Work Package will exceed the maximum time limit (tolerance) set by the Project Manager, what should the Team Manager do?

❑ a) Report the matter as a 'lesson identified' when the Work Package is delivered, to help with more accurate estimation on future projects.

❑ b) Send an issue to the Project Manager, unless some other notification procedure has been specified in the Work Package.

❑ c) Do nothing until the next Checkpoint Report is due, at which point the details of the problem and the new estimated completion date should be put on record.

❑ d) Do nothing for the time being, but try to make time savings during the remaining work to minimise the delay.

8. Which of the following are part of the objective of the process Managing Product Delivery?

A. To ensure that work on products allocated to the team is authorised and agreed

B. To ensure that accurate progress information is provided to the Project Manager at an agreed frequency, to ensure that expectations are managed

C. To ensure Team Managers, team members and suppliers are clear as to what is to be produced and what is the expected effort, cost or timescale

D. To ensure that any delays in executing the Work Package do not impact the agreed delivery targets of the stage or of the project, as set down in the plans

❑ a) A, B and C

❑ b) A, B and D

❑ c) A, C and D

❑ d) B, C and D

9. Which of the following is NOT an activity within the process Managing Product Delivery?

❑ a) Accept a Work Package.

❑ b) Execute a Work Package.

❑ c) Review Work Package Status.

❑ d) Deliver a Work Package.

10. During work on a Work Package, which PRINCE2 management product should be reviewed regularly by the Team Manager?

❑ a) Daily Log

❑ b) Risk Register

❑ c) Quality Register

❑ d) Project Brief

Practitioner-level questions

Have a go with these questions and try to do them in 18 minutes. That will be going at the same speed as the exam where you'll have 10 questions in a section instead of our generous 12, but then about 15 minutes for answering them. So, read the additional scenario, then set your timer and go for it with the questions.

When looking to find out what is wrong with a sample product, it helps to glance first at Appendix A of the PRINCE2 manual to be clear in your mind how it should be. Then you have the contrast and you can spot many of the errors more rapidly.

Additional scenario

Please take into account the following additional project scenario information to supplement the main project information at the end of Chapter 2.

Extract from Work Package WP2-2 for delivery stage 2

1. Checkpoint Reports for this project will be produced daily.

2. Three teams are working in this stage, so there are three Work Packages – one for each team. This Work Package covers all the products being developed in the second delivery stage by the Works Team (Team 2).

3. The Checkpoint Reports for this Work Package will be produced by the Project Manager with assistance from Project Support, using information supplied by Team Managers and team members, including forward projections of 'estimated time to complete' for the work.

4. The five products in this Work Package will be worked on in turn by the team, and as each is completed it will be returned to the Project Manager, or completion notified by email.

5. This Work Package includes a copy of the Stage Plan covering this part of the development. Based on the Stage Plan, the Project Manager has also produced a series of Team Plans, each one covering the construction of a product in the Work Package. Team Managers should check the Team Plans when they first receive them to ensure that they fit the current staff allocations to their teams. They should also ensure that timescales are realistic and that the plan fits in with team members' other commitments outside the project.

6. Any problems with the structural alterations when the new doorways are being made in delivery stage 1 may cause a delay in the start of delivery stage 2 and the work of all teams involved in the stage.

Warning: This information may contain errors

Classic style questions

Answer the following question about the Work Package content given in the additional project scenario for this section. Remember to limit your answers to the number of selections requested in each section.

1	Paragraph 1 is about the frequency of Checkpoint Reports. Which **1** action should be taken with this paragraph?	
	A	The entry is correct because daily reporting would be sensible due to the tight timescales which represent a high risk for the Works Team in this Work Package.
	B	Reduce the frequency to weekly Checkpoint reporting.
	C	Reduce the frequency to monthly Checkpoint reporting.
	D	Replace the paragraph with the words 'A Checkpoint Report will be submitted by the Team Manager at each product delivery 'milestone'.
	E	Remove the paragraph completely as it is incorrect for a Work Package entry.
2	Paragraph 2 is about the packaging of stage products into Work Packages. Which **1** action should be taken with this paragraph?	
	A	Leave the paragraph in place, but list the products which are included.
	B	Delete just the first sentence which is explaining the way the stage work is being structured, not the detail of the specific Work Package.
	C	Delete the whole paragraph as it is incorrect and reveals a misunderstanding of the correct use of Work Packages in a PRINCE2 project.
	D	While the approach is acceptable move the statement to the Project Initiation Documentation (PID) to update it, as the approach affects the whole project not just one particular Work Package.
	E	The entry is correct as written, so leave it as it is.
3	Paragraph 3 is about the responsibility for producing Checkpoint Reports for the Work Package. Which **1** action should be taken with this paragraph?	
	A	Leave the paragraph in place as it correctly reflects an option for progress reporting in a PRINCE2 project.
	B	Remove the words 'with assistance from Project Support' since support staff should not carry responsibility for progress reporting, but leave the rest of the paragraph intact.
	C	Replace the paragraph with the words 'Progress reporting will be by team members submitting time sheets to the Project Manager on a weekly basis'.
	D	Replace the paragraph with the words 'The Team Manager will produce Checkpoint Reports but these will only cover equipment purchases since the time of team members is paid for by the company anyway so doesn't need to be recorded or reported'.
	E	The entry is incorrect and should be removed completely.

4	Paragraph 4 is about the return of products. Which **1** action should be taken with this paragraph?
A	Remove the entry as it reflects a misunderstanding of a Work Package in a PRINCE2 project.
B	Leave the paragraph as it is because this is an acceptable application of the process in a PRINCE2 project.
C	Leave the paragraph in place, but remove the words 'will be worked on in turn' because it may be acceptable for some products to be created in parallel.
D	Remove the words 'or completion notified by email' since the PRINCE2 activity 'Deliver a Work Package' requires that all products should be returned to the Project Manager.
E	Remove the reference to 'five' as authorised changes could alter the number of products allocated to the Works Team in Delivery Stage 2.

5	Paragraph 5 is about the provision of plans. Which **1** action should be taken with this paragraph?
A	Remove the paragraph except for the first sentence.
B	Remove the paragraph completely since the Project Manager should not produce Team Plans.
C	Change the entry to show that the Team Manager will produce a Team Plan for each product in the Work Package.
D	Change the entry to show that Project Assurance will provide a Team Plan for each product in the Work Package
E	The entry is correct as written as this is an acceptable application of PRINCE2 to a Work Package, so leave it as it is.

6	Paragraph 6 is about possible delay resulting from structural work in Delivery Stage 1. Which **1** action should be taken with this paragraph?
A	Leave the paragraph in place as it warns of a potential problem with the timing of the Work Package that the Team Manager needs to be aware of.
B	Remove the words 'when the new doorways are being made' since any other works in Delivery Stage 1 could also cause delay.
C	Remove the paragraph altogether and put the information into the Risk Register.
D	Remove the paragraph altogether and put the information into the Quality Register.
E	Remove the paragraph altogether and put the information into the Lessons Log.

Assertion–reason style questions

A long-serving electrician on the Works Team is more familiar with the cabling throughout the old HQ building than the Team Manager. The Team Manager thinks that this team member's knowledge of existing cable routes will be invaluable in speeding up the planning of the cabling alterations for the new offices.

Each row in the table below consists of an assertion statement and a reason statement. For each row identify the appropriate selection from options A to E that applies. Each option can be used once, more than once or not at all.

Selection	Assertion	Reason	
A	True	True	AND the reason explains the assertion
B	True	True	BUT the reason does not explain the assertion
C	True	False	
D	False	True	
E	False	False	

	Assertion		Reason
1	The electrican should develop the Team Plan for the cabling Work Package	BECAUSE	the electrician has better detailed knowledge of this part of the work than the Team Manager.
2	During the cabling work, the Project Manager should refer any changes to the Work Package directly to the electrician	BECAUSE	once the work is underway on a Work Package, team members will report progress directly to the Project Manager as it will affect the running of the stage.
3	The Team Manager should discuss the cabling Work Package with the Project Manager when receiving it	BECAUSE	it is important that the Team Manager is clear on what is to be delivered and understands controls such as the reporting requirements.
4	If the electrician hits an unforeseen problem with the cabling work, this should be reported to Quality Assurance	BECAUSE	Quality Assurance have responsibility for quality standards and procedures throughout the customer organisation.
5	A Checkpoint Report should be produced by the Team Manager when the cabling work is complete	BECAUSE	in PRINCE2, the Checkpoint Report is used to notify that a Work Package is finished and that the team is ready to take on another one if it has another to do.
6	The electrical work will be tested according to the Product Description and the team member who creates a product must always have responsibility for tests	BECAUSE	the Product Description sets down the quality method to be used to ensure that the product meets the specified quality criteria.

Answers to the Foundation-level questions

1. **b.** Lessons may be reported by a Team Manager, but this is done by putting them on the Checkpoint Report, not by producing a Lessons Report. The Lessons Report is always produced by the Project Manager in PRINCE2. There's no such thing as a Work Package Report, and the Highlight Report is the progress report from the Project Manager to the Project Board, so is not created in this process, which is to do with the Team Manager's work.

2. **c.** They all sound possible don't they? This admittedly nasty question is to make the revision point that you need to be familiar with the purpose statements, not merely understand them. The key to knowing the correct answer in this instance is remembering that it's the summary of the three activities that make up the process.

3. **b.** This is the only process that covers the work of the Team Manager.

4. **b.** When accepting a Work Package, no products have been built yet, so they can't be tested. In delivering the Work Package, the products are being reported complete, so it's far too late to start testing them. What if they fail a test?

5. **d.** It's the Team Plan that may be created in this process. But it's 'may', because Team Plans are optional.

6. **d.** It's back to lessons learned, and again stressing that a Team Manager will report lessons in the Checkpoint Report. Team Managers don't submit Lessons Reports, neither do they make notes in the Lessons Log, which is the Project Manager's document. Project Assurance are primarily concerned with audit, not active project work such as collecting lessons. You'll find 'Lessons identified' in the 'This reporting period' section of the Checkpoint Report. [**Manual** A.3.2]

7. **b.** Under the exception management procedure, projections that a Work Package will exceed the defined limits must be reported immediately. If not, why have limits? The whole purpose of them is to act as a reporting trigger.

8. **a.** The giveaway that statement D is wrong is that it's describing stage and project control, which can't be within the control of a Team Manager concerned with an individual Work Package. So the correct parts of the objective are A, B and C. [**Manual** 16.2]

9. **c.** Review Work Package Status is a PRINCE2 activity, but it refers to the Project Manager's check of the Work Package as part of the process Controlling a Stage. It might have looked like a tough question if you weren't sure of the answer, but then again there are only three activity names to remember for this process, so it's not too unkind.

10. **c.** The Team Manager should be aware of what quality activity is needed on the products in the Work Package and be checking to ensure that those activities are being carried out. The Daily Log and Risk Register are the Project Manager's responsibility, while the brief was left behind long ago when the Product Initiation Documentation (PID) was created. The Team Manager may also check the Risk Register, but this is not as central as the checks on the Quality Register, so 'c' is a better answer.

Answers to the Practitioner-level questions

You should have had some fun with the first six Practitioner questions, if there is such a thing as fun when revising for a PRINCE2 exam. The extract from the Work Package is all horribly wrong, and hopefully you'll have found some of the possible answers entertaining as you looked for the right ones. The objective of these questions is to get you to focus first on what the product should be, as suggested in the 'Remember' note at the start of the section. When you're clear on the right use of the product, then for each question it's easier to filter out most – if not all – of the wrong answers, so that you quickly get to the right one, or at least reduce the field so you can focus in on a smaller number of possibilities. If you were really clear on the Work Package, you might have been able to go straight for the right answer to each question with limited attention to the other possibilities. It's always worth a quick look at the other answers though, just in case one of them looks sensible and warns you that your first shot at the right answer may be incorrect and need checking.

Classic-style questions

1 **E.** The entry is incorrect because it relates to the whole project, not to this particular Work Package. The default in PRINCE2 is that requirements for Checkpoint Reports are set down in the 'Reporting arrrangements' section of the Work Package, so that requirements can be varied between one Work Package and another. For example, a high risk Work Package may justify more frequent reporting than a low risk one being done at the same time by a different team.

2 **C.** Paragraph 2 is a complete misunderstanding of the correct use of Work Packages. A Work Package is an instruction to build a product or a group of perhaps two or three products, if it makes sense to build them together and it's the same team doing it. Work Packages are not written team by team, but product by product. Each team, potentially, may work through many Work Packages in each stage. [**P2FD** Ch7 Figure 7-2]

3 **E.** Again, a big misunderstanding of PRINCE2 is reflected in the paragraph. The Checkpoint Report is the regular progress report created by a Team Manager and sent to the Project Manager at the intervals specified in the Work Package – which may or may not be weekly.

4 **A.** More misunderstanding, and you should have identified this quickly because the statement runs counter to the three activities in the process. The 'delivery' activity is done when all the products in that Work Package are complete and have successfully passed the test (unless they have been approved off specification). The whole point of the Work Package is that it's a single unit of work and may comprise one product or more than one. If there are several products in the package, they will be delivered, or reported complete, in one go at the end, and not individually. If delivery is to be product by product in sequence, then each product should be in its own Work Package.

5 **B.** Still more misunderstanding of the planning and control in PRINCE2. This Project Manager is clueless, was clearly trained by an inferior training company (not mine) and passed the exam by fluke (it happens), so you can be encouraged that there's hope for you yet! The Team Manager produces Team Plans, normally on receipt of the Work Package, if they are required at all. It's an option that Team Plans are produced at the same time as the Stage Plan, but this is not done independently of the Team Manager, as seems to be the case in the scenario paragraph.

6 **C.** The statement describes a risk. The Team Manager needs to know about risks and will look at the Risk Register as well as discuss these risks with the Project Manager. However, the Work Package does not contain risk information. There's a good practical argument for saying that the Work Package should contain risk information, but at the moment, as Appendix A of the manual shows, it doesn't. [**Manual** A.26.2]

It's unlikely in the exam that you'll get a set of questions based on a product that's so completely wrong. This Work Package example, hopefully, gave you a bit of light relief in your revision and some confidence that you can spot errors because you know how PRINCE2 works in this area. It was also to break you out of any assumption that because one section of a product contains an error, the next one is more likely to be correct. If you think something is the right answer, then select it and don't be swayed by thoughts that 'they wouldn't have set the questions like that in the exam'. Keep your focus on PRINCE2, not on any assumptions about how the paper may or may not have been constructed.

Assertion–reason style questions

1 **D.** The scenario information at the start of the question panel shows that the second statement is correct. The Team Manager should draw on that knowledge when constructing the Team Plan, but it doesn't mean that the Team Manager should abdicate responsibility for the plan. It's the Team Manager, not a team member, who owns the plan.

2 **E.** Rubbish! The team members are not part of the PRINCE2 project management team, and the Project Manager wouldn't bypass a Team Manager. Equally, progress for the whole team is reported by the Team Manager with Checkpoint Reports. Progress is not reported by individual team members.

3 **A.** The Team Manager will indeed discuss the Work Package with the Project Manager, and the reason statement gives just two items from the list in the PRINCE2 manual. [**Manual** 16.4.1]

4 **D.** Problems are dealt with in the project not by consulting Quality Assurance, which is involved with standards in the organisation, not operational work in a project. If you're a bit unclear on Quality Assurance, in terms both of what it is and how it differs from Project Assurance, be sure to check it out. [**Manual** 6.2.6, **P2FD** Ch12 Understanding Organisational Assurance]

5 **E.** More rubbish! The Checkpoint Report is a time-driven control, typically produced weekly, to notify progress while the work is underway. It isn't used as a completion notification after a deafening silence throughout the work.

6 **D.** Did you read the question carefully? The question said that the testing responsibility 'must always' be given to the team member who creates the product. It's usually the case that it's better to have different people testing the product to the ones who created it. It may sometimes be better for the same people to both build and test a product, but that's a judgement for a particular product, not a general requirement. Five areas of quality are covered in a Product Description, and the 'quality method' is indeed one of them.

Chapter 9

Managing a Stage Boundary

*T*he management stage boundary is a crucial control in PRINCE2 – in fact it's the most important control. The stage boundaries form key points where the Project Board will check that the project is okay and then specifically authorise the next 'block' of work – the next stage.

Going through PRINCE2 processes can be a bit overwhelming. You may find that all the process and activity boxes begin to blur together and march around inside your head, rather like the pink elephants in the Walt Disney film *Dumbo*. However, if you can stand back and see the logic, then everything is easier both to understand and remember, and you can send the pink pachyderms packing.

Managing a Stage Boundary is straightforward – really it is. It doesn't look it, especially with the rather unhelpful way that the diagram in the manual has an entry point at the bottom, so that the main flow is upwards. So, put the diagram out of your mind for a moment. Instead, imagine yourself as a Project Board member on a significant and expensive project. The Project Manager has come to ask you to authorise the £3.5 million spend on the next stage and to sign the authorisation. The Project Manager holds the authorisation in front of you, and you're more than a bit nervous: if this all goes badly wrong, your name will be on the authority, despite your clever scheme to sign it with such an awful signature than nobody will be able to recognise it.

As a Project Board member, what would you want to know before giving the authority to proceed? You would probably take the following views of the project:

✔ **A look back:** For the stage that's just finishing, how did it go? Did it deliver smoothly or were there problems with warning signs of more severe things to come? Was the spending according to plan? Did the plan accurately reflect the work, or was extra essential work found that had been missed off the plan, which in turn resulted in lots of changes and recasting of estimates?

✔ **A look at where the project is now:** Is it still justified – is the Business Case still sound? Are the benefits projections still as they were at the start, or better? How about the risk position? If the negative risk has shot up and the benefits projections have fallen through the floor, perhaps you shouldn't sign and instead you should be thinking about shutting the project down.

> ↳ **A look ahead:** What about the Stage Plan for the next stage? Is it sensible, complete, realistic and achievable? If you sign it but you don't believe it's achievable, then you're just asking for project failure.

If all three views are okay – the look back, the present position and the look forward – you start to relax and reach for your pen to sign the authority. Well, the three views sum up what Managing a Stage Boundary is all about. The process covers the work of the Project Manager getting exactly that information together to present to the Project Board. Given that logic, the activities are straightforward enough.

The pattern in PRINCE2, as in most staged approaches to projects, is that the stage planning is done towards the end of the previous stage, using the very latest information available. It doesn't make sense in most projects to plan everything in fine detail at the beginning, because so much can change as the project progresses. Such change can be in the business environment, with technology, with resourcing or in the light of what happens in the earlier parts of the project. There's a slight difference when the process is triggered by an exception, but you'll find more on that in the next two sections.

Revising the Managing a Stage Boundary Process

There are two product-related areas of work for the Project Manager in the process. The first is producing new management products, notably the Stage Plan for the next stage. The second area is to update ongoing project documentation such as the Project Plan and the Project Approach.

As you revise the process, watch out for poorly named activities. The most misleading is the activity 'Update the Project Plan', which actually covers much more than updating the Project Plan. It involves checking the Project Initiation Documentation (PID) and updating anything that needs it, including the strategies. In the list of recommended actions for the activity, the manual gives a few examples of changes that may be needed, but be aware that the changes can go wider than the examples given. [**Manual** 17.4.1]

Those who already know PRINCE2 appreciate the need to update the PID on the stage boundary anyway, so in practice it doesn't cause too much of a problem. The manual is very much harder to follow if you're learning PRINCE2 and you find the text hard to follow or find that it assumes prior knowledge. If you get confused, try *PRINCE2 For Dummies*, where the style is more relaxed than the official PRINCE2 manual can be and there's more explanation. [**P2FD** Ch6, Understanding the Process of 'Managing a Stage Boundary']

A second activity with a rather misleading name is 'Update the Business Case', which indeed performs that update, but also the related product, the Benefits Review Plan. For good measure, the activity can update a couple of registers as well: the Risk Register and the Issue Register.

Revision checklist – Foundation

Scan down this revision checklist and, if you can't tick any item confidently, that warns you to look at the point again as part of your revision:

❑ The purpose and objective statements for the process – predictably

❑ The two triggers of a stage boundary – this is an important point, and there's more on it in the section 'Clarifying Some Key Points'

❑ Understanding that the process is not used at the end of the last stage in the project – the Closing a Project process is used instead; there's more on this in Chapter 19

❑ The activities of the process and the suggested sequence of them – as shown by the arrows in the process model

❑ Who's doing what in the activities – it's mostly the Project Manager

❑ What management products are being input into the process and what products are being created – in the manual, the activity summary tables, one for each activity, make a good reference

❑ That an Exception Plan may include an adjusted Project Plan, and possibly Team Plans, as well as a revised Stage Plan

❑ That where the process is happening part-way through a stage because of an exception, work done to date is not re-planned and included in the Exception Plan – instead it's closed down and there's an End Stage Report for it

❑ The interaction of Managing a Stage Boundary with PRINCE2 principles and themes

Revision checklist – Practitioner

For the Practitioner exam, make sure you're clear on the points in the Foundation checklist above, then add these four areas to your revision check:

❑ The exact way in which PRINCE2 themes are called into play on a stage boundary – this is fairly intuitive, but make sure that you're clear.

❑ What products are created and updated on a stage boundary, and why; as noted in the Foundation revision checklist, you'll find the products listed for each activity in its activity summary diagram in the manual. You'll also find a reference panel at the end of the relevant chapter in *PRINCE2 For Dummies*, which lists the major products and explains why they're updated or created [**P2FD** Ch6 Checking out the major stage boundary products].

❑ The content of the products used on a stage boundary – that you know what each section of each product is about and can spot errors in 'critique' questions.

❑ How the process can be adjusted to suit different situations in a project – but don't get too worried about this, because the exam doesn't expect you to be able to deal with a complex project situation.

Clarifying Some Key Points

The process Managing a Stage Boundary isn't actually very difficult to understand, but it can seem so at first until you get the idea of the overall structure. Your understanding hinges on appreciating the two triggers. The triggers are covered in the first clarification point below. Have a glance at each point in the section and, if you're confident that you already understand it, skip it and move on to the next one.

Understanding the two triggers

The normal trigger of the process is when the Project Manager is checking out the status of the current stage and sees that the end of the stage is getting close. The Project Manager realises that it's time to start preparing for the next stage and getting ready for the Project Board check of the project at the End Stage Assessment. Effectively, the Project Manager fires off the stage boundary process and starts work on the next Stage Plan.

The second trigger is when a stage has gone into exception part way through, and the Project Manager realises that the stage is going to breach one or more of the limits such as time and cost set by the Project Board (the *tolerances*). To get out of the problem, everyone realises that the rest of the stage – and perhaps the project – is now going to have to be done differently from how it was originally planned. Clearly, then, the existing Stage Plan will be of no use. The Project Board instructs the Project Manager to prepare an Exception Plan. That instruction forces a stage boundary that wasn't originally intended. The work done up to this point in the stage is closed down as an end stage, and there's an End Stage Report for it. The remaining work in the stage is re-planned by creating an Exception Plan. Because the plan is at stage level (and may also include an update to the Project Plan), it must be approved by the Project Board, so it goes to the board in the same way as at any end stage. The main difference is that this time the board meeting is called an Exception Assessment.

Seeing why exception doesn't always need the stage boundary process

An exception need not lead to re-planning. It's a fairly common misunderstanding to think that every exception forces a stage boundary. That misunderstanding can result from focusing on the PRINCE2 documents and mechanisms to the exclusion of day-to-day reality. A good trick here is to try to think 'real life', and you'll see that PRINCE2 actually fits, and its mechanisms come into a better context. For example, if the stage goes slightly over cost tolerance, the Project Board may decide that it had been a little tight on tolerance in the first place, and simply increase it a bit. Or if the overspend is due to some unforeseen complexity, the board may just authorise a small increase to the stage budget. In that case, the Project Manager would carry on with the work in line with the original plan, perhaps working to a revised tolerance. Or the Project Board may decide that the project is no longer viable. In that case, the Project Board wouldn't instruct that a new plan be prepared, but rather that the project should be shut down – so the Closing a Project process would be triggered instead.

Knowing what gets created and what gets updated

The products created on a Stage Boundary are those associated with planning. Remember that a plan is a comprehensive beast in PRINCE2, containing, as it does, product plans, activity plans and resource plans. It also has to include financial plans, although the method remains very strangely quiet on this vital element of planning and only mentions it out of the corner of its mouth. Having said that the plan includes product plans, I should remind you not to forget that in turn that means the planning diagrams at stage level and also Product Descriptions for the stage-level products. Some, or perhaps all, of the products at this new level of detail will need to be version-controlled ('configuration managed' to use the PRINCE2 term) so Configuration Item Records will need to be set up to hold version information about the products. As you start to think the process through, you'll realise that there are indeed a lot of management products created in the process.

For the exams, be sure that you understand what products are created – not forgetting the End Stage Report, but also the wide range of products that may get updated. Most of those updates involve things within the PID, so to help get to grips with this you can simply think of the work as mostly updating any parts of the PID that need it. However, it's not just the PID, so don't forget things such as the registers. Have a look at Chapter 5 if you need to brush up on the PID and its contents, and also *PRINCE2 For Dummies*. [**P2FD** Ch5]

You may still feel a bit overwhelmed as you consider all the products in play, but remember that PRINCE2 is logical, so the use of products is actually rather straightforward. Clearly if work on the new stage plan reveals a couple of significant risks that hadn't been previously spotted, details of those risks should be entered into the Risk Register, so the register will be 'updated'. Then again, the stage planning may reveal the need for a product which will have to comply with a company, industry or legal standard. Perhaps up to this point in the project it wasn't realised that any products would need such compliance, so the standard wasn't mentioned in the Quality Management Strategy. Now that the need has been identified, the strategy will, logically enough, require updating. You may have detected, from various passing comments, that I'm not a fan of the 2009 edition of the manual. Happily, however, the method has the inheritance of the logic and careful thinking of previous editions, even back to Version 1 of the method and actually before that to its predecessor, the method PROMPT II. That underlying logic will help you as you learn and revise.

Practising With Some Questions

This next section gives some questions to practise with. All the questions are based on the stage boundary process, so you can have a go with them as you progress with your learning of PRINCE2 or revise this area after you've learned the whole method.

If you're studying for just the Practitioner exam having already passed Foundation, you may still like to have a quick go with the Foundation questions – which, of course, you should now get completely right, and very rapidly too. However, in the extremely unlikely and almost unimaginable event of you getting a Foundation question wrong, it can warn you of a gap in your knowledge which it's best to find now, before the Practitioner exam, while there's still time to do something about it.

Foundation-level questions

Test your knowledge of Managing a Stage Boundary with these Foundation-level questions. Set your timer for eight minutes. You can find answers and explanations at the end of the chapter.

1. Which of the following is an activity in the process Managing a Stage Boundary?

❑ a) Reporting stage end

❑ b) Updating the Project Initiation Documentation (PID)

❑ c) Updating the Stage Plan

❑ d) Reporting exception options

2. When should the process Managing a Stage Boundary be performed?

❑ a) During Initiation to produce a Stage Plan for each stage in the project

❑ b) Only if a stage goes into exception and requires an Exception Plan

❑ c) Only when instructed by the Project Executive, based on exact control needs

❑ d) At, or close to the end of, each management stage except the last stage

3. PRINCE2 expects the Business Case to be updated as part of the work of Managing a Stage Boundary. Which PRINCE2 principle does this primarily support?

❑ a) Focus on benefits

❑ b) Tailor to suit the project environment

❑ c) Continued business justification

❑ d) Learn from experience

4. Which role is responsible for updating the Benefits Review Plan, if required, at the end of a stage?

❑ a) Executive

❑ b) Business Assurance

❑ c) Project Manager

❑ d) Project Support

5. Why is the Quality Register updated in the process Managing a Stage Boundary?

❏ a) To enter the results of all the tests performed in the stage just finishing

❏ b) To record any changes in the responsibilities for achieving the required quality levels in the project

❏ c) To enter details of quality management activities required in the following stage

❏ d) To enter the total cost of quality activity in the stage just finishing

6. In the process Managing a Stage Boundary, which of the following is NOT part of the stated purpose of providing the Project Board with information?

❏ a) So the board can review the success of the current stage

❏ b) So the board can confirm continued business justification

❏ c) So the board can review Team Plans to ensure that they're achievable

❏ d) So the board can confirm that the risks remain acceptable

7. Within the PRINCE2 process Managing a Stage Boundary, which of the following activities should be done immediately after the activity 'Update the Project Plan'?

❏ a) Report end stage

❏ b) Plan the next stage

❏ c) Review product status

❏ d) Update the Business Case

8. Which other PRINCE2 process is triggered by the process Managing a Stage Boundary?

❏ a) Directing a Project

❏ b) Closing a Project

❏ c) Controlling a Stage

❏ d) Managing Product Delivery

9. Which of the following events can trigger the process Managing a Stage Boundary?

A. Nearing the end of a delivery stage, except the last stage in the project

B. Ad hoc direction from the Project Board

C. Nearing the end of the Initiation Stage

D. Nearing the end of work in the process Starting Up a Project

❑ a) A, B and C

❑ b) A, B and D

❑ c) A, C and D

❑ d) B, C and D

10. Which of the following plans is created in the process Managing a Stage Boundary?

❑ a) Project Plan

❑ b) Team Plan

❑ c) Benefits Review Plan

❑ d) Exception Plan

Practitioner-level questions

Read through the additional scenario and then try to answer the 12 questions in 18 minutes or less. In the exam itself, you won't get a whole section on just one process, and a section involving Managing a Stage Boundary will also include questions on Closing a Project and Directing a Project. Also in the exam, you'll have 10 questions and about 15 minutes to deal with them. Because there are 12 questions to practice with here, allow yourself slightly longer – 18 minutes – for answering. The 18 minutes includes any re-reading of the scenario information and looking anything up in the PRINCE2 manual.

Additional scenario

For the Practitioner questions in this chapter, please take into account the following additional project scenario information as well as the original information at the end of Chapter 2.

Extract from the Daily Log

Entry 23. 14 May. The Works Team has once again been called away from its project work to do maintenance work elsewhere – this time it's for work in the new Managing Director's office to replaster two walls and then redecorate. The new Managing Director has ordered that this be done as a top priority, so that he can settle in quickly after his appointment to the company. This is now the third time that works staff have been called away to do other things.

Entry 24. 16 May. Called the furniture supplier at 3 p.m. this afternoon to confirm everything is okay. Delivery of most new furniture will be on time, but there's a problem in getting enough side tables of the same design as the desks in the time available before it's necessary to furnish the office. The supplier can get enough side tables for three of the offices, but not for all four. A few other similar-looking side tables can be provided in time, but they aren't exactly the same design as the desks.

Entry 25. 16 May. Checked with Kath Orford, the new manager of the e-business unit, about the side table supply matter (see log entry 24). She says that provided the tables look similar to the desks and are the right size, and the side tables within each of the four offices are the same design, she doesn't have a problem if they don't match the desks exactly. I've just emailed the Senior User as a heads up on this and am now recording an issue with a view to asking for a few side tables to be accepted off spec. See Issue Report 2/12.

Entry 26. 17 May. 11.15 am. Claire from the Works Office phoned to say that a few minutes ago two members of the Works Team handed in their resignations. These staff have been poached by a transport company which is moving into large office premises on the other side of town. The team members have given a month's notice, but unfortunately each has two weeks' annual leave owing, which means they'll actually leave in two weeks. That will be before the end of the project and leave the Works Team short-staffed for the painting and wallpapering work, unless replacement staff can be recruited very rapidly. The impact of these resignations needs to be determined quickly, because we're near stage end. I'm more than half way through preparing the next Stage Plan, and that will be affected.

Classic style questions

	Answer the following questions about the the use of the project's Daily Log when managing a stage boundary in the e-business unit project .	
1	Entry **23** is about the redecoration of the Managing Director's office. Which **1** answer option indicates why the Project Manager would take note of this on the stage boundary, or if he wouldn't need to?	
	A	The entry indicates that the scope of the project should be extended to control other refurbishment work in the company and the Project Plan and PID will need adjusting accordingly.
	B	It represents a new risk that the project will be cancelled if the new Managing Director decides on a new strategy that doesn't require an e-business unit.
	C	The entry is just a point of information and the Project Manager would not have to take note of it on the stage boundary.
	D	The repeated loss of Works Team time needs checking out since if it is expected to continue it will affect the resourcing on the next Stage Plan.
	E	The Works Team matter is a major problem, and on a Stage Boundary the Project Manager should transfer all major problems from the Daily Log to the Issue Register.
2	Entries **24** and **25** in the Daily Log are about a problem with getting enough matching side tables. Which **1** answer option correctly identifies the Project Manager's interest in these entries when doing the work of 'Managing a Stage Boundary'?	
	A	The side table situation would require a change to the Project Product Description.
	B	The side table problem would need to be resolved before the Senior User would be in a position to authorise the next Stage Plan because it is not yet clear exactly what furniture will be delivered.
	C	An Off-specification must be authorised by the Project Manager and passed to the Project Board at the same time as the new Stage Plan for the next stage.
	D	The side table problem described in Entries 24 and 25 would not be of interest to the Project Manager in relation to work in the PRINCE2 stage boundary process.
	E	The failure to meet the required quality critieria for an essential product (the side tables are a necessity, not a luxury) means that the project should be cancelled and the process 'Closing a Project' should be used instead of 'Managing a Stage Boundary'.
3	Entry **26** is about the resignation of two of the Works Team. Which **1** action should be taken by the Project Manager as part of the work involved in 'Managing a Stage Boundary'?	
	A	Do nothing, since the team members haven't actually left yet.
	B	Change the next Stage Plan, currently being created, and the Project Plan to allow for a longer duration because of the reduced Works Team resource.
	C	Transfer the information to the Risk Register as the transport company could attract further works staff, but take no other action.
	D	Before finalising the next Stage Plan and updating the Project Plan, check the position with the Team Manager of the Works Team on the probability of losing further works staff and if suitable new staff can be recruited quickly enough to fill the gaps.
	E	Instruct the Works Team not to carry out any other work elsewhere in the company but only do project work from now on so that the next Stage Plan is not disrupted.

Assertion–reason style questions

Each row in the table below consists of an assertion statement and a reason statement. For each row identify the appropriate selection from options A to E that applies. Each option can be used once, more than once or not at all.

Selection	Assertion	Reason	
A	True	True	AND the reason explains the assertion
B	True	True	BUT the reason does not explain the assertion
C	True	False	
D	False	True	
E	False	False	

	Assertion		Reason
4	The Executive should recalculate the costs of the e-business unit project at each end stage to update the Business Case	BECAUSE	the Executive represents the business viewpoint and so is personally responsible for updating the Business Case throughout the project.
5	With the exception of the Business Case, The Project Initiation Documentation (PID) for the e-business project must not be changed on a stage boundary	BECAUSE	the PID was 'baselined' when it was approved by the Project Board at the end of the Initiation Stage as it accurately described the requirements for the new e-business unit accommodation.
6	In the new e-business unit project, the work of 'Controlling a Stage' will stop when the work of 'Managing a Stage Boundary' begins	BECAUSE	except in very small projects, PRINCE2 does not require the Project Manager to continue managing a stage at the same time as doing the extensive planning work on the stage boundary.
7	On a stage boundary, no use will be made of the configuration management content of the Change theme	BECAUSE	the Works Teams will have finished work on the current stage and will not yet have started work on products in the following stage.
8	Where an exception occurs part way through a stage and an Exception Plan is required, an End Stage Report will not be produced	BECAUSE	in the case of an exception part way through a stage, the stage will not have reached the scheduled end as shown on the current Stage Plan.
9	The project management team structure for the e-business unit project will be checked by the Project Manager on a stage boundary	BECAUSE	some roles may have changed and the structure should be kept up-to-date to accurately reflect roles and responsibilities in the project.

Further classic style questions

	Answer the following question about the stage boundary within the e-business project.
	Remember to limit your answers to the number of selections requested in each section

10		Which **2** PRINCE2 management products would or might be updated by the Project Manager of the e-business unit project on a stage boundary?
	A	Project Brief, to show any adjustment of the project scope
	B	Business Plan, to reflect any changes in the e-business growth forecasts
	C	Risk Register, to show any changes in risk status after risk review
	D	End Stage Report, to record final metrics (such as time and cost) from the last stage
	E	Project Approach, to record any changes in things that constrain the final deliverable or the way that the project must be run
	F	Project mandate, to keep the overview of the project up to date with any changes

11		Which **2** items of information would be relevant to include in the End Stage Report?
	A	The plan for the next stage
	B	Planning assumptions for the next Stage Plan
	C	A summary of Daily Log entries for the stage just finishing
	D	A list of all issue received in the stage just finishing
	E	A review of team performance in the stage just finishing
	F	A report of lessons learned in the stage just finishing

12		Entry 26 of the Daily Log supplied at the start of this section has an entry about the resignation of two members of the Works Team. The resignations occurred after the Project Manager had started the PRINCE2 stage boundary work. If the impact of the problem is to increase the time needed to run the project, which **2** management products being worked on by the Project Manager would need to be adjusted to reflect this impact?
	A	Project Plan
	B	Project Product Description
	C	Business Case
	D	Project management team structure
	E	Project approach
	F	End Stage Report

Answers to the Foundation-level questions

1 **a.** This is the last activity in the process, as a look at the process model reveals.

2 **d.** At the end of a stage, just before the next one begins. The exception is the last stage where the Closing a Project process is used instead. The exclusion of the last stage in a project is a significant point but one the manual forgets to mention, thereby making that part of the purpose statement very misleading; so be careful you don't get misled! [**Manual** 17.1]

3 **c.** The Business Case must be reviewed at least at the end of every stage. Be careful with 'Focus on benefits'. It sounds rather good, but it isn't one of the seven PRINCE2 principles.

4 **c.** The Project Manager is responsible for most of the updates of products on a stage boundary; this information provides good grounds for guessing if you weren't absolutely sure.

5 **c.** The Quality Register lists all the quality activities in a stage so that each can be signed off when it's done – it acts as a sort of checklist. The stage boundary is where that list gets put into the register for the following stage.

6 **c.** You can get to the right answer in one of two ways. The first is by being familiar with the elements of the purpose statement, and the second is by remembering that the Project Board members don't see Team Plans; the team plans are too low a level of detail for the board to be concerned with.

7 **d.** Again, the process model reveals the answer. For the exam, it helps if you have a photographic memory – but, if not, the logic of the process should help. After the plans have been updated, there may be new forecasts of time and cost, and both of these are included in the Business Case.

8 **a.** This is for the Project Board activity 'Authorize a Stage or Exception Plan' in the process Directing a Project.

9 **a.** Remember that Start Up isn't a stage. Instead, the work of stage planning (for the Initiation Stage) is covered by one of the activities of Starting Up a Project, not by calling the stage boundary process to do it.

10 **d.** The key word here is 'created'. The Project Plan and Benefits Review Plan are updated, not created. Team Plans are created in the first activity in the process Managing Product Delivery.

Answers to the Practitioner-level questions

Classic-style questions

1 **D.** Project resource is getting depleted. This needs checking out with the Senior Supplier, because the promised resource is not forthcoming. If resource levels can't be met – and it's quite hard to argue with a Managing Director – then the plans must be rebalanced to take account of the lower level of resource. That might be by extending the time needed to complete the project or by spending money to buy in additional help from a decorating company. It looks serious enough to justify handling as a formal issue.

2 **D.** The matter will need to be resolved, and as an issue which is probably going to be an Off-specification. However, it's not a huge problem and won't have an impact on the stage planning for the next stage or the End Stage Report. If a concession is made to accept a few side tables off specification, then remember that according to the manual, a concession can only be authorised by the Project Board and not by the Project Manager, as suggested in answer C.

3 **D.** This question is slightly messy and is to stretch you a bit in your understanding of PRINCE2. The process Controlling a Stage doesn't stop while the stage boundary work is being done; and that's the subject of a later question. Inevitably, then, there's going to be some crossover between the two. The issue will be dealt with as part of the stage control, but it does have an impact on the preparations for the next stage. In projects, of course, you don't think to yourself, 'Ah, I'm now going back to the process Controlling a Stage before I return to continue my work in Managing a Stage Boundary'! Instead, you just get on with it. But if you analyse what you're doing, then in PRINCE2 terms you're actually dealing with the two processes in parallel, using appropriate activities from each.

Assertion–reason style questions

4 **E.** The Project Manager updates the Business Case on a stage boundary, although he or she should consult the Executive. [**Manual** Table 17-3]

5 **D.** The baselined version is kept for later comparison, but it doesn't mean that the documentation is frozen. A lot of the updating in the process is to do with the Project Initiation Documentation (PID).

6 **E.** A nice thought, but sadly multi-tasking goes with the territory in project management. Make sure that you understand how some processes run in parallel; for more on this, have a look at Chapter 19.

7 **D.** Configuration Item Records must be created for newly identified products, but in any case some management products are being configuration managed, not just the specialist products that the teams are involved with.

8 **D.** Where an Exception Plan is being produced at a point part way through a stage, there's no point in re-planning work that's already done. That part of the work is shut down as an end stage and has an End Stage Report.

9 **A.** Really the team structure should be kept up to date all the time, but the manual does show it being checked and updated in the stage boundary process.

Further classic-style questions

10 **C and E.** Again take note of the word 'updated'. There's no Business Plan in PRINCE2, and the mandate and brief are long gone by the time of the delivery stages.

11 **E and F.** Check out the report in Appendix A of the manual. [**Manual** A.9.2]

12 **A and C.** Both the Project Plan and Business Case include project duration information, and the Project Plan also contains resource plans. Team members aren't be in the project management team structure, because they're not in the project *management* team.

Chapter 10

Closing a Project

....

....

So, to the last of the PRINCE2 processes: Closing a Project. Closure is easy to follow in PRINCE2 if you keep in mind that it's an orderly shut down. The closure will usually be the planned one at the end of the project, but it may also be a 'crash stop' (premature close) if, for example, something goes badly wrong or someone in authority decides that the project isn't needed any more. Either way, planned close or premature close, it's an orderly and conscious process, not a fizzling out of the project.

The Project Board will make the final decision as to whether the project can be closed, and the process Closing a Project is where the Project Manager does the shut-down work and prepares for that final board decision.

Revising the Closure Process

Although closure is a fairly straightforward business, you need to cope with a surprising amount of content for the exams, not least because there are a large number of management products flying about. Be sure then to allow time for revising the process, especially for Foundation where all the information has to be in your head. For Practitioner, you have the relative luxury of being able to look things up in your PRINCE2 manual. However, you still need to remember a lot of this stuff, so that looking something up in the manual during the exam is just a fast check to confirm something, not reading big chunks of the closure chapter to find out large amounts of information.

Revision checklist – Foundation

Scan down this revision checklist and if you can't tick any item confidently, that warns you that you need to look at the point again as part of your revision:

❑ Yes, it's the process objectives and the purpose statement again. Are you sure that you'll be able to recognise the different parts if they come up in a question?

❑ The two triggers for the process: detecting the end of the last stage when checking the stage status in the process Controlling a Stage, or as a Project Board instruction for a 'crash stop' – a premature close.

❑ That a premature close instruction can come from the Project Board at any time out if its activity 'Giving ad hoc direction' or at a fixed point by it choosing not to authorise work on a following stage or part stage and ordering project closure instead out of the activity 'Authorize a Stage or Exception Plan'.

❑ The two aspects of the Project Manager's work: shutting down the project itself and then preparing information such as the End Project Report for the Project Board.

❑ The five activities in the process, what's happening in each, and who's responsible for the work in each – that's mostly the Project Manager with Project Assurance then checking things, but there's occasional involvement of Project Support.

❑ The End Project Report as the Project Manager's record of how the project went, and reporting out-turn figures such as the final cost of the project.

❑ That the process, and the End Project Report, compare achievements to date with the objectives set down in the original *baselined* Project Initiation Documentation (PID) as it was agreed at the end of Initiation, not just the latest PID version which will include changes made during the delivery stages.

❑ That any benefits that come on stream at the end of the project are measured now and reported now.

❑ That there's no End Stage Report for the final stage. Instead there's the End Project Report, which covers the whole project including the final stage.

❑ What a *follow-on action recommendation* is and what sort of work may be passed on as a follow-on action recommendation.

❑ The way in which the process is associated with the seven PRINCE2 principles. There's more on this in Chapter 19.

❑ How the process uses the management products feeding into it; there are a lot. Have a look in the manual at the products shown as inputs into the activities of the Closing a Project process, and in *PRINCE2 For Dummies*. [**Manual** Ch18 activity summary diagrams for the five activities, **P2FD** Ch9 final panel – Checking out the CP products]

Revision checklist – Practitioner

Do check out the items on the Foundation revision checklist above to be sure that you're still clear on them, and then have a look at the following additional points to be ready for Practitioner questions:

❑ Understanding that there's basically no difference in management products between a premature close and a planned close. Both go through similar close-down work in terms of the management products used.

❑ The nature of the key closure products of the Benefits Review Plan, End Project Report and Lessons Report, and what the sections within each are about. Do you know them well enough to be able to spot errors quickly in a faulty example?

❑ That acceptance of the project by the customer is based on the Acceptance Criteria in the Project Product Description (PPD), and that handover also follows what is set down in the PPD.

❑ The nature and content of the management products which feed into the process, how they're used and where, if necessary, they're updated.

Clarifying Some Key Points

The following points are ones which people studying PRINCE2 don't always get clear the first time around. Have a look through the section. If you read a sentence or two of an item and decide that you already know the point well, just skip the rest of that item and move on to the next one.

Having a closure stage . . . or not

PRINCE2 used to be very keen on having the closure work as just work that you carried out towards the end of the last delivery stage. Other approaches, such as the PRIME project management method and the Project Management Institute (PMI) approach have a dedicated closure stage. One of the improvements to the method in the 2009 edition of the PRINCE2 manual is that the door's been left open to have a closure stage in a PRINCE2 project. That makes sense, because although products have been handed over, team members often still need to be on hand to make final adjustments and to assist operational users who are learning to use what the project has delivered. In larger projects, this can be a significant stage of some length. In the project to build Hong Kong airport – my favourite international destination – the support period lasted for some weeks after the move of operational flights to the new airport site at Chek Lap Kok. Project staff remained involved until they were sure that everything had settled down in this highly successful project.

Understanding follow-on actions

To be precise, this section is about follow-on action *recommendations*. The follow-on actions relate to things that the organisation is being asked to do after the project has shut down. The project is in no position to dictate to the organisation what it should or shouldn't do, so the action is 'recommended'. The Project Manager prepares the follow-on action recommendations and passes these to the Project Board, which in turn distributes them to the appropriate people in the organisation.

Follow-on action recommendations may include:

✔ Suggested changes to project management procedures in the organisation.

✔ Ongoing risk management actions concerned with the operational life of deliverables such as dangerous machinery.

✔ Ongoing requirements for configuration management (version control) of working products – especially, but not solely, in engineering and IT environments.

> ✔ Issues that were not dealt with in the project. For example, a team member may have had a great idea, but there wasn't time to implement it during the project. The idea is passed forward as a follow-on action recommendation so that it isn't forgotten. The organisation can then consider it for implementation as part of day-to-day work or add it to a future project.

In PRINCE2, the benefit reviews held after closure are, strictly speaking, follow-on actions, because the project has shut down and the review will be conducted by organisational staff who may or may not have been involved in the project.

Seeing why benefits reviews can come later

Most projects deliver business benefits such as higher sales, cost savings and staff time savings. These benefits may be seen – *realised* – at different points, as covered in Chapter 11 on the Business Case. One of those points is after the project. In some cases, it will be a while before the benefits build up to their full level or are clear enough to be measured.

An example of the need for a benefits review post project is with a project that introduces a new business procedure. When the products are handed over and the project closes down, staff are still unfamiliar with the new procedure and so are working more slowly than will be normal. It makes sense to measure the benefit six to eight weeks after the project. At that time, staff should be familiar with the new procedure and an accurate measure can be taken of just how much faster it is (hopefully) than the old one and what the saving in staff time is.

There may be more than one benefits review post project if, for example, different benefits are coming on stream at different times.

Updating the Benefits Review Plan

This is a slightly strange update in Closing a Project, because the manual refers to checking that the plan includes the reviews which are to happen post project. Checks aren't exactly an update, and if post-project reviews were found to be missing it would mean that something had gone awry with the preparation and checking of the plan earlier in the project. If it's sensible for the plan to be checked though, then why not the Business Case as well to ensure that the benefits section is clear and understandable for review staff to use? A bit confusing then, but for the exams just bear in mind that the Benefits Review Plan is 'updated'.

Practising With Some Questions

Have a practice with some questions to check out your knowledge of the closure process. Remember that these aren't live exam questions, so it's no good just learning the answers and hoping that'll be enough get you through. Even the official sample papers don't contain live questions. The pool of questions from which your exam questions will be drawn is extensive, so you need to make sure you're well prepared across all parts of each subject.

Foundation-level questions

Check out your knowledge of the Closing a Project process with these Foundation-style questions. Try to do them within a time limit of eight minutes, but if you can go a bit faster and still be accurate, then that's good.

1. Which report(s) may be created by the Project Manager using the Closing a Project process?

❑ a) End Stage Report and Exception Report

❑ b) Highlight Report and End Project Report

❑ c) Only an End Project Report

❑ d) End Stage Report and End Project Report

2. If, part way through a delivery stage of the project, the Project Board instructs the Project Manager to shut down the project prematurely:

❑ a) The Closing a Project process would not be used, because the project would stop immediately.

❑ b) The Project Manager would make a decision on whether to use the Closing a Project process.

❑ c) Project Assurance would make a decision on whether the Closing a Project process should be used.

❑ d) The Closing a Project process would always be used.

3. If the Closing a Project process is being used for a premature close of the project, then:

❑ a) There will be no handover of products at all, because the project is being abandoned.

❑ b) All products worked on to date will be handed over, including incomplete ones.

❑ c) Some products may be handed over to salvage anything of value from the project.

❑ d) Only management products will be handed over, because these may be of value in planning any subsequent project.

4. Which role is mostly responsible for the work in the process Closing a project?

    ❑ a) The Executive

    ❑ b) Project Support

    ❑ c) Project Manager

    ❑ d) Project Assurance

5. In any project, important lessons may be learned that will be of value to the organisation when running further projects. How is the process Closing a Project used to ensure that such lessons from a project are passed on into the organisation?

    ❑ a) The Lessons Log is submitted to the Project Board for onward transfer to corporate or programme management.

    ❑ b) The Project Manager sends the Lessons Log to the Project Office or person responsible for project standards within the organisation.

    ❑ c) Project Support files the Lessons Log in a place where other organisational project staff will be able to access it easily in the future.

    ❑ d) The Project Manager prepares a Lessons Report based on entries in the Lessons Log.

6. Which of these products is NOT an input into the process Closing a Project?

    ❑ a) Risk Register

    ❑ b) Issue Register

    ❑ c) Project Initiation Documentation (PID)

    ❑ d) Project mandate

7. Which of these activities is included in the process Closing a Project?

    ❑ a) Hand over products

    ❑ b) Plan the next stage

    ❑ c) Report highlights

    ❑ d) Authorize project closure

8. Which of the following statements are included in the objective of the process Closing a Project?

    A. Assess any benefits that have already been realised

    B. Review the performance of the project against its baselines

    C. Keep the Business Case under review

    D. Verify user acceptance of the project's products

    ❏ a) A, B and C

    ❏ b) A, C and D

    ❏ c) A, B and D

    ❏ d) B, C and D

9. In the process Closing a Project, the Project Plan is updated. Why is this?

    ❏ a) To change the plan to reflect what the teams actually did in the project instead of what was planned for them to do in the Work Packages

    ❏ b) To enter 'actuals' of things such as time and money spent in the final stage of the project

    ❏ c) To make sure that the plan format complies with organisational standards

    ❏ d) To delete time and cost information, which may be confidential

10. If a risk will continue into the working life of a product, such as an ongoing biological hazard, how is this handled in the process Closing a Project?

    ❏ a) A copy of the relevant Risk Register entry is forwarded to the person who'll be responsible for ongoing risk management.

    ❏ b) The risk is transferred to a follow-on action recommendation.

    ❏ c) Project Assurance will enter the risk into the organisation's risk management system.

    ❏ d) PRINCE2 doesn't cover this, because it concerns the ongoing operational use of products and so is outside the management control of the project.

Practitioner-level questions

There are two sets of questions for Practitioner practice. The first are a matching type and effectively 'true/false'. You need to identify whether project closure is being handled in the way that the PRINCE2 manual sets down. Note carefully that the best way or the most logical way doesn't always line up with the PRINCE2 way. Remember that the exam is about PRINCE2, not about project management. Other project methods and approaches may be different and better in some places than PRINCE2, but how those methods and approaches handle things won't get you the mark in the PRINCE2 exam.

The second set of questions are in the assertion–reason style. You may think there are rather a lot of examples of assertion–reason questions in the book, and that's right; but it's no accident. Most people find the style rather awkward to deal with, so there are more examples to give you more practice. Added to that, they're dangerous. There may be three steps to go through before you arrive at the answer, and if you get any step wrong you'll lose the mark. Have a look at Chapter 2 for advice on tackling the different styles and for the three-step approach to assertion–reason questions.

The questions in this chapter are based on the project scenario set down at the end of Chapter 2, the project to refurbish offices for a new e-business unit at Princess Projects. There's no block of additional scenario information to read for the questions in this chapter, although a small amount of extra information is embedded in some questions.

When starting a new section of the PRINCE2 exam, always, always, *always* check the scenario part of the paper, which is a separate section, to see whether there's information there. Some sections of the exam have additional information in the scenario paper, and some don't. The original scenario information still applies as well though, so don't forget that either.

You should allow 18 minutes to cover the 12 practice questions, and they're all on Closing a Project to help you revise this process. In the Practitioner exam, there are just 10 questions in a section and you have around 15 minutes to answer, so the pace is the same. Also in the exam, you won't ever have a whole section on just one process; again it's done here to help you with topic based revision. In the exam, if Closing a Project comes up it will be in a section which also covers Managing a Stage Boundary and Directing a Project. So, because there's no additional project scenario information to read before you start these questions, set your timer for 18 minutes and get stuck right in.

Matching style questions – true/false

	For each statement about project closure of the office refurbishment project in column 1, please select the correct option in column 2 to say if that action is a correct application of PRINCE2. An option in column 2 may be used more than once or not at all.	
	Column 1	Column 2
1	The telecoms supplier must come back after the project is finished to replace a faulty phone socket. It is going to take a couple of days to get the replacement done and by then the project will have closed. The Project Manager has recorded this as a follow-on action recommendation and is sending it straight to the Works Team Manager to instruct him to ensure the socket is fixed by the supplier.	A This action is a correct application of PRINCE2 for the project. B This action is not the correct way of performing project closure according to PRINCE2.
2	The Issue Register is being passed on to the new manager of the Business Unit for her to deal with the three remaining issues that the project didn't have time to deal with. A fault has been reported with a drawer in a new desk, there's a request to change the position of one of the phone sockets and someone has asked that the layout be altered to have desks in one room in a different place.	
3	It was not possible to get enough matching side tables in the time available. In one of the four offices the tables are similar to the desks but not exactly the same range as was specified on the order. The Project Board agreed at the time that the alternative tables would be okay and should be accepted, and the Project Manager is now recording this in the End Project Report.	
4	The Project Manager needs to confirm to organisational managers in Princess Projects Plc that their staff are about to be released from the project as it is coming to the planned close. The Project Manager has asked the Project Board for permission to send out these notices.	
5	In order to produce the End Project Report, the Project Manager will look at the original PID, as agreed at the end of the Initiation Stage, as well as the latest version that includes all approved changes.	
6	In the section of the End Project Report on team performance, the only entry the Project Manager has made is to record the names of two team members who performed particularly well.	

Assertion–reason style questions

Each row in the table below consists of an assertion statement and a reason statement. For each row identify the appropriate selection from options A to E that applies. Each option can be used once, more than once or not at all.

Selection	Assertion	Reason	
A	True	True	AND the reason explains the assertion
B	True	True	BUT the reason does not explain the assertion
C	True	False	
D	False	True	
E	False	False	

	Assertion		Reason
7	The Executive is responsible for producing the End Project Report	BECAUSE	the Executive is ultimately accountable to Princess Projects Plc for the e-business unit project.
8	The Project Manager should ask Project Support for a Product Status Account during the work of 'Closing a project'	BECAUSE	the Product Status Account is included in the End Project Report to prove that all products have a state of 'complete'.
9	Configuration Item Records may be passed on into the organisation at the end of the project	BECAUSE	some specialist products may need to be subject to ongoing configuration management control in their operational lives.
10	All logs and registers for the e-business unit project will be closed down as part of Closing a Project	BECAUSE	all outstanding matters in the logs and registers must be resolved before the Project Board can authorize closure.
11	Things that went badly in the project may be reported in a Lessons Report	BECAUSE	the only function of the Lessons Report is to ensure that project mistakes never happen again.
12	When closing down the e-business unit project, the Project Manager will not review the achievement of quality	BECAUSE	specific quality criteria for each product are set down on its Product Description which is used for testing and approval at the time the product is created, not at the end of the project when it's too late.

Answers to the Foundation-level questions

1   **c.** Only the End Project Report is created in the process. It's important that you know which reports come out of which processes. Go over this area in your revision if you're still a bit unsure. As a quick reference you may find Table 18-1 useful in Chapter 18 of this book. Just look for the reports in the table and you'll see the process named where each report is created.

2   **d.** A PRINCE2 project always uses the closure process. In a premature close, the activities may be performed faster than in a normal planned close, but they're still done. There's also a specific activity to prepare a premature close, as well as the other option which is to prepare the originally planned close.

3   **c.** If you look at the process model for Closing a project it shows a dashed line from the activity 'Prepare premature close' to the activity 'Hand over products' to show that some products may be handed over. The text of the manual also makes clear that useful things should be salvaged. [**Manual** 18.4.2]

4   **c.** The Project Manager will consult other members of the project management team, and there's some work by Project Support and Project Assurance, but the vast bulk of the closure work is down to the Project Manager.

5   **d.** The Lessons Report is included in the End Project Report, and the Project Board is charged then with distributing the lessons to the relevant people in the organisation. I can't see Project Board members ever actually doing that – and certainly have never experienced it – but again it's what the book says and is another minor area where the method is perhaps a little out of touch with reality. In practice, it's more likely that the board will ask the Project Manager to distribute the lessons after it's approved them, but always remember that the exam is about the book.

6   **d.** The mandate was left behind long ago. Reviewing original objectives is achieved by looking at the original ('baselined') Project Initiation Documentation (PID) as agreed at the end of Initiation.

7   **a.** Obviously there isn't going to be a next stage if this is the end of the project, and there's no progress to report, because the process concerns only closure products. If there's a closure stage, then this is being managed in parallel with the closure work and any highlight (progress) reporting is being done out of the process Controlling a Stage. The activity 'Authorize project closure' is a Project Board activity which comes after the work of Closing a Project and is part of the process Directing a Project.

8   **c.** Keeping the Business Case under review is, in fact, part of the objective of the process Controlling a Stage. It was actually hard when writing this question to find part of an objective from another process that couldn't also be applied to closure. Even now, it's a tough question because logically you could review the Business Case in closure to help write the End Project Report, even though the manual doesn't specifically mention it (just the PID) and it isn't listed as part of the objective. This question is to emphasise the revision strategy point that you need to be familiar with the purpose and objective statements in the manual, and logic alone isn't enough.

9   **b.** Remember that in PRINCE2, there's no End Stage Report for the final stage, and instead there's just the End Project Report. The PRINCE2 approach here is debatable on more than one front, which may cause you a problem when revising if your logic or your experience takes you, justifiably, in a direction other than the PRINCE2 direction. One problem here is that you may be used to a computerised project tool where actuals are automatically entered into the Project Plan when they're entered into the stage plan, because it's the same file in the software. The update will therefore happen in the activity 'Review Work Package status' in the process Controlling a Stage. PRINCE2 has always been a bit strange on this point, and there's a similar issue when updating the Project Plan on a stage boundary. Just take this point on board as a matter of rote learning then: on a stage boundary, and here at project closure, the Project Plan is updated with actuals. At closure, the update happens in the activity 'Prepare planned close' and also in the alternative activity 'Prepare premature close'. [**Manual** 18.4.1 and 18.4.2]. In passing, I was rather pleased with the wrong answer 'a', because I suspect it happens in more than a few cases, although often disguised with high sounding terms such as 'iterative development'!

10   **b.** Follow-on action recommendations cover anything the organisation is being asked to do after the end of the project. Among other things, that includes configuration management (version control) and, in this case, ongoing risk management.

Answers to the Practitioner-level questions

Check out your answers below. I include a few references to help you locate where the PRINCE2 manual gives specific information on a point.

Matching-style questions – true/false

1   **B.** Follow-on action recommendations are routed through the Project Board as part of closure, for the board members to pass them on to the relevant people out of their activity 'Authorize project closure'. The Project Manager doesn't act independently and bypass the board with follow-on actions. It's also a 'recommendation' not an instruction, and the Project Manager has no authority to instruct staff to do things after the project, even if those staff were under his or her control during the project. [**Manual** Table 13-5]

2   **B.** This is incorrect. The Issue Register is closed, and each outstanding issue is either closed with it, or is made into a follow-on action recommendation. The Issue Register doesn't have a life after the project.

3   **A.** In my opinion, the authors of PRINCE2, 2009 edition, have gone way over the top with the detail in some reports which had already prompted widespread accusations of the method being bureaucratic. However, as pointed out in the note at the start of the Practitioner questions, the exam is about PRINCE2 and not about what I – or you – happen to think is a good idea. The End Project Report includes a section for reporting on products, and that includes confirmation of any concessions granted where products were accepted off specification. [**Manual** A.8.2 Review of Products]

4   **A.** PRINCE2 gets terribly formal around closure time. It is indeed the case that the Project Manager shouldn't circulate information about the release of staff until the board has said it's okay to do that. That's sensible in some settings, although unnecessary in nearly all project environments I've been involved in. However, as always, the exam is about the default in the book. [**Manual** 18.4.1]

5 **A.** This is correct, because the assessment of whether objectives have been met needs to refer to the project's 'original intent' as well as the objectives in any revised state after authorised changes during the project. The original Project Initiation Documentation (PID) is said to be 'baselined' to preserve what was agreed when it was first authorised. [**Manual** 18.4.4 first action]

6 **A.** Sad, but a correct use of the report section. The 2009 edition of the PRINCE2 manual includes a really valuable section in the End Project Report (and a similar one appears in the End Stage Report) to comment on team performance. All sorts of useful performance metrics could be included in the section, but the only thing the manual can find to suggest is mentioning people in dispatches – commenting on good team member performance. So, it's in line with PRINCE2 that this is the only information included by the Project Manager in the new business unit project. In terms of exam strategy, this question demonstrates the need to work at some depth. You need to be aware of what products are in use at different points in PRINCE2, but also what those products are all about in order to know whether they're being used appropriately. Don't forget that you have Appendix A to turn to in order to check things out if you can't quite remember the fine detail – just don't spend too long doing so. By the way, there's a place to make some comment on performance metrics, but weirdly it's in the Lessons Report – performance metrics aren't exactly a lesson any more than financial and quality metrics are.

Assertion–reason style questions

7 **D.** The Project Manager is responsible for the End Project Report. He or she will consult the rest of the project management team, and that includes the Executive, but remains responsible for producing the report.

8 **C.** The wording of the manual suggests that getting a Product Status Account is always necessary. That's not true for live projects, but as always stick with what the manual says when dealing with exam questions. However, that account isn't included in the End Project Report, as Appendix A confirms. [**Manual** A.8.2]. Don't confuse the review of products in the End Project Report with a Product Status Account, which is something the Project Manager uses for management control, not for reporting to the Project Board.

9 **A.** The thing to remember about configuration management (version control) is that it continues after the end of the project. That's easier to appreciate in an engineering or IT environment. Clearly with an operational computer system, for example, it's important for maintaining that system to know which versions of which programs make up the current 'release'. The 'baseline' of versions (release) will almost certainly change in the working life of the system, because some parts are upgraded over time while other parts may not change at all.

10 **C.** The logs and registers are indeed closed down in the last activity of the process. However, there may be outstanding actions needed, and these will be passed on as follow-on action recommendations.

11 **C.** It's true that the organisation doesn't want to repeat bad stuff, but the Lessons Report also records good things that may be of use to later projects. For example, a team member may have discovered a better and faster way of doing something. The key word in the reason statement is 'only'. Remember, read every word in the question and take particular care if you're under time pressure.

12 **D.** Closure does involve reporting on quality, but that's now at a project level. The Product Descriptions, and quality checking of individual products, are at a lower level of detail, and obviously that quality work is needed throughout the project as products are being generated and tested. The process Managing Product Delivery with its activity 'Execute a Work Package' deals with the majority of product testing against Product Descriptions, because this deals with the specialist products.

You may have noticed that there were more 'A' correct answers than 'B' correct answers in the first set of questions, and a disproportionate number of 'C' correct answers in the assertion–reason set, and that some answer options in the assertion–reason set were never used at all. Remember, focus on what you believe to be the right answer and don't try to play structure games and think that one answer option is more likely than another because that answer letter option hasn't been used much, or at all, yet.

Part III

Revising the Themes

The 5th Wave   By Rich Tennant

REVISING THE ORGANIZATIONAL THEME

I'm thinking maybe scones! Let them eat scones!

In this part . . .

Part III of this book works through the PRINCE2 themes in the same way as Part II covers the processes – with a chapter on each. You'll find revision checklists, clarification of the trickier themes and a solid bank of practice questions to get you into the exam zone.

The practice exam questions here, as in the previous part, help you to familiarise yourself with the demands and different styles of test you'll need to get through.

Chapter 11

Business Case

....

In This Chapter

▶ The key word to understand the Business Case

▶ Knowing how the Business Case is maintained through the project

▶ Getting the tie in with the Benefits Review Plan

▶ Understanding what a benefit is . . . and isn't

....

Understanding the Business Case in PRINCE2 hinges on a single word. That word is *justification*. A focus on justification gets you away from thinking solely about benefits, which is a common point of confusion. While most projects are indeed justified by the business benefits that will result from them, some are not and need other types of justification. For example, the project may not lead to any business benefits at all, but may still be fully justified because it's necessary for legal compliance or because it's being carried out as an instruction from headquarters.

The Business Case is particularly important in PRINCE2, because the business focus is the primary emphasis in the method. The good news when you're revising is that while there are one or two tangles to work through, overall the theme shouldn't cause you much difficulty. The Business Case theme still has a fair amount of content though, so be careful to allow plenty of time for revising it before the exams.

Revising the Business Case Theme

Watch out for three areas in particular as you revise the Business Case theme. The first is to be clear on what the Business Case contains. Have a look in the PRINCE2 manual or in *PRINCE2 For Dummies*. [**Manual** A.2.2, **P2FD** Ch11 Writing a Business Case]

The second area to check up on is where the Business Case is developed and then where it's used throughout the project. The 'quick and dirty' – 'outline' – Business Case is developed in Start Up then that case is refined into a full Business Case during Initiation, where it then forms part of the Project Initiation Documentation (PID). If you're unclear on how the case goes on to be used throughout the project, have a look at the next main section in this chapter, 'Clarifying Some Key Points'.

The third area to watch out for in revision is how the Business Case relates to the Benefits Review Plan. Again, there's more on this in the next main section in this chapter.

As you plan your revision, and to help make sure that you understand the detailed content of the Business Case theme, have a look at the following checklists, one for each exam.

Revision checklist – Foundation

Read through this checklist and tick off the items that you're confident that you know about and understand. If you don't feel confident on any item, don't tick it until you have done a bit more work to revise that area.

- ❏ What's in the Business Case – do you understand each of the headings?
- ❏ Responsibilities for the Business Case
- ❏ The purpose and objective statement of the theme – are you sufficiently familiar with them to be able to recognise them as belonging to this theme?
- ❏ The difference between the Outline Business Case (as developed in Start Up) and the full Business Case (as 'refined' in Initiation)
- ❏ The different types of justification – there's more on this in the next section of this chapter, if you're unsure
- ❏ The PRINCE2 processes in which the Business Case is created and then, throughout the project, updated
- ❏ How the Business Case is used by the Project Manager and the Project Board to ensure that the project continues to be justified – so fulfilling the PRINCE2 principle of 'continued business justification'
- ❏ The terms 'output', 'outcome' and 'benefit'
- ❏ The definition of a benefit as a 'measurable improvement'
- ❏ The term 'disbenefit' – a disadvantage of running the project, not to be confused with what happens if you don't run the project
- ❏ The Benefits Review Plan and how it's used

Revision checklist – Practitioner

For the Practitioner exam, do have a look through the Foundation exam checklist to be sure you're still fluent in those aspects of the Business Case. Then have a look at these additional areas to check that you're confident and to find where you need to brush up.

- ❏ The concept of a 'nested' Business Case where a project's Business Case may be part of a larger programme Business Case
- ❏ The detailed contents of the Business Case
- ❏ The detailed contents of the Benefits Review Plan
- ❏ Exactly where the Benefits Review Plan is updated and used
- ❏ Clarity on outputs, outcomes and benefits so that you can tell them apart if you're given examples in an exam, perhaps in a matching style question

Clarifying Some Key Points

This section covers some points you may be unclear on while learning PRINCE2. The section covers things that people often find difficult or confusing. Have a look through each area and if, after reading a few sentences, you're sure you understand it, then skip the rest of that item and move on to the next one.

Understanding project justification

Most projects are justified on the level of benefits that will result from them – or that people claim will result from them! Most projects are justified on the basis that they will lead to business benefits which are of greater value than the cost of the project. For example, a three-month project costing £150,000 may lead to savings worth £1 million a year. Another £150,000 project may lead to additional sales of a commercial product, leading to increased profits of £750,000 a year.

PRINCE2 does recognise other types of project justification, though. Some are fair enough, while you may find others hard to understand. The 2009 edition of the PRINCE2 manual lists different justifications, but sadly doesn't offer clear explanation or examples. The following list may help if you aren't clear on the different types of project justification:

- **Benefits:** Although not listed in the PRINCE2 manual among the other types of justification, because it's covered in the main manual text, most projects are benefits driven.

- **Compulsory project:** This is the 'compliance' type of project, mentioned earlier in the chapter. The project must be run because of an instruction or perhaps because it's a legal requirement.

- **Not for profit:** The term is a little weird, because it normally refers to organisations such as charities, where even though the organisation doesn't make a profit, the projects must still show clear justification and, usually, benefits. However, it's possible that an organisation simply has to do something such as a buildings maintenance project that doesn't show business benefit, so the project is 'not for profit'.

- **Evolving project:** This is a project, such as in research, where people believe that the project will deliver benefit, or that it may do, but don't yet know how much or when.

- **Customer/supplier project:** I really can't help you with this one, because even a customer/supplier project has to show some justification such as benefits. Why else do it? It's true that costs can be affected, such as a supplier offering to work for free in exchange for gaining experience in running a type of project, but that's more a matter of cost sharing than a 'type' of business case.

- **Multi-organisation project:** Again slightly weird, because there should still be some justification for running a project, even if several agencies are sharing it. A multi-organisation project will, however, affect the format of the Business Case: it may be segmented, with each partner organisation having benefits in its area of interest.

Quick quiz – is it a benefit?

To check out your understanding of business benefits, try this quick quiz. For each item, the question is simply: is it a benefit or not? Answers are at the end of the chapter.

1. The project will deliver a fully automated, self-levelling flange mechanism.

2. The new computer system will go a lot faster than the old one.

3. The saving in staff time of the new business procedure to be delivered by the project is expected to be £410,000 a year.

4. The project involves staff training, and using the organisation's own human resources staff to do this training will be £8,500 cheaper than buying it in from a specialist outside training company.

5. The new display, installed by the project in the call centre, will allow operators to see how long the next caller has been in the queue waiting for the call to be answered.

6. There will be some disruption to the production line while machines are replaced as part of this upgrade project. Over the life of the project, the down time for replacement and testing will result in an estimated production loss of 12,500 units worth £343,750.

7. The product improvements delivered by the project are expected to lead to £750,000 a year in increased sales. This estimate is based on the market research set out in the consultant's report to the senior management team last February.

8. Customers visiting the company will have a much better first impression of the organisation after the project to modernise the reception and waiting area.

9. The new computer system will have a fully integrated database.

10. The Managing Director has instructed that this project be carried out, after a major customer complained to the Managing Director personally, expressing strong dissatisfaction.

Seeing the Business Case as a living document

The 'living document' phrase reflects a report some years ago into troubled UK Government projects. The report emphasised that projects must continue to be justified right the way through and that the Business Case should not be used to get funding at the start and then forgotten about. PRINCE2 has taken that on board in two ways: first in the regular updates and checks of the Business Case, but now also with one of the principles of the method, 'continued business justification'.

To help you be clear on checks and updates of the Business Case, I set the key ones down in the 'Life of the Business Case' panel below.

Life of the Business Case

The Business Case is developed in Start Up and then progresses right through the project. Make sure you're crystal clear on the following key points in that lifespan:

✔ **Start Up:** The Business Case is created in rough-and-ready form as an Outline Business Case. The Executive is responsible for the production of the Outline Business Case, although others may help. The Outline Business Case forms part of the Project Brief.

✔ **Initiation:** The Outline Business Case is refined into a detailed Business Case. The responsibility for the document itself remains with the Executive, although production of the full Business Case is now down to the Project Manager, again with possible input from others. From here on, the Business Case forms part of the Project Initiation Documentation (PID).

✔ **Management stages:** The Business Case is checked and possibly updated as part of the activity 'Review the stage status'. The wording of the PRINCE2 manual is particularly poor in this section: it hints that the Business Case may be updated, because it refers to it being 'impacted', but the manual doesn't actually say that it will be updated. Clearly if an issue has an impact – in either direction – on the Business Case, then an update is called for even if a benefits limit (tolerance) set by the Project Board has not been breached. If benefits are coming on stream during the project, the Project Manager will also refer to the Business Case in order to check the exact level of benefits expected.

✔ **Stage boundaries:** A routine updating of the Business Case occurs at end stage using the activity 'Update the Business Case'. The Project Board will then have the very latest projections available (cost, time, benefits) when deciding whether the project remains viable and whether to authorise a following stage. Responsibility for the update of the Business Case lies with the Project Manager.

✔ **End project:** Any benefits immediately visible at the end of the project will be measured and reported in the End Project Report. As with the stage boundary, measurement may involve consulting the Business Case on the expected benefit levels.

Realising when benefits may be realised

In the latest, 2009, edition of the manual, PRINCE2 has recognised that benefits may come on stream before the end of a project. If products are being taken into operational use throughout the project, then often benefits will start to come on stream during the project as well. Those benefits may not reach their peak until later, but even lower-level benefits are worth measuring earlier to give some indication of whether the project will turn out to be the success that everyone hopes.

Benefits coming on stream, such as savings starting to be seen, is known as them being *realised* – if you're not already familiar with that bit of business speak.

Benefits can be measured at three points:

✔ **During the project.** For example, early on in the project, an old and high maintenance machine is replaced by a new, low maintenance machine. The savings in maintenance costs will start to be seen soon after, and there's no need to wait until the end of the project to check whether the savings are there.

✔ **At the end of the project.** In many projects, benefits will be seen at the end, when products are delivered. The benefits may not have reached a peak yet, but they're still visible.

✔ **After the end of the project.** Some benefits may not be visible at all until some time after products have been taken into operational use and the project closed down. Other benefits may have been seen earlier but won't have reached their peak until some time after the project. The organisation should therefore run one or more benefit reviews after the project to measure what the actual benefits were. The PRINCE2 project can't run the reviews, because the project has shut down.

Deciding when to measure benefits, and who will do it, needs planning. Lights, music, enter stage right: the Benefits Review Plan. The plan covers the period of the project but also the time after the project, for any benefits coming on stream after the project has shut down. The Benefits Review Plan is passed on into the organisation at the end of the project so that an organisational manager can take responsibility for the measures. That person is often the manager who acted as the Executive for the project, because he or she had overall responsibility for the project, including the Business Case. However, it may be a different manager.

Practising With Some Questions

Have a go with some practice questions on the Business Case theme.

If you get a question wrong and when you look at the correct answer you say to yourself 'Oh yes, of course,' then don't worry too much that you got it wrong. Clearly you know the method if you can immediately see why you didn't get the mark. Perhaps you got the wrong answer because you didn't read the question carefully enough; if that's the case, take note to be extra careful in the exam to RTFQ – Read The Flipping Question. If you got the answer wrong and you can't immediately see why, it's probably because you don't know PRINCE2 in that area. In that case, take your wrong answer as a cue to do a bit more revision on the point until you're more familiar with it. Unlike in the exams themselves, it doesn't matter too much whether you get questions in this book right or wrong, although it's encouraging to get a lot right. For each question you'll either confirm that you know something or pinpoint an area you need to brush up on – it's win–win.

You'll find some Foundation-level questions and some Practitioner-level ones in the following sections. Even if you already have the Foundation Certificate and are reading this book to help prepare for Practitioner, it's still worth running through the Foundation practice questions. Being an acknowledged and certified expert at Foundation level, it shouldn't take you many moments to answer the questions. If any do happen to reveal a gap in your knowledge, then you can target those areas as part of your Practitioner revision.

Finally, do try to answer the questions within the time limit suggested at the start of each section. One of the keys to exam success is answering not only accurately but fairly quickly. Timing out is a common cause of failure, and if you've had lots of practice in keeping to time you're less likely to encounter that particular problem when you sit the exam for real.

Foundation-level questions

This section has ten questions in the 'classic' style used for the Foundation exam. Try to answer the questions within eight minutes.

1. In a PRINCE2 project, which role is responsible for the Business Case?

❏ a) Corporate or programme management

❏ b) Executive

❏ c) Business Assurance

❏ d) Project Manager

2. Which of the following is a section in a PRINCE2 Business Case?

❏ a) Executive summary

❏ b) Summary of benefits achieved to date

❏ c) Responsibilities

❏ d) Sensitivity analysis

3. Which of the following statements about the Business Case is correct?

A. The Business Case is included in the Project Brief.

B. The Business Case forms part of the Business Management Strategy.

C. The Business Case forms part of the Project Initiation Documentation (PID).

D. The Business Case should be updated at the end of each stage except the final stage.

❏ a) A, B and C

❏ b) A, B and D

❏ c) A, C and D

❏ d) B, C and D

4. Which of the following statements is correct?

  ❏ a) A Business Case is not needed if the project is very low risk.

  ❏ b) A Business Case is not required if the project is compulsory and must be done.

  ❏ c) A Business Case is not needed if the project is part of a programme.

  ❏ d) A Business Case is always required in a PRINCE2 project.

5. Which variant of the Business Case is produced in the process Starting Up a Project?

  ❏ a) Summary Business Case

  ❏ b) Outline Business Case

  ❏ c) Detailed Business Case

  ❏ d) Provisional Business Case

6. In PRINCE2, who's responsible for specifying and subsequently realising benefits through the use of products?

  ❏ a) Executive

  ❏ b) Senior User

  ❏ c) Senior Supplier

  ❏ d) Project Support

7. In which process is the Benefits Review Plan created?

  ❏ a) Starting Up a Project

  ❏ b) Initiating a Project

  ❏ c) Directing a Project

  ❏ d) Managing a Stage Boundary

8. The Business Case refers to a timescale. What does this timescale refer to?

❑ a) Just the timescale of the project

❑ b) The timescale of the project and the period over which benefits will be realised

❑ c) Just the period over which benefits will be realised

❑ d) The staff time taken to prepare the detailed Business Case

9. Once the Business Case has been approved by the Project Board as part of the Project Initiation Documentation (PID), when must it be updated?

❑ a) At regular intervals during each stage, to provide detail for Highlight Reports.

❑ b) Only if there's a related lesson to be learned requiring a Lessons Report.

❑ c) As part of the work of Managing a Stage Boundary, at the end of each management stage except the last stage in the project.

❑ d) The Business Case is 'baselined' in the PID, so it mustn't be updated.

10. Which of the following options completes the wording of the purpose statement of the Business Case theme?

The purpose of the Business Case theme is to establish mechanisms to judge whether the project is (and remains) desirable, viable and achievable as a means to support:

❑ a) Effective judgement on the favourable balance of costs and benefits

❑ b) Informed decisions on financial risk exposure

❑ c) Decision making on the project's (continued) investment

❑ d) Continued business justification

Practitioner-level questions

Have a go with these Practitioner-level questions. As there are 12 questions for you to practice with, allow yourself 18 minutes for answering after you've read the additional project scenario information. That's the same pace as the exam where you'll have about 15 minutes, but then just 10 questions for a section.

Additional project scenario

Management overview

The balance of benefit will be negative in terms of costed benefits (the savings will be less than the expense). However, the Board of Directors considers that the operational advantage of having the new unit at headquarters fully justifies the modest costs involved.

Reasons

The refurbishment of the headquarters office will allow members of the new e-business team to be accommodated together. Creating this e-commerce unit is part of the five-year plan.

Options

1. Have a virtual team where members work from home rather than in one office.

2. Leave staff where they are in their present regional offices rather than have everyone together at headquarters, and use video conferencing for team interaction.

3. Refurbish office space at headquarters to make a new base for the e-commerce unit where all staff can be together. This was the preferred option and is the basis of the project.

Benefits expected

1. A better team identity with staff being together in this new e-business unit.

2. Better career development opportunities for staff by being at headquarters.

3. Saving of travelling time and costs, because our headquarters is close to 80 per cent of our major customers, and staff actually had to travel further when doing customer visits from other offices.

4. Provision of improved offices at headquarters.

5. An additional 10 per cent lift in sales, because e-business staff will work closely together, as opposed to the staff being split over different locations or working from home.

Costs

The creation of the unit, including costs of staff moves, is as instructed by the Board of Directors of Princess Projects Plc, so project costs are not a factor.

Timescales

The work is not expected to take very long, and a lot of the time involved will be in waiting for the furniture to be delivered after it's been ordered.

Investment appraisal

To be provided in the full Business Case when it's developed during Initiation.

Warning: There may be inaccuracies and errors in this Outline Business Case

Classic style questions

Using the main project scenario and the Outline Business Case provided as additional scenario for this section, answer the following questions. Remember to limit your answers to the number of selections requested in each section

1	\multicolumn{2}{l}{Which **2** changes would you make to the 'Benefits' section?}
	A	Delete benefit 1
	B	Delete benefit 2
	C	Delete benefit 3
	D	Delete benefit 4
	E	Delete benefit 5
2	\multicolumn{2}{l}{Which **2** changes would you make to the 'Costs' section?}
	A	Delete the existing entry
	B	Add 'It is estimated that the project will cost £20,500 but this will be adjusted or confirmed during project Initiation'
	C	Add 'The exact costs of the project will not be known until the furniture has been ordered'
	D	Add 'Costs are not relevant as Directors have instructed that the project should go ahead anyway'
	E	Add 'Most of the project benefits are operational, not financial'
3	\multicolumn{2}{l}{Which **1** action would you recommend for the 'Timescale' section?}
	A	Leave it as currently written as it is correct
	B	Replace the entry with 'The project timescale is not known and will depend on how quickly the furniture can be delivered after the order is placed'
	C	Replace the entry with 'Sensitivity analysis has shown that the project is not sensitive to time delay unless the delay is greater than two weeks'
	D	Replace the entry with 'At this point it is estimated that the project will take five weeks'
	E	Replace the entry with 'This section will be completed later as the project timescale can only be determined after the activity planning in the Initiation Stage'
4	\multicolumn{2}{l}{Which **1** action would you recommend for the 'Investment Appraisal' section?}
	A	Leave it as currently written as it is correct
	B	Replace the entry with 'The cost-benefit will be negative'
	C	Replace the entry with 'The project is an investment in operational effectiveness rather than financial investment gain'
	D	Replace the entry with 'The project costs will be met from central funds'
	E	Transfer the entry to the Daily Log to record that the investment appraisal must be done in the Initiation Stage of the project

Matching style – true/false

	For each entry about the Business Case for the e-commerce unit project in column 1, please select the correct option of true or false in column 2. An option in column 2 may be used more than once or not at all.	
	Column 1	**Column 2**
5	The Outline Business Case for the new e-business unit project should go on to be included in the Project Initiation Documentation (PID), together with the full Business Case. This is because the 'outline' version will be used at the end of the project to check against the initial – baseline – cost estimates.	A True B False
6	The benefits section of the Outline Business Case should be changed to only include benefits for which there is a currently calculated value and that benefit value must now be added.	
7	The Outline Business Case for this project need not contain the options as these are only needed for the development of the full Business Case when project funding is being requested.	
8	An Outline Business Case has been developed for this project, and this is required in PRINCE2 even though the project is being done on the specific instruction of the Board of Directors of the company.	
9	In this project, the Project Board should still review the Business Case at the end of each stage even though the project is included in the company's five-year plan.	
10	The Executive of the project should make the Senior User responsible for the Business Case as this is how PRINCE2 ensures that the Senior User is made accountable for specifying and delivering benefits.	
11	In line with the PRINCE2 standard, staff costs for the project should not be included in the Business Case as the company will pay the staff anyway, whether the project goes ahead or not.	
12	The Benefits Review Plan should include measures after the project to check if having e-business staff located together has given the increase in sales set down in the Business Case.	

Answers to the quick quiz

How did you get on with the benefits quiz? Here are the answers.

1 **No.** Did you notice, this is an 'output'. It describes something that the project is delivering, not a benefit.

2 **No.** The system going faster won't necessarily be a benefit. The computer running your word processor is capable of carrying out millions of instructions each second, but if you can only type with two fingers and key ten (short) words a minute, there isn't much benefit gained from that considerable processing power. Added to that, PRINCE2 says that a benefit should be measureable, and what does 'a lot faster' mean?

3 **Yes.** At last, a measurable benefit. It's a saving in staff time that can be expressed in cash terms.

4 **No.** This isn't a benefit resulting from the project. Rather it's an option for doing part of the project, which will be £8,500 cheaper than another option. It will be included in the Business Case as part of the costs, but it isn't a benefit.

5 **No.** This is an 'outcome'. Hopefully it will lead to the benefit of staff answering customer calls more quickly (a measurable improvement in customer service) when they see that callers have been on the line for hours and hours listening to canned music interrupted at 30-second intervals with a message telling them that 'Your call is valuable to us.'

6 **No.** This isn't a benefit, but did you spot what it actually is? A disbenefit. You get a bonus point if you realised that when you saw the question.

7 **Yes.** And let's hope the consultants were right.

8 **No.** You might argue about this one, as delegates on my courses often do. But I'd say that it isn't a benefit, even though you can measure the customers' impression of the 'improvement' with a questionnaire and get them to rate the 'improvement' on a scale of 1–10. However, what's the real benefit? Customers admiring the décor? The real benefit is surely an increase in sales, and can you prove the degree to which a sale was influenced by the new reception area? If the area had still been dark and dingy, would the company have lost that order from a particular customer? The look of the reception area will be an influence. Dark, faded paint and worn out, dated furniture may well put people off the company, but the impact of a bright, modern reception area cannot be quantified meaningfully. It therefore doesn't fit the PRINCE2 expectation of a 'measureable improvement'.

9 **No.** This is a technical feature. It may or may not lead to benefits. If the integrated database means that staff will no longer have to key the same information into three different databases, then there will be a saving in staff time, and that will indeed be a benefit. In the current form though, it isn't.

10 **No.** It may be a justification (a mandatory project), but it isn't a benefit. Actually this example is based on a real project, only the setting was a police force and a Chief Constable's instruction, and the 'customer' was a judge!

Answers to the Foundation-level questions

1. **b.** Tricky one this, because the PRINCE2 manual is rather confusing. In the responsibility panels, the manual shows the Project Manager as responsible for *producing* the full Business Case during Initiation, so you may be tempted to think that the Project Manager is now responsible for the Business Case itself. However, the text of the manual makes clear that the Executive continues to be responsible for the Business Case overall, even though others are charged with extending and updating it. The question is here to emphasise that you need to take on board the precise wording of the exam question to be sure to hit on the right answer.

2. **a.** No argument on this, because the exact section names are listed in Appendix A of the PRINCE2 manual. [**Manual** A.2.2]

3. **c.** PRINCE2 includes four strategies, and Business Management Strategy isn't one of them. Quick check – what are the four then? Look them up if you're not sure. You should have got this question right by knowing that there isn't a business strategy or by knowing that the other three statements are clearly correct. The Business Case is a part of the brief and also a part of the Project Initiation Documentation (PID) at different points of its development. In the brief, the Business Case is still in a rough 'outline' form.

4. **d.** Even if a project is mandatory, information must be recorded on any benefits, costs, timing and the fact that the justification is indeed 'mandatory'.

5. **b.** Tricky if you work on extremely large projects, because the PRINCE2 language conflicts with the terminology used in very large scale project environments. Remember to forget! Forget, for your revision and the exams, any normal practice which is different, and focus hard on the PRINCE2 terminology and meanings.

6. **b.** The Senior User represents those who will *use* the project deliverables (products) and go on to generate benefits such as increased sales and cost savings.

7. **b.** It's too much work for Start Up. The plan is created during Initiation at the same time as the Business Case is worked up into full detail.

8. **b.** This is where Appendix A of the manual comes in useful with its short explanations of the section headings in management products such as the Business Case. As you revise the management products, quickly look up any explanations where you find you're unsure of what a section is about. [**Manual** A.2.2]

9. **c.** The Business Case is routinely updated as part of the process Managing a Stage Boundary so that the Project Board can have the very latest forecasts available for its decision on whether to authorise the next stage.

10. **c.** Just rote learning I'm afraid, and there's no short way out of that. You just have to know which phrases fit where, or you make a decision not to worry too much about them, put your revision effort elsewhere, and risk losing the odd mark if you get an awkward question in the exam. Answer option 'd' is particularly nasty, because it's the exact words of a PRINCE2 principle. Were you familiar enough with the wording of the principles to recognise it and so realise it couldn't be part of the purpose statement? If you haven't revised the principles yet, don't worry too much. If you have revised the principles and still chose 'd', then perhaps it's time to have another look at them!

Answers to the Practitioner-level questions

Classic-style questions

1 **Two answers out of A, B and D.** However, B and D are best. Occasionally there are more 'right' answers than the number you are asked for. In this case, any two of the three correct answers is okay and get you the mark. However, if you selected all three, you'd be wrong because the question clearly asks for two answers. By the way, both of your answers need to be correct to get a mark. Sadly the days seem to be past where you were credited with half a mark if you got one of the answers right and the other wrong.

2 **A and B.** The existing entry is clearly wrong. Even mandatory projects have a cost, and the Project Board – and others – should know what that cost is.

3 **D.** It's accepted that the project timescale (and cost for that matter) is a high level estimate during Start Up, but it should be given. By the way, did you spot that you're now only being asked for one answer, not two? That's sneaky and won't happen in the real exam – or at least it hasn't happened yet. I've switched the number on you here, part way through the block of questions, to highlight the point that you must be very careful to check how many answers you're being asked for.

4 **A.** The entry is correct. Investment appraisal takes both good information and time. In the fast-paced work in Start Up, there just isn't time for such detailed work, but in any case the full information needed to make the investment appraisal sensible won't normally be available until the more detailed planning work in Initiation. You won't be asked to do any investment appraisal in the Practitioner exam, because PRINCE2 doesn't cover the techniques. However, you're expected to know what investment appraisal is by virtue of the fact that it forms a section in a PRINCE2 Business Case. In turn, that should lead you to the right answer that the level of work involved just isn't appropriate to Start Up. In case you're not sure what investment appraisal techniques are, they include things like Discounted Cash Flow (DCF), seen on spreadsheets with the formula @NPV (net present value). This requires exact costs and savings and then 'discounts' the value of money as you go further into the future. So, if there's a £1 million project that saves nothing for five years but then makes a one-off saving of £1 million, it won't actually pay for itself. That's because £1 million will be worth less in five years' time than at today's values when the project is being run and the expense is being incurred. Have a look at Inspirandum's *The Project Techniques Toolbox* if you want to know more on appraisal investment techniques for your live projects.

Matching-style questions – true/false

5 **B.** It's the full Business Case that forms the 'baseline' for reference at the end of the project. The Outline Business Case is a stepping stone, and the full or 'detailed' Business Case will be developed for the Project Initiation Documentation (PID). The PID as a whole is 'baselined' at that point, including the Business Case within it. That simply means a copy is kept. The PID will be updated throughout the project, again including the Business Case within it, and at the end of the project both the latest PID and the original baselined version will be checked out. If there's a big discrepancy, in either direction, between the benefits claimed in the original detailed Business Case and the latest one at the end of the project, the reasons for the discrepancy can be examined and reported in the End Project Report.

6 **B.** In both the main text and the glossary, the PRINCE2 manual defines a benefit as 'a measurable improvement'. However the text of the manual is then rather contradictory where it mentions 'intangible benefits'. It's not the case in the Outline Business Case that exact benefits levels need to be stated, and work may be done to establish those levels during Initiation. Remember that the *Outline* Business Case is 'quick and dirty' and just enough to show whether it's worth starting the project and doing the more detailed work of Initiation.

7 **B.** The context of the project should be given in all versions of the Business Case, including the Outline Business Case.

8 **A.** Yes, there should always be a Business Case in the Project Brief.

9 **A.** The need for an e-commerce unit is in the five-year plan, but the option to have it based at headquarters may turn out to be unfavourable if, for example, costs rise steeply. In that case, the project may cease to be viable and the company will choose to implement the e-business unit another way, perhaps using the different option of having a virtual team with staff working from home.

10 **B.** Back to responsibilities and a rather tough question to be sure that you're crystal clear on who's responsible for what. Yes, the Senior User is responsible for specifying benefits and then delivering them, but the Executive remains responsible for the whole Business Case.

11 **B.** Staff costs are often the most expensive part of a project, and the Business Case would be distorted and incomplete without them. PRINCE2 makes no such statement on the exclusion of staff costs.

12 **A.** Quantification may be difficult, because it'll be hard to prove that sales were due to staff being located together, but it should be attempted to get as good a measure as possible.

How did you find the questions – straightforward or tough? You should have found them challenging and that they took you into areas of exact detail. Don't feel too bad if you tripped on a few of the questions. While you're reading this book, there's still time to look at any difficult areas again; it's better that you pick up on these now, not hit a wall in the exam itself and have to start reading large parts of the manual to try and find answers.

Chapter 12

Organization

- -

In This Chapter

▶ Knowing the difference between roles and jobs

▶ Knowing where people are appointed to the project management team

▶ Key revision areas to watch out for

- -

*U*nderstanding the Organization theme is fundamental to understanding PRINCE2. At the time of writing this book, there aren't too many questions on roles in the Foundation exam question pool, but there's always a full section on it in the Practitioner exam. However, if the examiners ever read these words they may decide to boost the Foundation pool, so don't think you can safely leave the area out of your revision.

For the Practitioner exam, you'll be facing a full section of 12 questions on Organization, and it's highly likely that you'll have additional project scenario information to read. What's more, the additional scenario is likely to be substantial and longer than in any other section of the exam. The size can be up to about one and a half sides of A4; the large amount of text is because often you're given a list of people with a paragraph of information about each person. From that list, you may be asked to select suitable people to fill roles in the project. In many instances, you're asked to select just one person for each role, but occasionally you may get questions where you're asked to select two people who may be suitable to consider for a particular role. Such questions, obviously enough, are to check whether you understand the PRINCE2 roles and the suitability of people to fill them, such as the Senior Supplier on the Project Board being a manager who is in a position to allocate staff resource for the project teams.

Revising the Organization Theme

Along with revising the roles themselves, you need to be clear on four related areas, so include them in your revision if you're currently unsure of them. The areas are:

✔ BUS: the business, user and supplier viewpoints (which you'll see in the Project Board and Project Assurance appointments)

✔ The four management levels and how the roles map on to these

✔ The Communications Management Strategy

✔ The impact on project roles and responsibilities if the project is part of a programme (such as the impact on reporting lines, but also where programme staff may also cover project roles, such as the Programme Director also being the Executive)

For a full explanation of how the roles work, have a look at the companion book *PRINCE2 For Dummies*. This has a chapter on the roles and responsibilities, but also a whole chapter on running the Project Board. [**P2FD** Ch10 and Ch12]

In this book, cross references to a section in the PRINCE2 manual are shown like this: [**Manual** 3.2.1]. Cross references to a section in *PRINCE2 For Dummies* are shown like this: [**P2FD** Ch11 Justifying the Project].

The next two sections are checklists to help you look for areas where you need to revise. If you can't tick off an item with confidence to indicate that you understand it, then put it on your list for revision. If you only have a very few ticks, then look out: it's going to be a long day – or night.

Revision checklist – Foundation

Check out these areas to think through whether you understand them. The checklist covers the exam syllabus, but also a bit more to deal with general points of understanding.

❑ The purpose and objective statement for the theme (sorry, even though I'm not responsible for pedantic Foundation exam questions)

❑ The significance of roles as opposed to jobs

❑ The use of role descriptions to back up role allocation

❑ The theme fulfilling the PRINCE2 principle of 'defined roles and responsibilities'

❑ The roles on the project management team – management roles only, so not team members or corporate or programme management

❑ The use of the project management team structure – usually a simple organisation chart – to record role allocations in the project, first in the Project Brief and then in the Project Initiation Documentation (PID)

❑ Which roles can be covered by the same person, and which can't

❑ Which roles can be shared between more than one person, and which can't

❑ In terms of the process model, where people are appointed to roles and where the role allocation may be adjusted

❑ Who's responsible for appointing people to roles and also for keeping the project management team structure up to date – the latter is the Project Manager

❑ The 'BUS' viewpoints – business, user, supplier – and how they map onto Project Board and Project Assurance roles

❑ The four management levels – corporate or programme management, then three within the project – and how the roles map onto those levels

❑ The significance of the Project Board in 'owning' the project – in PRINCE2 it isn't the Project Manager's project

❑ The term 'stakeholders' and how the Communications Management Strategy is used to list stakeholders and note how they are to be kept informed

Revision checklist – Practitioner

If you're reading this book after you've already taken and passed the Foundation exam, don't ignore the Foundation checklist in the previous section. Have a quick run through that as well to ensure you're still fluent in the Foundation areas. In the exam, you won't have time to start looking things up in your manual to refresh your memory, just to confirm occasional points. If you need to start reading a lot because you've forgotten the detail, you'll almost certainly time out.

❑ The Organization-related products of project management team structure, Communications Management Strategy and Role Descriptions

❑ Use of the theme in PRINCE2 both in terms of where – processes and activities – and how, such as to record stakeholder management

❑ The detail of the Communications Management Strategy – are you confident that you understand all of the sections and could spot errors in a wrong one?

❑ How to adjust the allocation of roles appropriately to fit a project – back to one person having more than one role and some roles being shared between more than one person

❑ The characteristics of each role – so you can spot who'd be suitable to take on a role in a project and who wouldn't

Clarifying Some Key Points

For each sub-section, read a few sentences. If you're confident that you fully understand the point, then skip the rest and move on to the next sub-section. If you realise that you aren't so sure of the area, read the sub-section in full and perhaps put the topic on your revision hit list for a bit more attention.

Understanding the project organisation structure

There are two key areas to check out to be sure that you understand how the PRINCE2 organisation structure works: the management levels and the 'great divide' for role sharing.

Mapping roles to the management levels

There are four management levels. So what are they? Hopefully you'll know these by heart. Above the project is corporate or programme management. Normally it'll be corporate management, but if the project is part of the programme of projects, then the Project Board will report to programme management rather than directly to corporate management. Within the project, there are the three levels of 'directing', 'managing' and 'delivering'. These last three are covered by the PRINCE2 project management team roles. The Project Board is at the 'directing' level, the Project Manager at the 'managing' level, and the Team Manager(s) at the 'delivering' level. A diagram in the manual makes the levels very clear. [**Manual** Figure 5.2]

Understanding the 'great divide' for multiple role allocation

The key to understanding the basics of where someone can have more than one role is to appreciate 'the great divide' between the Project Manager and the Project Board. Anyone covering one or more of the roles of Project Manager, Team Manager(s) and Project Support can't also take a role on the Project Board or do Project Assurance. The Change Authority is a bit more murky due to some rather odd wording in the PRINCE2 manual, but happily that isn't a big factor in the context of the exams.

To make sense of the 'great divide', just think about Project Assurance. Project Assurance is primarily an audit function. Taking the parallel of financial audit, you don't have someone writing the accounts and then auditing those accounts; that would be pointless and would take away any hope of impartiality. So too with Project 'audit' – the Project Assurance. The Project Manager, Team Manager(s) and Project Support have been the people 'writing the accounts' so they can't also have a role responsible for checking that work. Remember too that the board members may choose to do some or all of the assurance themselves.

So, can the person who is the Project Manager also be the Executive? No, because that would cross the great divide. Can the person who is the Senior User also do some or all of User Assurance? Yes, because that doesn't cross the great divide.

You may find it confusing that the Project Manager attends meetings of the Project Board – such as the End Stage Assessment meetings at the end of each stage. It makes sense, though, when you remember that the Project Manager is accountable to the Project Board, but isn't a member of it. The Project Manager attends the meetings and can recommend things, but doesn't share the decision-making authority.

Appreciating the significance of roles

You need to be very clear on the difference between a role and a job on the project. Even the manual is a bit fuzzy in places, which may have lead to you misunderstanding this important core point.

To check your understanding, answer this question. Is it acceptable for the Senior User to attend a Quality Review (QR) as a reviewer for the specialist product 'New Office Plan'? The answer is a resounding 'no'. If you think that's wrong, then you haven't quite grasped the concept of roles. Suppose that Peter Graham is the Senior User on the project. Why shouldn't Peter be a reviewer on a QR if he happens to know all about the requirements for the new office? Well, he can be a reviewer; I have no problem with that at all. 'But,' I hear you say, 'you just said that he couldn't be.' Well, no I didn't actually, and that's the point. The Senior User is not involved in a QR of a specialist product, but a reviewer is. Peter can be involved in the QR in the capacity of a reviewer, but that's nothing whatever to do with his role as Senior User. One person can have more than one role, but everyone must only 'wear one hat at a time'.

The use of roles is actually very powerful in any project setting, including PRINCE2. One person can have more than one role, and with a couple of exceptions in PRINCE2, roles can be shared by more than one person. This gives huge flexibility in project organisation. A very small PRINCE2 project can be run with just two people, both of whom are part-time on the project, and that includes all of the teamwork! Read *PRINCE2 For Dummies* if you want to know more about how that can be.

Jobs do map one to one to people. So one person's job may be part of a role, a whole role or more than one role. Peter, in the example above, has a job on the project which is made up of two roles. He's the Senior User and also a reviewer for one or more specialist products that will be put through QR. If the project is formal, Peter may well have a role description that states that these are his two roles. But the two roles are entirely separate. It would be wrong for Peter to go into the QR saying, 'Well I insist that it's done this way, because I'm the Senior User.' That would be wearing two hats at once and is a confusion of the roles. A mistake like this can be damaging in some circumstances in the project. (Peter – who is actually a real person – is very familiar with PRINCE2, so I know he wouldn't really make that mistake.)

So, be clear on roles and jobs. One person's project job may be a single role, part of a role (for example if two people are sharing the role of Senior User), or more than one role, such as with the example of Peter.

Understanding the roles

You should be familiar with each of the roles in the project management team and the basic responsibilities of each one. There's no need to list them here with any explanation, because they're all in Appendix C of the PRINCE2 manual. Use the appendix as a checklist: tick off those roles where you're confident you understand them, and read more about that role where you're not so sure.

To check out your knowledge of the roles and responsibilities, try the quick quiz. Unlike the sample Foundation questions, the quiz doesn't give you options to choose from. The questions only probe a few areas, so don't think that learning the answers will get you through the exams – you wish. You'll find the answers at the end of the chapter.

Quick quiz – who does what?

1. Who sets up and then maintains project files?

2. Who carries out configuration audits to ensure that the version control information is both complete and accurate?

3. Who verifies that the project will deliver something that provides value for money?

4. Who authorises Work Packages (work assignments given to project teams)?

5. Who is ultimately in charge of the project?

6. Who should secure project funding?

7. Who should refer (*escalate*) something to corporate or programme management if it goes beyond the financial authority or limits delegated to the project?

8. Which Project Board role is particularly significant in any decision making concerning the safeguarding of expected benefits?

9. Which Project Board role represents the teams working on the project?

10. Who keeps the project management team structure up to date during the project?

Seeing where stakeholders fit in

As a bit of a comfort in case any training course that you're doing didn't cover it: you won't be asked exam questions related to the actual management of *stakeholders*. You're expected to know, however, where PRINCE2 records stakeholder information, notably in relation to communications with them, and to know what a stakeholder is. Stakeholders are people who can affect or be affected by the project, or who think they will be. Those taking project roles, such as the Executive, are clearly affected by the project and so are stakeholders. Other stakeholders may be outside the project, such as people in other departments or the company's customers and suppliers, and won't have any powers to make decisions about running the project.

Knowing when appointments are made

Be sure that you know at what point people are appointed to roles. For the most part, that's in Start Up, but remember that Team Managers may be identified and appointed later on in the project. In Start Up, two activities are involved. The Executive and Project Manager are appointed first, and then the rest of the project management team are appointed later in the activity 'Design and appoint the project management team'.

Knowing when appointments can be changed

PRINCE2 is slightly weird about the whole area of changing appointments, and always has been. The method talks of the project management team structure being updated on the stage boundary, as if it can't be changed at any other time. There's no need to get into a debate here though, because the purpose of this section is just to draw your attention to the recommended update action in the activity 'Update the Project Plan' in the process Managing a Stage Boundary. [**Manual** 17.4.2]

It may also be that after initial appointments are made in Start Up, some completion or update is carried out in Initiation. This is alluded to in the manual text for the activity 'Create the Project Plan' rather than specifically stated, but it's shown clearly on the activity summary diagram together with an update of any role descriptions. [**Manual** Figure 14.7]

Practising With Some Questions

Have a go with some exam-style questions on the Organization theme. If you're reading this to study for the Practitioner having already passed the Foundation exam, still have go with the Foundation exam questions. It will either confirm that you still have good recall of the Foundation-level material or warn you that you have got a bit rusty and need to revise those areas a bit more to get back up to speed.

Foundation-level questions

Try to answer these Foundation-level questions in eight minutes and, to mimic the real exam, answer them from memory without looking anything up.

1. Which of these roles cannot be shared and must be filled by one person only?

❑ a) Project Support

❑ b) Team Manager

❑ c) Project Manager

❑ d) Senior User

2. Which Project Board roles commit staff resource to the project?

❑ a) Executive and Senior Supplier

❑ b) Senior Supplier and Senior User

❑ c) Executive and Senior User

❑ d) None of the above

3. Which of these roles is optional and need not be filled in a PRINCE2 project?

❑ a) Senior User

❑ b) Senior Supplier

❑ c) Project Manager

❑ d) Team Manager

4. Which of these roles is *not* part of the PRINCE2 project management team?

❑ a) Team Manager

❑ b) Project Manager

❑ c) Quality Assurance

❑ d) Supplier Assurance

5. In which PRINCE2 process is the project management team designed?

❑ a) Starting Up a Project

❑ b) Initiating a Project

❑ c) Directing a Project

❑ d) Controlling a Stage

6. Which of these statements is correct?

❑ a) Stakeholders are appointed to the project in the process Starting Up a Project.

❑ b) The Project Manager is normally from the customer side, not the supplier side.

❑ c) The Project Manager role is optional and need not be filled.

❑ d) For stability, once a role is filled the appointment cannot be changed.

7. Who should appoint a suitable person to the role of Project Manager if this is not done by corporate or programme management?

❑ a) The Executive

❑ b) Project Assurance

❑ c) Quality Assurance

❑ d) Project Support

8. Who's responsible for the preparation of the Communications Management Strategy?

❑ a) The Executive

❑ b) The Senior User

❑ c) Project Assurance

❑ d) The Project Manager

9. What are the three types of Project Assurance?

❑ a) Directing, managing and delivering

❑ b) Financial, quality and progress

❑ c) Business, user and supplier

❑ d) Project, stage and team

10. Which of these is *not* an acceptable set of roles to be covered by one person in a PRINCE2 project?

❑ a) Project Manager and Project Assurance

❑ b) Executive, Senior User and Senior Supplier

❑ c) Project Manager and Project Support

❑ d) Executive and Senior Supplier

Practitioner-level questions

There's some additional project scenario to check out for the Practitioner questions. After you've read through the scenario, allow yourself 18 minutes to answer the 12 questions. To help you revise and practise, there are more questions here than you will have in an exam section. In the exam there will be only 10 questions in an Organization section, but then about 15 minutes to answer, so the pace is the same. The 18 minutes includes any time you need for re-reading either the additional project scenario, or the original at the end of Chapter 2, and for looking anything up in your PRINCE2 manual.

Additional project scenario – some of the Princess Projects Plc staff

John J Johns. Managing Director of Princess Projects Plc. John Johns is a highly experienced and successful business manager, newly appointed to the company. John's particularly concerned that the e-business unit will be set up quickly, because he sees that this is the most promising area for fast growth in the company.

Mary Li. Mary is a long-serving member of staff who has a reputation for getting things done. She knows nearly everyone at headquarters and is both liked and respected because of her hard work and open-door policy to help her staff excel in their roles.

Mary James. One of Mary Li's own administrative staff, Mary James is experienced in project management, risk management and PRINCE2.

Ed Strong. Ed is the Deputy Head of the Sales Department and will have overall responsibility for the new e-business unit. He's very concerned to ensure that the accommodation being prepared for the unit will be functional and will facilitate rather than hinder the work of the new unit. He can be forceful, but has a track record of success.

Michelle Rew. A junior accountant, Michelle has great skills in budgeting and budget control. Michelle has project experience and a very analytical mind. Others value her input on projects to check that the thinking behind each Business Case is sound as well as that the calculations are accurate. She always achieves high professional standards and while always trying to be positive, she has no time for anyone 'cooking the books' to make project benefits artificially high.

Fabio Kapelo. A new middle manager of good reputation in the company. Fabio's management experience was mostly gained in a sports-focused organisation where he worked for some years before coming to Princess Projects Plc. He has extensive, practical knowledge of project management, and is PRINCE2 Practitioner qualified.

Alec Trician. Alec is a member of the Works Team and is both smart and keen to get into project management. He studied PRINCE2 from Wiley's *For Dummies* books in his own time and has recently passed both the Foundation and Practitioner exams with great marks and in a single sitting. At Alec's last annual review, his manager noted the interest and said he would look for openings on projects to provide some experience.

Saif Hans. Saif has worked in the Sales Office for the past two years, having come to the company with limited sales experience. He has found his niche though, and in 8 of the last 12 months has had the highest monthly sales total. Four months ago, Saif moved over to the e-business side of sales, and is keen to see that area develop into a strong and successful part of the company. Saif wants the new office to be set up well to allow good communications between sales staff, because he knows that even minor communication problems can cause misunderstandings and delays that can lose sales.

Amit Ghosh. A surprising member of staff, Amit joined the company as a general administrative assistant but quickly showed imagination and flair for developing new business. During his eight months with the company, he's put forward no less than 16 business-related staff suggestions, of which 14 have been adopted. Two months ago he was moved over to sales, where his technical skills alongside his business flair have led to growing success on the e-business side.

Try to answer the following questions within 15 minutes. You can look things up in your manual where you need to, but try to limit such checking or you'll slow down.

Classic style questions

<table>
<tr><td colspan="3">Answer the following questions about the allocation of people to management roles in the project to prepare offices for the new e-commerce unit.

Remember to limit your answers to the number of selections requested in each section</td></tr>
<tr><td>1</td><td colspan="2">Which **1** of the following is a correct statement about the allocation of staff to roles in the project?</td></tr>
<tr><td></td><td>A</td><td>John J Johns, the Managing Director, should take over as Executive if Mary Li, the appointed Executive, has to leave the project as he has most authority in the company.</td></tr>
<tr><td></td><td>B</td><td>There should only be one person in the Senior Supplier role unless there is to be a big change of team resource part way through the project that will need staff resource authority from a different area of the company.</td></tr>
<tr><td></td><td>C</td><td>The staff resource for the project has already been approved by the company's Board of Directors in the project mandate, so in this project PRINCE2 should be tailored to leave out the Senior Supplier role from the Project Board.</td></tr>
<tr><td></td><td>D</td><td>Because work by outside supplier companies is limited to phone line installation, there is no need to have a Senior Supplier from outside Princess Projects Plc.</td></tr>
<tr><td>2</td><td colspan="2">The project management team structure may be amended by the Project Manager at the end of the first delivery stage when work on the structure of the building to create the new doorways has been completed. Which **1** statement correctly gives the reason for this?</td></tr>
<tr><td></td><td>A</td><td>To record the names of the supplier staff who will be coming in to install the new phone lines as this information should now be known.</td></tr>
<tr><td></td><td>B</td><td>From the newly created Stage Plan for the next stage, to record the names of team members allocated to work in that following stage.</td></tr>
<tr><td></td><td>C</td><td>To enter details of any new stakeholders who, when work started and they found out about the project, said that they could be impacted by it.</td></tr>
<tr><td></td><td>D</td><td>To reflect any necessary changes in role descriptions or the allocation of management roles within the project as the project continues.</td></tr>
<tr><td>3</td><td colspan="2">Which **1** of the following statements describes an option for appointing Project Assurance to the project that would comply with the PRINCE2 approach to managing projects?</td></tr>
<tr><td></td><td>A</td><td>The Project Office in Princess Projects Plc is now experienced in using PRINCE2 so the staff member allocated to the project can provide both Project Support and Project Assurance. This will help minimise the number of people involved.</td></tr>
<tr><td></td><td>B</td><td>Mary James does not have any involvement in the project management or teamwork of the project. She would be suitable to carry out the Business Assurance function.</td></tr>
<tr><td></td><td>C</td><td>The project will be fast moving to meet the deadline for the launch of the new e-business unit. To save time Ernest Wise, the Project Manager, could carry out the Project Assurance work himself before passing information to the Project Board.</td></tr>
<tr><td></td><td>D</td><td>Because the project is short at just five weeks, the Project Board members must cover the assurance function and cannot appoint separate Project Assurance.</td></tr>
</table>

Assertion-reason style questions

Answer these questions about the possible appointment of staff to Project Management Team roles in the e-business office preparation project.

Each row in the table below consists of an assertion statement and a reason statement. For each row identify the appropriate selection from options A to E that applies. Each option can be used once, more than once or not at all.

Selection	Assertion	Reason	
A	True	True	AND the reason explains the assertion
B	True	True	BUT the reason does not explain the assertion
C	True	False	
D	False	True	
E	False	False	

	Assertion		Reason
4	Alec Trician would have been a suitable alternative to Ernest Wise as Project Manager	BECAUSE	Alec has a strong interest in project management
5	Michelle Rew would be suitable as Executive should Mary Li, the appointed Executive, leave	BECAUSE	Michelle is an accountant with an analytical mind
6	Saif Hans would be suitable for consideration as Senior User	BECAUSE	Saif understands the requirements for good usability of the new suite of offices
7	Alec Trician would be suitable as Senior Supplier	BECAUSE	Alec is employed as an electrician in the Works Team which will be doing a lot of the work in this project
8	Amit Ghosh would be suitable for the role of Supplier Assurance	BECAUSE	Amit has flaire for new business and could check that the layout of the new office area is suitable
9	Fabio Kapelo could be considered for the role in Project Assurance	BECAUSE	Fabio has project background in sports

More classic style questions

	Answer the following questions about the preparation of the project management team structure for the project to prepare the office accommodation for the new e-commerce unit. Remember to limit your answers to the number of selections requested in each section

10	Which **1** statement describes a factor that the Executive should take into account when considering the Senior Supplier role on the project?	
	A	Because the Works Department will be doing most of the work of the project, the Senior Supplier should be a manager from that department, authorised to commit resource.
	B	There should only be one person in the Senior Supplier role because, in this project, more than half of the work is to be done by Princess Projects Plc's own staff.
	C	The staff resource for the project has already been approved by the company's Board of Directors in the project mandate, so in this project PRINCE2 should be tailored to leave out the Senior Supplier role from the Project Board.
	D	Because of the significant risk of complications during the structural work, the Princess Projects Plc Risk Manager should take the role of Senior Supplier in the project.

11	After a serious problem with old wiring in another part of the building that nearly caused a fire, Mary Li, the Executive, is concerned that new electrical circuits in the offices should fully comply with the latest safety standards as set down in the Quality Management Strategy. From within the Project Management Team for the project, who should she ask to check that the that the quality control procedures in the project are being applied correctly to ensure that the electrical standards are met?	
	A	Ernest Wise, the Project Manager, as the person responsible for the day-to-day management of the project and the activity 'Receiving completed Work Packages'
	B	The Team Leader of the Works Team who will be doing the electrical work
	C	Supplier Assurance, part of the Project Assurance
	D	The Quality Assurance staff of Princess Projects Plc

12	Which of the **1** of the following statements describes when a Team Manager appointment should be made for the project team made up of staff from the Works Department?	
	A	At the start of the stage when that team will first be involved in the project, in this case the first delivery stage after Initiation when structural work is done
	B	During the stage when the team is involved and at the point when the team arrives and needs to get organised
	C	Before PRINCE2 starts, as part of the project mandate, because the organisation should ensure that the right managers are available before starting PRINCE2
	D	During the process 'Starting Up a Project' because it is clear that the team will be needed and because Ernest Wise, the Project Manager, will not be leading the team himself

Answers to the quick quiz

1. Project Support. [**Manual** C.9.1]

2. Project Support. [**Manual** C.9.1]

3. Business Assurance within Project Assurance. [**Manual** C.7.1]. The key word in the question is 'verifies', and verification falls to Business Assurance.

4. Project Manager. [**Manual** C.5.1]

5. Executive. [**Manual** C.2.1]. Yes, it's the whole Project Board, but within that it's the Executive acting as a 'head of department'. [**P2FD** Ch12 Examining the Project Board]

6. Executive. [**Manual** C.2.1]. If your own organisation does this differently, remember the exams are PRINCE2 exams, not exams on your organisation's practice.

7. Executive. [**Manual** C.2.1]. The name PRINCE2 uses for the limits is 'tolerances'.

8. Senior User. [**Manual** C.3.1]. The Senior User is responsible for benefits, both determining what they will be and then delivering them.

9. Senior Supplier. [**Manual** C.4]

10. Project Manager. This update forms a part of the activity 'Update the Project Plan' in the process Managing a Stage Boundary. [**Manual** 17.4.2]

Answers to the Foundation-level questions

1. **c.** PRINCE2 allows only one Project Manager (and only one Executive).

2. **b.** The Senior Supplier authorises specialist resource, and the Senior User authorises any user resource (such as to help specify requirements and take part in testing).

3. **d.** The work can be covered by the Project Manager, usually in a small project.

4. **c.** Quality Assurance is an organisational function, external to the project.

5. **a.** Specifically in the activity 'Design and appoint the project management team'.

6. **b.** You can have a supplier-side Project Manager, but the default is that the Project Manager should be from the customer side; it's the customer's project, not the supplier's. Stakeholders are identified, not appointed – read *every* word in the question.

7. **a**. [**Manual** Table 5-1]

8. **d.** Others may contribute and help, but the Project Manager is responsible.

9   **c.** [**Manual** Appendix C.7.1, **P2FD** Ch12 Looking at Project Assurance]

10   **a.** Project Assurance must be independent of the Project Manager. On a very small project, it's fine for one person to be the Project Board and cover all three board roles.

Answers to the Practitioner-level questions

In the PRINCE2 exams, it's sometimes apparent that the person setting a question has seized on a point in the manual and built a question around it, irrespective of whether that point reflects something important in PRINCE2 or is obscure, insignificant in real projects or plain weird. That makes life tough for you, because no matter how hard you revise, you're not going to remember every part of every sentence in every chapter of the PRINCE2 manual. What does help is to think where that point may be addressed in the manual. For appointments to roles, focus on three areas in the PRINCE2 manual for quick reference:

1. **The Organization theme chapter**, and particularly the section that works through the roles in the project management team. [**Manual** 5.3.2]

2. **Activities in processes** where people are appointed to roles (mostly in Start Up). So, for the Executive, the activity 'Appoint the Executive and Project Manager' notes that someone who is a 'decision maker with appropriate authority' is needed as Executive. [**Manual** 12.4.1]

3. **Appendix C** with its role descriptions and lists of responsibilities for each role.

As you check the manual, if you happen to hit on the phrase that the person who wrote the question based it on, then you have an advantage.

The area of the Organization theme is tricky in a second sense, and that's because it's more prone than nearly all the others to having answers based on opinion. In your opinion Rachel Smith may be a good choice for project Executive, but in my opinion Wu Ling would be better, and I set the question. As with any area of the Practitioner exam that has a judgement call, you just hope that your view coincides with that of the people setting the questions. Having said that, it's important to bear in mind the point in the previous paragraph. Those setting the questions are likely to have selected a particular person as the best appointment because of some factor stated in the manual, so that they can then point to that phrase in defence of their answer.

So, here we go with the 'right' answers. How did you get on?

Classic-style questions

1   **D.** The Senior Supplier represents those doing the work of the project – the teams. Having phone lines put in is not exactly teamwork and is more likely to be simply external supply with an telecoms engineer visiting for three or four hours. Such limited involvement by an outside supplier does not need representation on the Project Board.

2   **D.** You may think that answer C is a possibility here, but option D is a better answer and reflects the wording in the manual. The question illustrates one of the revision points set down at the start of the Practitioner questions earlier in this section. It sometimes helps to look at the process involved and the relevant activity within that process. In the activity 'Update the Project Plan' in the process Managing a Stage Boundary, a recommended action includes the words 'Any changes within the Project Initiation Documentation (e.g. . . . project management team structure or role descriptions.) [**Manual** 17.4.2]

3   **B.** Mary James has an existing management link with the Executive, and this working relationship can carry forward effectively into the project. However, tackling the question from the other direction, the other answers are wrong. Project Assurance, for example, must be independent of the Project Manager – and that also means independent of Project Support, which is helping the Project Manager. Even though the project is short, separate assurance staff can still be appointed.

Assertion–reason questions

4   **D.** A Project Manager should have suitable experience, not just a strong interest.

5   **D**. Michelle Rew looks to have sufficient business understanding, but doesn't seem to have sufficient decision-making authority, as a 'junior accountant'.

6   **A.** A bit of a judgement call, but certainly Saif looks worthy of consideration and like he would be a safe pair of hands.

7   **D.** Alec is not in a management role in the Works Team and so would not have authority to commit staff resource.

8   **D.** Amit may be considered for appointment as Senior User, but doesn't have the background needed for Senior Supplier.

9   **B.** The sports project experience isn't a deciding factor, but the extensive project understanding means that Fabio should know what to look for when checking a project out.

More classic questions

10   **A.** This is a straightforward question but it also illustrates the strategy of ruling out wrong answers to arrive at the right one, or at least eliminating some answers to focus more clearly on the possible ones. In this case, three of the four answers are nonsense, so the question is relatively kind.

11   **C.** Supplier Assurance, as recorded in Appendix C of the PRINCE2 manual. [**Manual** C.7.1 Supplier assurance responsibilities]. Quality Assurance from Princess Projects Plc may also have an interest, but the question was focused on staff within the project and specified the project management team.

12   **D.** It's only in very small projects, normally, that a Project Manager will run the team and Team Managers are not needed. However, the question makes clear in any case that Ernest Wise won't be leading the team. Sometimes it's not until later in the project that the team requirements and resourcing become clear, so appointments may be made on a stage boundary, but in this project it's clear. The appointment of the Team Manager of the Works Team is therefore appropriate to the activity 'Design and appoint the project management team' in the process Starting Up a Project. [**Manual** 12.4.3]

Chapter 13

Quality

. . . .

In This Chapter

▶ Getting to grips with the management products related to quality

▶ Checking that you understand Quality Review

▶ Knowing the place of the Product Description within quality management

▶ Having a go with a quick quiz and some practice exam questions

. . . .

*L*ike the other themes, the Quality theme has a whole section devoted to it in the Practitioner exam and is the subject of quite a lot of questions in the Foundation question pool from which the 75 in your Foundation exam will be drawn.

The chapter on Quality in the official PRINCE2 manual is a little strange, and always has been. As a result, you may feel unsure about the theme to the point that you think you don't 'get' it. Also, if you have any professional experience in the area of quality, you may feel uncomfortable and think that everything seems rather off beam. If you experience either or both of these two reactions, don't worry . . . it's not you. PRINCE2 is actually pretty good when it comes to quality, it's just that the chapter explaining it is rather focused on procedures and definitions, and that tends to obscure the quality approach.

Your approach to revision then should be to put aside any unease and instead ensure that you understand the individual components of quality management in PRINCE2. So, for example, what exactly is the Quality Management Strategy and just how does a Product Description figure when it comes to quality management in a project?

A particular area to watch out for is Quality Review (QR). A common misconception is that every product in a PRINCE2 project must go through QR. This formal type of review is actually only needed, usually, for a small number of products, and in a particular project may not be used at all. If you don't see why, dip into the 'Clarifying Some Key Points' section later in this chapter.

Revising the Quality Theme

When planning your revision, run through the checklists below to see where you feel confident and where you think you should highlight a point to go through again in revision. If you already have the Foundation Certificate and are reading this book to prepare for Practitioner, still go through the Foundation list to make sure you remain up to speed on the basics, and then check out the Practitioner list in addition.

Revision checklist — Foundation

This list takes in the official syllabus for the Foundation exam, but also some other key points essential to your understanding of the theme. Don't tick off an item unless and until you feel confident that you understand it. The items you need to grasp are:

❑ The purpose and objective statements for the theme

❑ The three steps in a Quality Review (QR), and the four roles

❑ In the context of QR, the difference between a producer of a product and a presenter in the QR — the person who created a product may or may not be suitable to present it to others in a QR

❑ The objectives of a QR, as set down in the PRINCE2 manual — in order to be able to recognise them rather than recite them from memory [**Manual** Quality Review Technique panels in 6.3.2.1]

❑ How roles are combined in a minimum form of QR — one person is Chair and Reviewer, a second person is Presenter and Administrator

❑ Quality planning and the place, content and purpose of the Quality Management Strategy

❑ How quality planning picks up lessons from the past (Lessons Log), and the management of quality within the project then involves recording lessons learned to pass back into the organisation to contribute to continuous improvement

❑ The difference between Customer Quality Expectations and Acceptance Criteria — the expectations tend to be a bit woolly, while the project's Acceptance Criteria are precise and can be measured to say whether they were achieved

❑ The tracking of quality down to the level of Product Descriptions — the sections in a Product Description that are focused on quality (the final five)

❑ What quality control is (basically testing) and the types of quality method — 'in-process' and 'appraisal', and then within appraisal, 'testing' and 'quality inspection'

❑ The contents and purpose of the Quality Register — and the fact that it's used to record the outcome of a QR, just like it is for any other quality action

❑ What a Quality Management System (QMS) is in the organisation — and how this can have a bearing on setting up quality management within the project

❑ The difference between Project Assurance and Quality Assurance

❑ Where quality is specified in PRINCE2: the Project Product Description (PPD) within the Project Brief then in the Project Initiation Documentation (PID), the Quality Management Strategy, also in the PID, and then individual Product Descriptions. How this 'trail' can be followed through [**Manual** Figure 6.1]

Revision checklist – Practitioner

Make sure that you're fluent with the areas in the Foundation checklist, then go through this one for additional Practitioner revision points.

❑ The detail of the quality audit trail, to be sure that you understand every element and how the diagram goes down through the levels of the project to individual products. [**Manual** Figure 6.1]

❑ The detail of interaction with the organisation's Quality Management System (QMS)

❑ Where quality requirements are recorded and then maintained in terms of the process model. This may be a useful list to write into your PRINCE2 manual for reference during the exam. So, to start you off: Customer Quality Expectations and project Acceptance Criteria in the Project Product Description (PPD) within the Project Brief – activity 'Select the project approach and assemble the Project Brief' in the process Starting Up a Project.

❑ The detail of the Quality Management Strategy – do you understand each section in the strategy and could you spot errors in a faulty one?

❑ Where Product Descriptions are created and used, and by whom – not forgetting the PPD and the fact that Product Descriptions can be used for management products as well as specialist (team) products.

❑ Who does what in quality management in PRINCE2 – mostly easy, because it's in the responsibilities table in the manual, which, of course, you can consult during the exam. Just don't forget that it's there. [**Manual** Table 6-3]

Clarifying Some Key Points

This section runs through a few areas that those learning PRINCE2 sometimes misunderstand or find hard to follow. For each point, have a look at the first few sentences and if you understand the area well, leave the rest and move on to the next point. If you don't understand the area, the text may help, but you'll also benefit from putting the point on your revision list, digging into *PRINCE2 For Dummies*, and reading the relevant part of the PRINCE2 manual.

Understanding the focus on appropriate quality

PRINCE2 doesn't insist on the very highest level of quality for every project. A project to refit the stationery cupboard doesn't have safety-of-life implications – well, not usually. However, a new computer system to control air traffic across the southern part of the UK does have implications for human safety. The quality level is going to be very different for the two projects, then. In PRINCE2, the difference between projects is reflected in the fact that there are Customer Quality Expectations, project Acceptance Criteria and a Quality Management Strategy for each project. The important things are to determine what quality level is appropriate for each individual project, how that quality will be achieved (the *strategy*), and to check that it's been achieved. PRINCE2 covers all of those things with an approach that maps through to the acceptance of products.

Planning the quality management

Planning quality is focused on achieving the required quality – it's about implementing the Quality Management Strategy. The Project Manager checks the strategy when creating the Project Plan, and then repeatedly when planning successive stages, to build in the correct quality. This includes meeting any specified standards.

Appreciating the place of the Product Description

The PRINCE2 approach to quality is tied in with product-based planning, so the quality is very specific indeed. The final five sections of the Product Description are quality related. Check that you're clear on each one: 'Quality criteria', 'Quality method', 'Quality tolerance', 'Quality skills required' and 'Quality responsibility'.

It's worth commenting briefly on the last of the sections, 'Quality responsibility', because it isn't well thought through or explained clearly in the PRINCE2 manual. According to the manual, the section lists who will produce the product, who will check it and who will approve it – and approval of a product may be by the same person who checked it. Unfortunately, the manual talks of who will 'review' a product rather than who will check it, leading to the common misconception that every product needs to go through Quality Review (QR). Don't be fooled: *review* doesn't necessarily mean Quality Review. Also, the producer of the product isn't always involved with the quality management; often it's important that the producer isn't involved, so that checks are independent.

Understanding the Quality Register

The *Quality Register* is a brilliant device used in a number of approaches to project management, not just PRINCE2. However, the PRINCE2 name – Quality Register – isn't so good, in my biased opinion. Neither is the description in the PRINCE2 manual that the register functions like a quality diary. Actually the Quality Register functions more as a checklist. The concept of a checklist is a key one, because that's where the strength of the register lies. The register is primarily a list of product tests that are to be made in a stage; when each test is carried out, it's signed off in the register. It's therefore very easy to see whether a planned test or any other quality action has been forgotten, because it won't have been ticked off on the checklist.

The Project Manager puts the list of tests into the Quality Register during stage planning. The Project Manager works with the stage-level Product Descriptions, each of which has a 'Quality method' section to say how that product will be tested. The tests from all the Product Descriptions for that stage are simply copied into the register, ready to be signed off when they're done. Should a product fail a test during the stage, then of course it's has to be put right and re-tested. That additional test work must now be entered into the Quality Register so that it too can be signed off once it's been done. Most entries in the register, then, are made during stage planning, but some are made during the stage itself as the need for additional quality work is identified.

In the context of the Quality Register, the method refers to *quality actions* rather than tests or checks. The term 'quality actions' is appropriate, because other quality work above and beyond the testing needs to be put into the register. For example, quality audits may be planned for the stage, and the register needs to show that they've been done too. The outcome of all quality actions in a stage will go in the Quality Register. Don't forget that a Quality Review (QR) is just a type of test; the QR outcome goes in the register just like the outcome of any other test.

Understanding Quality Review

The *Quality Review* (QR) is often misunderstood, but the concept is actually straightforward. A QR is simply a test; it's one sort of test that you might apply to a printed product such as an office design, a specification or even to management products such as the Project Plan. The QR is a formal meeting which is a structured walkthrough of a product, a section at a time, so that people can say whether it's okay. In fact, although the method claims QR as a PRINCE2 technique, it was around long before PRINCE was thought of, and is sometimes still known as a *quality walkthrough*.

It's important to take on board that not every product is suitable for QR; a QR is usually for paper-based products. If you want to test that the new bridge is strong enough, you drive heavy lorries or a tank over it rather than hold a meeting to talk about it.

Who does what in Quality Review?

Check out your knowledge about who does what in a QR with this quiz. The answers are at the end of the chapter.

1. What are the QR roles?

2. Who plans the QR for a specialist (team) product?

3. Who makes administrative arrangements for the review, such as booking the room?

4. Before the review meeting, who should circulate the product to be reviewed, together with its Product Description?

5. Before calling the review, who should check that the product is ready for review?

6. Who should check that the reviewers are available?

7. During the meeting, who records details of any errors found in the product?

8. In PRINCE2, which QR role chairs the QR?

9. Which role should introduce the product at the start of the review?

10. At the end of the review, who should read back any required actions to confirm them and also to confirm who is responsible for taking each action?

Practising With Some Questions

Have a go with some exam-style questions to try your hand at the theme of Quality. Don't forget that before your exam you can and should also practise with the official sample papers available from the exam authority or through your training supplier. For the Foundation exam though, the official sample papers won't help much until you have all of the method under your belt, because the questions cover subjects in random order. In this chapter, you have ten Foundation-level questions solely on Quality; what joy.

Foundation-level questions

Try to answer these questions in eight minutes, without looking at any reference material. If you don't know the answer, then guess; after you've been studying PRINCE2 for a while, surprisingly often your gut reaction is correct. For more on exam technique, including more on how to set about guessing, see Chapter 2.

1. It's important to think through and record how a project will achieve its required quality level. Which product records that detail in PRINCE2?

   ❑ a) Quality Plan

   ❑ b) Quality Management System (QMS)

   ❑ c) Project Approach

   ❑ d) Quality Management Strategy

2. Which Project Board role is responsible for ensuring that the project delivers things that are fit for purpose?

   ❑ a) Executive

   ❑ b) Senior User

   ❑ c) Senior Supplier

   ❑ d) Programme representative

3. In which PRINCE2 product are Customer Quality Expectations first recorded?

   ❑ a) Project Product Description (PPD)

   ❑ b) Project Initiation Documentation (PID)

   ❑ c) Project Quality File

   ❑ d) Quality Management Strategy

4. Which phrase completes the purpose statement for the Quality theme? The purpose of the Quality theme is to define and implement the means by which the project will create and:

❑ a) Deliver products that meet the specified quality standards.

❑ b) Test products to deliver a workable solution that is value for money.

❑ c) Verify products that are fit for purpose.

❑ d) Assure products that meet the customers' quality expectations.

5. Which of these is NOT a role on a PRINCE2 Quality Review?

❑ a) Executive

❑ b) Administrator

❑ c) Presenter

❑ d) Reviewer

6. What name does PRINCE2 give to quality control while a product is still being developed to ensure that quality is 'built in'?

❑ a) Developer tests

❑ b) Pre-emptive quality control

❑ c) In-process methods

❑ d) Live testing

7. When is the Quality Management Strategy prepared in a PRINCE2 project?

❑ a) During 'Starting Up a Project' to form part of the Project Brief

❑ b) At the start of the stage in which the first major specialist product delivery will be made

❑ c) During the Initiation Stage

❑ d) During the delivery stages when the quality work is underway if it's then decided that a strategy will be helpful

8. Which of these statements are correct?

   A. Quality Assurance is from outside the project management team

   B. Quality Assurance is part of the project management team

   C. Quality Assurance is accountable to the Project Manager

   D. Project Assurance reports to the corporate or programme Quality Manager

   ❏ a) only A

   ❏ b) only B

   ❏ c) B and D

   ❏ d) A and C

9. When should those attending a Quality Review receive a copy of the product to be reviewed?

   ❏ a) As soon as the product has been created

   ❏ b) When the product has been created and handed back to the Project Manager by the Team Manager

   ❏ c) Before the review, but in good time to send in comments beforehand

   ❏ d) As part of the introduction at the start of the Quality Review meeting

10. Which of these would be a suitable entry in a project's Acceptance Criteria?

   ❏ a) The machine modifications must be done quickly to minimise production loss.

   ❏ b) The new system must have 99 per cent availability with 1 per cent maximum down time.

   ❏ c) The stage for this year's conference should look smarter than in previous years.

   ❏ d) The new website should include the normal facilities of a modern site.

Practitioner-level questions

Have a go with the 12 practice questions and allow yourself 18 minutes after you've read through the additional project scenario information. In the exam you'll have slightly less time, but also only 10 questions. Don't forget to take on board the original scenario information at the end of Chapter 2.

Product Description – office plan

ID: PD21 **Title:** Office Plan

1. Purpose: To help understand the detailed nature, purpose, function and appearance of the product.

2. Composition: Desks, side tables, chairs, visitor chairs, cupboards, filing cabinets, carpets, blinds, coat stand (one for each room).

3. Derivation: List of required furniture.

4. Format and presentation: Colour plan on one side of A3 paper, with any accompanying notes single-sided on A4.

5. Development skills required: An understanding of office layout generally, including health and safety aspects, and also an understanding of the communication needs within the new e-business unit.

6. Quality criteria:

6.1 The chairs must be comfortable.

6.2 The plan must be to scale.

6.3 The plan must show the location of all furniture and power and phone sockets.

6.4 The new doorways should be made before new carpets are laid, so that carpets remain clean and are not damaged by debris or made dirty with dust.

7. Quality tolerance: The project must be delivered in no more than six weeks, but could be delivered up to two weeks early, provided that this does not incur extra costs such as overtime payments to get work done faster and so deliver unnecessarily early.

8. Quality method: The plan will be checked against the standard checklist for headquarters offices, and against current legislation for offices, including checking ergonomic factors to ensure that the office will be both comfortable and safe to use.

9. Quality responsibilities:

The check against headquarters standards – Head of Works Department.

Health and safety and ergonomic standards – to be decided later, because the Health and Safety representative has just resigned, and the replacement is not known. It may have to be an external consultant if a new member of staff is not appointed in time.

Warning: There may be errors in this Product Description

Classic style questions

		Answer the following question about the supplied Product Description for the office plan. Remember to limit your answers to the number of selections requested in each section
1		Section 1 is the purpose section. Which **2** actions should be taken with this paragraph.
	A	Leave the paragraph in place as it correctly reproduces the purpose statement in the PRINCE2 manual for a Product Description
	B	Remove the paragraph as it gives the PRINCE2 manual purpose statement for a Product Description rather than states the purpose of the Office Plan product
	C	Add the words 'To show the proposed location of furniture in the four offices, allow checks to ensure adequate space and guide project staff on where to place furniture'
	D	Add the words 'To comply with project 'best practice' which requires plans'
	E	Add the words 'To comply with the PRINCE2 requirement that all plans are formally recorded so that they can be configuration managed (version controlled)'
2		Section 2 is about the composition of the product. Which **2** actions should be taken with this section?
	A	Leave the existing wording in place, but add more detail.
	B	Remove the entry because this is a list of things to be shown on the plan, not elements of the plan document itself.
	C	Add the words 'Plan drawing and accompanying notes as required'
	D	Add the words 'To be composed by a staff member with office design skills'
	E	Add the words 'To be decided later by the Team Manager after the rooms have been prepared and there is a clear view to see what furniture will fit in'
3		Section 6 lists quality criteria. Which **2** actions should be taken with parts of this section?
	A	Delete 6.1
	B	Delete 6.2
	C	Delete 6.3
	D	Extend 6.4 by adding the words 'to comply with the Board of Directors' requirement for good working conditions throughout the HQ building'.
	E	Add '6.5 The plan must show sufficient desks in each room to accommodate the staff who are allocated to that new office.'
4		Section 9 is about quality responsibilties. Which **1** action should be taken with this section?
	A	Delete the existing entries and leave the section blank as responsibilities will be decided by the Team Manager later as that part of the work is reached in the project.
	B	Delete the existing entries and replace with 'Project Manager'
	C	Delete the existing entries and replace with 'Quality Assurance'
	D	Delete the existing entries and replace with 'Senior User'
	E	The entries are correct so leave them as written

Matching question style – true/false

For each statement in column 1 about the application of the Quality theme, please select the correct option of True or False in Column 2. An option in Column 2 may be used more than once or not at all.

	Column 1	Column 2
5	The quality requirements for the e-business unit project should be listed in the Business Case as they will directly affect project costs and so affect the cost–benefit balance.	A True
6	The Acceptance Criteria for the project should not include a date since the exact date of the launch of the e-business unit is not yet known.	B False
7	The Senior User should be a reviewer for all products in the project as he or she has overall responsibility to ensure deliverables in the e-business project are 'fit for purpose'	
8	When the Office Plan is notified as complete, the Project Manager should check the Quality Register to ensure that all the quality actions for that plan have been taken.	
9	When the Office Plan is notified as complete, the Project Manager should NOT check the Quality Register as this will have been done by the Team Manager and it would be wasting time and also would undermine the Team Manager's authority.	
10	The Quality Management Strategy for the e-business project will be included in the Project Brief to ensure that quality is 'built in' from the very beginning, not 'bolted on' later.	
11	Unlike an engineering or scientific project, no product in the e-business unit project needs to be exactly right, so every quality criteria statement on the Product Descriptions for this project should have an accompanying quality tolerance.	
12	Because of the ultimate responsibility of the project Executive, he or she must attend all Quality Reviews in the e-business project.	

Answers to the quick quiz on Quality Review

1 Chair, Presenter, Reviewer, Administrator.

2 Project Manager – as part of Stage Planning for specialist products.

3 The Chair and Administrator both have responsibility for the administrative arrangements.

4 Presenter.

5 Chair.

6 Chair.

7 Administrator.

8 Chair – well, I have to let you relax now and again with an easy one.

9 Presenter.

10 Administrator.

Answers to the Foundation-level questions

1 **d.** The term 'strategy' is a giveaway for any aspect of 'how' something will be done, and in the context of PRINCE2 that's risk, quality, configuration management (actually, how all change will be managed) and communications.

2 **b.** A programme representative may attend board meetings, but that isn't a board role and so isn't defined in PRINCE2 for quality or any other responsibilities.

3 **a.** The Project Product Description (PPD) is developed early on – in Start Up. [**Manual** A.21.2]. The Customer Quality Expectations will go on to be included in the Project Initiation Documentation (PID), but the question specified 'first recorded'. By the way, in PRINCE2 there's no such thing as the Project Quality File. There are quality records, and while they may go into a file, that file isn't a PRINCE2 product.

4 **c.** Oh dear, they all sound so plausible don't they? That's why you need to be familiar with the purpose statements. [**Manual** 6.1]. Don't get excessively worried though. If you're strong across everything else and lose a mark or two on purpose statement questions you won't be in danger of failing. There's a balance to strike in revision, and your time may be better invested in places other than purpose and objective lists.

5 **a.** Don't confuse the 'Chair' role of the Quality Review (QR) with the chair of the Project Board. The Chair of a QR is someone with meeting skills.

6   **c.** More rote learning of terminology, I'm afraid, although this term is more readily understandable – and so memorable – than some others in the Quality theme.

7   **c.** The preparation of the strategy is covered by the process Initiating a Project, which in turn is part of the work done in the Initiation Stage.

8   **a.** Quality Assurance is from outside the project, while Project Assurance is inside the project and accountable to the Project Board – or board members do it themselves. Project Assurance is independent of the Project Manager, but Quality Assurance is independent of the whole project, including its Project Board.

9   **c.** Comments can be sent in before the review to be put on the agenda for discussion. That means people must get the product in good time.

10   **b.** Acceptance Criteria must be measurable, and the PRINCE2 manual gives examples. [**Manual** 6.3.1.2, **P2FD** Ch13 Specifying Criteria for Project Acceptance]. This question picks up on the 'availability' example.

Answers to the Practitioner-level questions

Classic-style questions

1   **B and C.** The purpose statement simply explains why the product is needed in the project.

2   **B and C.** It's easy to lose focus on the product. If you're confused, think about holding the finished product in your hand or, if it's too big for that, looking at it. What is the product itself made up of? What are its component parts?

3   **A and E.** Actually 6.4 is wrong too, so you wouldn't choose answer 'D' to extend it.

4   **E.** As in other chapters of this book, I've been unfair to you by switching the number of required answers part way through the block of questions. In the Practitioner exam, so far anyway, within a set of classic-style questions you'll always be asked for the same number of answers for each question. That number may be one or two, and hasn't yet been more (to my knowledge and recall). The rather sneaky switch here is to emphasise that you must stay vigilant to pick up on the number of answers you're being asked for. If you're asked for one answer but you select two, your answer will be invalidated. Similarly, if you're asked for two but only put one answer, your answer will be invalidated.

Matching-style questions – true/false

Don't expect true/false questions to be simple in the Practitioner-level questions. Some of them can dive deep into the method, and you require a really good understanding of PRINCE2 to answer them.

5   **B.** Yes, costs are in the Business Case, but there's no requirement to list out the quality elements in depth. That would make the Business Case excessively detailed.

6 **B.** A project of this sort should have an end date, irrespective of whether the launch date of the e-commerce unit is fixed. Remember that the Project Plan needs to be drawn up during Initiation, and that should show the expected duration. If the duration of the project fits with the launch date of the e-commerce unit, well and good. If it's then decided that the e-commerce unit will be launched earlier, and therefore the project needs to deliver earlier, this will come under the project's change control to decide how to speed things up.

7 **B.** Total nonsense; the Senior User is not involved in the day-to-day work of the project, and testing is day-to-day work. This question is to reinforce two important points. First, Project Board members are part of the 'management' of the project and don't do day-to-day quality work. And second, Quality Review (QR) is just another sort of test – one of the sorts you might apply to a document. If you're still confused by this, imagine another sort of test such as checking a computer program. Would you expect to see Project Board members sitting at screens checking programs against expected results as part of their standard responsibilities? Don't think of QR as anything more than a type of quality control – a test – because that's all it is. That's not to say a QR isn't valuable, it's just to clarify what it is.

8 **A.** Yes, the Project Manager should be sure that the quality has been delivered. That check of the register takes moments and is in addition to the check made by the Team Manager.

9 **B.** The reverse of the last question, to be sure you're clear on the point.

10 **B.** Don't confuse the comprehensive Quality Management Strategy produced in the detailed work of Initiation with the quality intentions set down in Start Up in the Project Product Description (PPD).

11 **B.** No, and in projects the criteria with a tolerance are likely to be a minority. Be careful here, because some people go a bit overboard with tolerances, and that may be reflected in any training material you have if you're on a PRINCE2 course. Don't fall into the trap of thinking that everything must have a tolerance. For example, if I want a text document to go in a standard physical file, I'll specify that it must be printed on A4 paper. That's it – no debate. I don't want it smaller and I don't want it larger. Am I really that fussed, and would it be such a problem if it was A3 or A5? Yes, it would be a problem, so print the wretched thing on standard A4 and let's get on with the project!

12 **B.** No, the role of the Executive is not involved in the QR of specialist products. The person who is the Executive may also be a reviewer for some specialist products where he or she has expertise. However, the person is a reviewer because of his or her expertise, and in the role of reviewer, not because he or she is the Executive.

Chapter 14

Plans

Planning is a core element of project management, so it's hardly surprising that PRINCE2 devotes a theme to it. Having said that, the approach in the current manual is a little awkward, and you may have found the planning aspect hard to follow. There are two areas to focus on in your revision. The first, which you'll need to know about for both exams, concerns the types of plan in the method, where they're produced (in terms of the processes) and who produces them. The second area, which you'll need mostly for the Practitioner exam, is the practicalities of the product-based planning approach – you should be able to produce the diagrams and forms involved.

This chapter in the book is a bit unusual, because the product planning content of PRINCE2 is so substantial on the one hand, yet there's so little information in the manual on the other. You do have the Plans theme chapter in the manual, but that's limited in content. There's also an appendix that gives a worked example, but that doesn't help you too much with learning product-based planning in the first place. The good news is that there's help in *PRINCE2 For Dummies*, where you'll find a substantial chapter on planning, and in this book have a look at Chapter 22 in the Part of Tens, where you'll find ten revision points that you can refer to in order to supplement the information in this chapter if you need to. [**P2FD** Ch14 whole chapter]

 In this book, cross references to a section in the PRINCE2 manual are shown like this: [**Manual** 3.2.1]. Cross references to a section in *PRINCE2 For Dummies* are shown like this: [**P2FD** Ch11 Justifying the Project].

Finding PRINCE2 Planning a Bit Unusual?

If you're finding product-based planning odd and hard to follow at first, don't worry because nearly everyone does. Most people are focused on activity planning with Gantt charts (bar charts) and perhaps even activity networks and the critical path method. Strangely, if you've been involved in projects for a while, and immersed in activity planning, you'll probably find product planning harder that if you're new to projects and project management. Some people are tempted to cast product planning aside and just try to learn enough to scrape through the exams with the intention of returning to their old 'activity led' ways immediately afterwards. But please don't take that path, or you'll miss out on something that's really good. Product-based planning is actually extremely powerful, it's just that it's not natural. If it takes you a while to get your head around it, don't worry; soon the logic of the approach will impress you. But another consequence is that if you're on a training course that rushed you through the subject (and one major PRINCE2 training company that I know covers product planning very, very fast – and awesomely badly), then you'll need to allow a good amount of time in your revision plan for going through it.

Just in passing, and to add a little bit of extra spice to your revision, when you do get to understand product planning well, be aware that not too many people do – including at least some of the authors of the manual and, dare I say it, some people who write exam questions. You'll find parts of the manual written in a way that shows that the person who wrote that section doesn't quite 'get' it. Now I don't mind criticising bad sections in the manual, as you may have detected already in other parts of this book. But my objective here isn't to criticise for the sake of it but rather to warn you that if you do understand product planning well and you read something odd in the manual, don't immediately think that you've got something wrong; it may not be you that's the problem. A small bit of good news is that while the manual problems can and do have an impact on learning, they don't affect the exams too much.

Revising the Plans Theme

Have a look at the checklists in this section as you plan your revision. If you know something well, tick it off the list. If you feel unsure of the point, don't tick it – yet – but put it on your revision list to go through again. The checklists cover what's in the official exam syllabus for each exam, but also some other key points that you need to have clear.

Revision checklist – Foundation

This list covers the official syllabus for the Foundation exam, but then adds some other points essential to your understanding of planning. Don't tick off an item unless you feel sure that you know it. The things you need to look at are:

- ❑ The purpose statement for the theme – as set out in the opening section of the Plans chapter in the PRINCE2 manual

- ❑ Levels of plan – Project, Stage and Team Plans, and who's responsible for each (Project Manager for the first two, Team Manager for the Team Plan)

- ❑ The use of the plan levels by the different management levels with appropriate information – for example, the Project Board doesn't need to see or approve the fine detail of a Team Plan

- ❑ The nature of an Exception Plan – and when one is and isn't needed

- ❑ Types of plan – product, activity, resource, financial (although PRINCE2 offers no significant help on the last of these)

❑ When plans are produced – including Stage Plans, generally, being produced at the end of the previous stage

❑ The fit of plans in the method and in support of the PRINCE2 principle 'focus on products' – starting with the Project Product Description (PPD)

❑ The fit of plans in support of other principles – 'manage by stages' with the use of Stage Plans, and 'manage by exception' with tolerances set on plans and the use of Exception Plans when needed

❑ The (alleged) steps of product-based planning – PPD, Product Breakdown Structure (PBS), Product Descriptions, Product Flow Diagram (PFD)

❑ The (alleged) steps in planning [**Manual** Figure 7.2]

❑ Following on from the last point, that the activity 'Analyse the risks' runs in parallel to most of the other planning activities

❑ What a product is and isn't – there's more on this in the next main section of this chapter, with a quick quiz to check your understanding

❑ The two types of product – management and specialist

❑ The three sub-types of management product – baseline products, records and reports, and what those names mean

❑ The technique of planning with products first (product-based or product-led planning) and what the diagrams are about – PBS and Product Flow

Revision checklist – Practitioner

Make sure that you're still up to speed with the areas on the Foundation checklist, then check this list out for additional Practitioner revision points:

❑ Product Flow Diagram (PFD) – that you can draw one and are confident enough with the technique that you could spot errors in a faulty one

❑ Product Breakdown Structure (PBS) – that you can draw one and, again, are confident enough with the technique that you could spot errors in a faulty one

❑ The difference between a PFD and a PBS, and how the diagrams give entirely different views of the products

❑ Product Descriptions – how they are used, when (in terms of the processes and activities), and what each of the sections on a Product Description is about

In the Practitioner exam, you'll get a whole section of the paper on the Plans theme, so don't be taken in by the apparently limited content of the exam syllabus in this area. You need to have a good grasp of product planning to be able to answer the exam questions. The checklist above mentions your ability to draw diagrams, and as a first reaction you may think that this is wrong, because in a multiple-choice format clearly you can't be asked to do any drawing. However, the skill is still needed, because you need to be able to interpret any diagrams given to you in the exam, perhaps to spot errors in faulty ones and to suggest correct substitute parts for diagrams to replace faulty elements.

Clarifying Some Key Points

This section is to set out some areas of product planning that people misunderstand when learning the technique. If that's not you, just skip the point when you've read a sentence or two and you remain confident that you know that area.

Quick quiz – is it a product?

Before getting stuck into the detailed points in this section, why not check out your understanding of products? For each of the items on this list, simply mark 'Y' or 'N" to say whether you think it's a product or not. If you think an item isn't a product, try to be clear on why and to think what the item actually is. You'll find the answers at the end of the chapter.

1. Office floor plan
2. Interview the stakeholders
3. FIX-IT-FAST Tool Hire Shop
4. Project funds of £300,000
5. Works Department staff
6. Trained user staff
7. Doorways completed
8. Desks
9. Risk Management Strategy
10. Training Plan

Seeing the difference between a PBS and a PFD

Because product planning is a bit unusual for most, some people find the diagrams a bit confusing and can think that one is just like the other but rotated or upside down. If that's you, read on. The Product Breakdown Structure and Product Flow Diagram are diagrams that show exactly the same products but in a very different way.

The *Product Breakdown Structure* (*PBS*), as its name suggests, is all about structure. It's simply the products grouped on the diagram in categories. To use a simple example, for a project to build a house, you might have 'category boxes' for brickwork, woodwork, electrics, decorating and so on. Under each of these boxes you'd have more boxes showing the actual products in that category. So, under the 'brickwork' category box, you might have foundation walls, main walls, garage walls and garden walls.

In contrast, the *Product Flow Diagram* (*PFD*) shows flow or sequence. It's the same products with the same symbols as on the PBS, but this time set down in a network diagram that shows the order in which the products will be created during the project. That's not the same order that's on the PBS. To take the brickwork category as an example again, the brickwork involved in the foundations of the house is going to be done early on in the project. However, the garden wall will be probably be built near the end of the project, because delivery lorries will be backing in during most of the project and won't want a garden wall in the way. The diagram is a network, not a straight sequence line, because some products can be built in parallel. While one team is hard at work putting in cables to create some of the electrical circuit products, another team may be busy on some of the woodwork products such the framing around the doorways.

Both the PBS and the PFD discriminate between external products – those coming from outside the project – and internal or team products, created by the project teams. The normal convention, and one which is followed in the Practitioner exam, is to show external products in an oval shape and internal or team products in a rectangle. In the Foundation exam, you may be asked about the diagrams, but there won't be any on the question paper – at least there haven't been any so far to my knowledge.

The other main difference between the diagrams is that the PBS has additional rectangles on the diagram which are the category boxes, under which products are grouped. Those category boxes do not appear on the PFD, because they'e not products but rather labels to show why a set of products are grouped together, such as under 'brickwork'.

Understanding why there are levels of plan

When writing a book, it's not generally a good idea to criticise authors of other books on project management. However, when explaining the next point, I always make an exception. Someone (and I won't name him) wrote a book claiming to set down the perfect way of planning a project. A key to success, claimed the author, is to plan the entire project in fine detail at the beginning. Well, I'd like him to try that on a research project. Actually I'd like to see him try it on an IT development project where it's not at all clear what the new system will look like until some investigation and requirements analysis has been done in the first part of the project. I'd even like to see him try it in a business environment where things are changing rapidly and the world is a rather different place at the end of the project to the way it was when the project started.

Seeing the logic of the staged approach

PRINCE2, and any staged approach to planning projects, is realistic. You plan the whole project to set out how you expect it to run, but that plan is not detailed; it's a high level view. You then plan in more detail for each stage, but only as you approach that stage (that is, at the end of the previous stage) – you don't try to do it all up front. That way, when doing the more detailed stage planning, you can take account of the very latest information, changing technology, changing business environments and even changing requirements because of modified business priorities. If that alters the overall plan, then well and good – the overall plan (Project Plan) can be adjusted in the light of the information gained while producing the latest Stage Plan.

The Stage Plan is detailed and in smaller projects especially, may be in enough detail for Team Managers to use to organise their teams and build the products. However, sometimes a Work Package is rather complex and the Stage Plan just doesn't provide enough detail for the Team Manager to exercise the required level of control. In that case, the Team Manager can develop a Team Plan based on the relevant part of the Stage Plan, to cover the work of that particular Work Package.

A *Work Package* is an 'instruction pack' from the Project Manager to a Team Manager to build a single product, or perhaps two or three products which it makes sense to build at the same time with the same team.

Understanding the different management interest

Even from understanding the nature of the three levels of plan, you should now see how the management interests differ. The Project Board may have authorised a stage, but really isn't interested in the fine detail of what team member Elizabeth Bloggins will be doing to test widgit 5 on day 8 of Work Package development. The Project Board is interested in the whole project and in what is happening in each stage, so will only see and authorise the first two levels of plan: Project and Stage.

The Project Manager is, of course, responsible for the Project and Stage Plan development. Having developed the Stage Plan, that's the one the Project Manager will mostly use for controlling a particular stage. The Project Board, too, will want regular information on the Stage Plan to know, for example, whether that stage is running pretty much to the expected time and cost. Often, managers on the Project Board like to keep track of the 'big picture' on the Project Plan too. Although the Team Plan is in the domain of the Team Manager, both the Team and Project Manager will want to be sure that it fits in with the Stage Plan. Consequently, once the Team Manager has created a Team Plan, he or she will check it out with the Project Manager.

Being clear on levels and Exception Plans

Please note very clearly, including for the Foundation exam, that an Exception Plan is not a planning level. The three levels are Project Plan, Stage Plan and Team Plan. You can think of an *Exception Plan* as a recovery plan. It's usually at Stage Plan level, but can also encompass the Project Plan level and may affect some Team Plans. If something goes significantly wrong during a stage, and to recover from the problem the rest of the stage must now be run differently, then clearly the existing Stage Plan won't be much use. So, a stage boundary is forced (it wasn't planned originally) and the Project Manager will produce an Exception Plan. It covers the stage from 'now' – the point of the problem – until the end of the stage. It's effectively a replacement Stage Plan but is called an Exception Plan to make it clear that it's not the original one. The work done up until 'now' in the stage isn't re-planned, because that would be pointless. Instead it's closed down and an End Stage Report is produced for it. The remaining work in the original stage, now covered by the Exception Plan, is treated as if it were a new stage.

Take note then, an Exception Plan is not a planning level. It's a replacement plan, normally at stage level, but also may take in the project and team levels. Basically it covers any and all plans that are affected by the exception.

Just occasionally, an Exception Plan may not result from a problem but from something good. If someone comes up with a brilliant idea, for example to save the organisation a fortune and deliver the project three months early, then adopting that idea may require re-planning the current stage and the rest of the project. The Project Board may be more than happy to authorise the re-plan because of the substantial benefit. It's like going into exception deliberately, and comes under the general area of change control and the Change theme.

Knowing how the Product Checklist works

The Product Checklist is a mystery to some people learning PRINCE2, particularly if the person delivering their training course doesn't really understand product planning (you'd be surprised how many don't!) and so glosses over it as something optional and hardly worth mentioning. Actually, the Product Checklist is both very simple and extremely powerful for progress control, which is a great combination.

The *Product Checklist* is simply a list of products that will be produced in a stage. The list is drawn from the Stage Plan. The target delivery date is entered against each product, and also the actual delivery date. It's then possible to see at a glance whether the project is on schedule. That progress check is based on fact – delivery to the required level of quality – not wishful thinking or estimates.

You can put additional information on the checklist, such as the planned and actual dates for testing, but the key information is delivery.

Checking Out Diagrams in the Practitioner Exam

If you're just focusing on the Foundation exam at the moment, you may prefer to skip this section and move on to the practice questions. If you're going for Practitioner, you may find this part helpful.

Some Practitioner exam questions on product planning are based on supplied diagrams of which one or more contain errors. You then have to answer questions to say whether there's an error in a particular part of the diagram. The lists here are to help you check that you really know how the diagrams should behave and so be sure that you can spot errors quickly and reel in the marks.

The most common exam approach, to date, has been to supply a Product Breakdown Structure (PBS) and a Product Flow Diagram (PFD) and say that the PBS is correct. You're then required to find errors in the PFD, some of which are based on inconsistencies with the correct PBS. However, be well prepared for a faulty PBS as well, so you can handle any question based on errors in either or both diagrams. To check the diagrams, make sure you understand each of the following lists.

Checking a Product Breakdown Structure

These are the key points you need to cover when you analyse a PBS to find errors:

❑ Is the top box the whole project – the 'project product'?

❑ Do the products correctly and completely reflect the project scenario? Don't forget to consult the original scenario information as well as any additional scenario information supplied for the 'plans' section of the exam.

❑ Are external products correctly shown as ovals (ellipses) and team products and category boxes as rectangles?

❑ Where the scenario clearly says that a product is coming from outside the project, is it correctly shown as external, and where it's clear that a project team is producing a product, is it clearly modelled in a rectangle?

❑ Are the products really products – not activities, resources, sources of supply, and so on?

❑ Does the PBS break down cleanly, or does the diagram join back up again lower down – an illegal and illogical structure?

❑ Are there any one-to-one connections where a group only has a single product – that is, there's a redundant level, because you can't have a group of one? A one-to-one structure is illogical and illegal in the technique.

Checking a Product Flow Diagram

Make sure you check these points when looking at a PFD with errors:

❑ Is the bottom box the whole project – the 'project product'?

❑ Do the products correctly and completely reflect the project scenario?

❑ Going by the information in the project scenario, are any dependency arrows incorrect?

❑ Again based on the scenario, are any dependencies missing?

❑ Are any elements of the sequence logical where they are not specified in the scenario? For example, you can't have the product 'cooked food' followed by a product 'raw food', because it's not possible to uncook food.

❑ Are internal and team products correctly modelled? Where a product is shown as 'external' on the PBS, has it mysteriously changed into a team product on the PFD? Similarly, has a team product on the PBS become an external product on the PFD?

❑ Have all of the products on the PBS been carried over to the PFD or have some been forgotten?

❑ Are all the products on the PFD worded identically to the corresponding box for the same product on the PBS – and that includes the project product at the top of the PBS and the bottom of the PFD? 'Identically worded' means exactly that, to the letter. 'Garden walls' on one diagram but 'Garden wall' on the other is an error.

❑ Have any new products mysteriously appeared on the PFD that weren't present on the PBS?

❑ Have any category boxes been included in the PFD by mistake (the PFD only shows products, not category boxes).

❑ Does the PFD flow smoothly through the project, with no loops joining a lower part back up to an upper part so that the project loops around forever and never finishes?

Practising With Some Questions

Have a go with some exam-style questions. These have two purposes. First, you gain familiarity with the styles and get used to working within time limits. Second, the particular points will help you with revision and with exam strategy.

In both exams, a vital strategy is to read the question! Clearly if you misread a question, you're highly likely to pick a wrong answer, so be especially careful – and all the more so if you find yourself under pressure of time.

There's advice on tackling the different question styles and more exam strategy advice in Chapter 2. You'll also find project scenario information for the Practitioner-level questions in Chapter 2.

Foundation-level questions

1. Who's responsible for approving the Project Plan?

❑ a) Corporate or programme management

❑ b) Project Board

❑ c) Project Manager

❑ d) Project Assurance

2. What approach does PRINCE2 take to planning?

❑ a) Activity led

❑ b) Financially based

❑ c) Product based

❑ d) Resource led

3. Which plan(s) out of the following are included in the Project Initiation Documentation (PID)?

❑ a) Just the Project Plan

❑ b) The Project Plan and all Stage Plans for the project

❑ c) The Project Plan and the Stage Plan for the first delivery stage only

❑ d) The Project Plan, all Stage Plans and any Team Plans that will be necessary

4. What are the three levels of planning in PRINCE2?

❑ a) Outline, full and detailed

❑ b) Project, Stage and Exception

❑ c) Stage, Team and Work Package

❑ d) Project, Stage and Team

5. Which words should replace [?] in the purpose statement for the Plans theme?

The purpose of the Plans theme is to facilitate [?] by defining the means of delivering the products (the where and how, by whom, and estimating the when and how much).

❑ a) Communication and control

❑ b) Accurate forecasting

❑ c) Clear accountability for project work

❑ d) Risk and quality control

6. Product descriptions are written:

❑ a) For management products only.

❑ b) For external products only.

❑ c) Only for high risk products that could be misunderstood.

❑ d) For all the identified products.

7. Which of the following shows the expected sequence of product development in a PRINCE2 project?

❑ a) Product Breakdown Structure (PBS)

❑ b) Project Product Description (PPD)

❑ c) Product Flow Diagram (PFD)

❑ d) Work Package

8. In a PRINCE2 project, when is a Stage Plan developed for a delivery stage?

❏ a) At the beginning of the project together with all other Stage Plans

❏ b) At the beginning of the stage to be covered by the plan

❏ c) During Starting Up a Project

❏ d) Towards the end of the preceding stage

9. Which of the following statements is correct?

A. Team Plans are not always needed in a PRINCE2 project.

B. The Senior User should check and approve all Team Plans.

C. PRINCE2 does not require activity planning to be done, only product planning.

D. An 'external' product is a product that's not needed on the project.

❏ a) Only A

❏ b) A and D

❏ c) B and C

❏ d) Only C

10. Within the PRINCE2 management product categories, which of the following is a report?

❏ a) Project Brief

❏ b) Benefits Review Plan

❏ c) Work Package

❏ d) Highlight Report

Practitioner-level questions

For the Practitioner-level questions, you'll find some additional project scenario material below, which you need for some answers, but don't forget the original scenario information at the end of Chapter 2. Once you've read through the additional scenario information, give yourself 18 minutes to answer the 12 questions. That gives you some extra practice since a Plans section in the exam will have just 10 questions, and you'll have about 15 minutes to answer. So, the actual exam will seem easy after going through this book won't it? Well no, not at all, but keep up with the practice anyway.

Additional scenario

Before the project started, it was decided who will work in the new e-business unit. A list of those staff is already available. This will be consulted in order to draw up a draft office plan showing who will sit where in the new offices, and where the furniture is to be placed. The draft plan will be checked by the new office manager and others, and after any minor changes the plan can be agreed, at which point it will be called the approved office plan. Clearly that plan will be needed to know where to put phone lines and also to determine what new furniture needs to be ordered. The plan will also give the final colour scheme; therefore once it's approved, paint can be obtained from the company stores and the painting can get underway. As soon as the painting is complete, the phone lines have been installed and the furniture has arrived and been put in place, the office will be completed.

Matching-style question

The Product Flow Diagram (PFD) for the project has yet to be finalised, but Figure 14-1 shows part of it, although the product names have not yet been entered.

The products, in no particular order, are:

A. New phone lines

B. Furniture list

C. Furniture order

D. Repainted office

E. Staff list

F. New furniture

G. Paint

H. Approved office plan

I. Completed office

J. Draft office plan

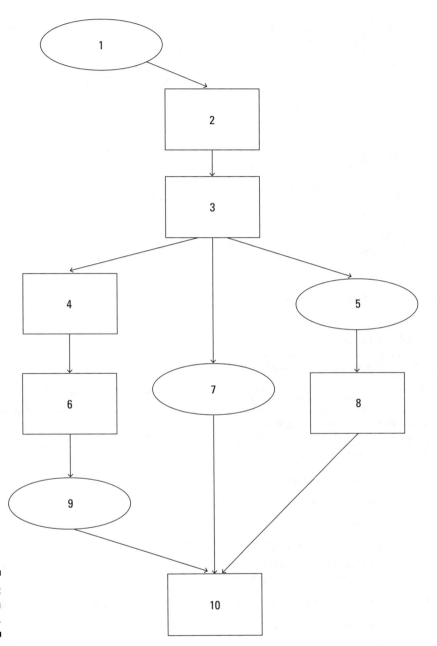

Figure 14-1:
Extract from
a PFD.

	Using the supplied extract from the PFD, say which product should go in each position on the diagram. For each numbered product position in column 1, select the correct product in column 2.	
	Column 1	Column 2
1	Product 1	A. New phone lines
2	Product 2	B. Furniture list
3	Product 3	C. Furniture order
4	Product 4	
5	Product 5	D. Repainted office
6	Product 6	E. Staff list
7	Product 7	F. New furniture
8	Product 8	G. Paint
9	Product 9	H. Approved office plan
10	Product 10	I. Completed office
		J. Draft office plan

Classic style questions

	Answer the following question about plans for the project.	
	Remember to limit your answers to the number of selections requested in each section	
11	Which **1** section of the project plan should explain that the plan is based on the expectation that staff will be released from other work and projects within Princess Projects Plc in time to take part in the e-commerce office project?	
	A	Plan pre-requisites
	B	External dependencies
	C	Planning assumptions
	D	Tolerances
12	Which **1** of the following accurately lists part of the content of the project plan?	
	A	The timescale to prepare the new offices ready for the e-business unit and the resource that will be required to carry out the project
	B	The risk that company policy might change so that the project is no longer required
	C	The requirement for new wiring to meet appropriate electrical standards
	D	The benefit of having offices big enough for the new e-business unit staff to be able to work together

Answers to the quick quiz

Products are mostly things that the project teams have built; you can hold them in your hand or, if they're too big for that, kick them. You may find it easier at first to think of products as 'deliverables', although you need to get used to the term 'product' as soon as you can. A few products aren't built by teams, and these are the ones coming in over the boundary of the project from outside – the 'external' products. Then there are the products used to manage the project, such as the Risk Register and Stage Plans, which are the 'management' products. So, on to the answers to the quick quiz:

1 **Yes.** It's a product and you can hold it in your hand.

2 **No.** This is an activity, not a product. Note the verb 'interview'. There may well be a product involved, such as 'interview records', but the item in the quiz is an activity.

3 **No.** This is a source of supply, perhaps where the product 'hammer drill' will come from. Remember, you're dealing with products here and not where the products came from. The only exception is if you thought the project involved setting up a tool hire shop, in which case it could be a product. However, because I believe that relatively few projects involve setting up tool hire shops, the answer 'no' is a better one.

4 **No.** Money is a resource, not a product that is made. I worked for a while in a security division of the UK Prison Service. Take it from me, unless you work for the Royal Mint (or your own country's equivalent if you're outside the UK), then literally making money is illegal. Sadly, that applies even if it's for the commendable purpose of providing a budget for your project, and you can visit my ex-colleagues for a very long time if you try it. A budget authority may be a product, but not the money itself.

5 **No.** The staff are a resource, not a product. Unless your project is quite long and very exciting, you don't make people. If you're hiring in people from outside, the people are still not really the product. In that case, the product is likely to be 'contracts'.

6 **Yes.** This may seem a strange answer in the context of the previous question, but the word 'trained' is key. The project won't deliver staff, but if it includes some training sessions it may well deliver trained staff.

7 **No.** A tricky one this, and pushing you a bit beyond the exams. This item is actually a point in time, not a product. It's when the doorways have been completed. I can't walk through 'doorways completed'. The correct product is 'completed doorways' or just simply 'doorways'. This isn't just playing with words either, because one isn't a product that you can kick and the other is.

8 **Yes.** However, the teams are unlikely to be making desks, so this is almost certainly an external product. A bonus mark if you spotted that it's external. Not that the bonus mark will do you any good at all, because I have no agreement with John Wiley to award prizes for the quick quizzes – or the practice exam questions either, before you ask. What a shame.

9 **Yes.** And it's a management product, as recorded in Appendix A of the PRINCE2 manual, which defines all the management products in the method. Another bonus mark if you identified the 'management product' bit.

10 **Yes.** You can print the Training Plan and hold it in your hand.

Answers to the Foundation-level questions

1 **b.** The plan may be checked by Project Assurance, but it's approved by the board. [**Manual** Table 14-6]. Any plan at project or stage level must have Project Board approval.

2 **c.** This supports the principle of 'focus on products'.

3 **a.** The Stage Plan for the first delivery stage accompanies the Project Initiation Documentation (PID) to the Project Board so that the Board can approve the project, whereupon work can start on the first delivery stage. The Stage Plan isn't part of the PID, though. The PID is about the whole project, not about individual stages, so Stage and Team Plans aren't put into it.

4 **d.** Exception Plans are not a level. An Exception Plan is normally at stage level, but may be at project level or involve more than one level.

5 **a.** Ugh! All so plausible, and you need to be familiar enough with the purpose statement to recognise the correct words.

6 **d.** Product descriptions are written for all identified products, and as soon as possible after the need for the product is identified. [**Manual** 7.3.3.3].

7 **c.** The key word is 'flow'.

8 **d.** Stage planning is covered by the process Managing a Stage Boundary, which is triggered at the end of each stage except the last stage in the project. When there isn't another stage to plan for, the process of Closing a Project is called instead.

9 **a.** PRINCE2 takes a product-based or product-led approach to planning, but that doesn't mean that other plans aren't needed, just that the products are done first. An external product is something coming over the boundary of the project from outside. An external product is needed on the project, or it wouldn't be included in the diagrams.

10 **d.** How kind, an easy one to finish with! Remember, all the PRINCE2 reports have the word 'report' in their title, with the sole exception of the Product Status Account. If you haven't learned as far as change control, don't worry about the Product Status Account . . . yet. The Highlight Report is the regular progress report sent by the Project Manager to the Project Board members and then to any other people designated in the Communications Management Strategy.

Answers to the Practitioner-level questions

Dealing with the 'fill in the diagram' type question requires both an understanding of product planning and some logic. On the understanding side of things, a particularly important point is to discriminate clearly between internal or team products and external products. The external products with their distinctive oval shape give you a good start to filling in the diagram. The logic kicks in when you see the relationship between external products and chains of team products and look for patterns in the dependencies. For example, the scenario mentions one product (the final 'completed office') that is created as soon as three others are complete. Well, on the Product Flow Diagram (PFD) there's only one box that has three others leading into it.

The completed PFD is in Figure 14-2, with the product list below it.

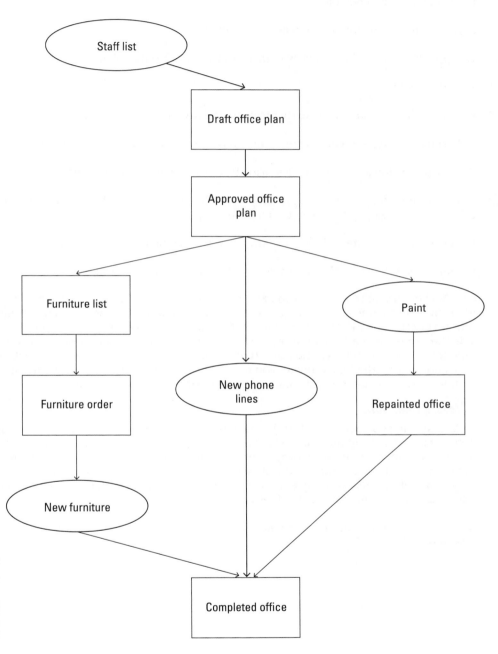

Figure 14-2:
Extract from
completed
PFD.

1. **E.** Staff list – external, and no prior dependencies because the additional scenario states that the list is already available

2. **J.** Draft office plan – drawn up using the staff list

3. **H.** Approved office plan – clearly comes after the draft office plan

4. **B**. Furniture list

5. **G.** Paint – an external, because the project staff aren't going to make paint

6. **C.** Furniture order – a team product, not to be confused with the furniture itself

7. **A.** New phone lines – the main scenario states that telecoms work is external

8. **D.** Repainted office – paint is a product on the list, so it's fairly obvious that this rectangle comes after an ellipse for the external product 'paint'

9. **F.** New furniture – external, because the team isn't going to make furniture

10. **I**. Completed office – final product, and with three products leading into it

One final comment to make on the PFD concerns the phone line product. The product is known to be an external one, even though it isn't mentioned in the additional scenario information at the start of the questions in this chapter. The fact that telecoms are to be provided from outside the project is made clear in the original scenario information set down at the end of Chapter 2. This emphasises the point that when answering all Practitioner questions in all sections, not just on the Plans theme, you need to bear in mind the original scenario information in addition to supplementary information given for that part of the paper.

Classic questions

11. **C.** A close call you may think. But the 'assumptions' section is the best place for this information, because the schedule will be based on that staff availability. If something goes wrong and the staff are not freed up from other work in time, it will affect the project. The plan states the assumption being made that staff will be there, so any impact will be readily understood if they're not. It can also draw attention elsewhere in the organisation to the importance of releasing staff on time for this business-critical project.

12. **A.** Time and resource are basic elements of any plan, and none less so than the Project Plan. [**Manual** 14.4.6]

Chapter 15

Risk

• •

In This Chapter

▶ Locking on to the key word in PRINCE2 risk management

▶ Some memory joggers for the Foundation exam

▶ Getting to grips with the risk management procedure

▶ Seeing where risk management fits into the method

▶ Getting in some practice with risk-based exam questions

• •

Risk management is a fascinating part of project management and, for the exams, the good news is that the content is mostly straightforward. However, don't mistake 'straightforward' for 'easy' when it comes to revision, because there's a lot of detail to get into your head. It's just that you shouldn't struggle too much over the thinking behind the theme.

The one concept you may find unusual is that of risk being positive – a good thing – as well as negative – a bad thing. If you're finding that idea difficult to get your head around because it flies in the face of a normal understanding of risk, and indeed the dictionary definition, then you'll find some extra help in the 'Clarifying Some Key Points' section later in this chapter.

Revising the Risk Theme

As you come to revise the Risk theme, do make sure that you allow plenty of time if you're heading for the Foundation exam. There's quite a lot to remember, and of course the Foundation is a closed-book exam. If you've already taken and passed the Foundation, you can relax a bit – you can have the PRINCE2 manual open in front of you in the Practitioner exam and you no longer need to memorise the fine detail.

In preparing your revision, have a look at the checklists in this section. They cover the exam syllabus, but also a bit more to make sure that you have a thorough grasp of the essentials. If, when you look at an item on the list, you feel confident you know it, then tick it off. If you don't feel you can tick it off, then put it on your hit list for extra attention in revision.

If you've already passed the Foundation exam, still have a look at the Foundation checklist to be sure that you've remained up to speed in key areas – but, as I've already pointed out, don't worry about memorising things any more.

Revision checklist – Foundation

Have a look at this list as you prepare to revise for the Foundation exam. Are you confident that you know each item?

- ❑ The PRINCE2 definition of risk

- ❑ The 'triggers' to risks – threats and opportunities

- ❑ What the management products related to risk are used for, who's responsible for them and when they're used – notably the Risk Management Strategy and Risk Register

- ❑ How risk fits in with the PRINCE2 principle of 'continued business justification' – notably that it's still worth the level of negative risk in order to secure the benefits made possible by the project

- ❑ The purpose statement for the Risk theme – you need enough familiarity to be able to recognise the parts of it if they're mixed in with similar-sounding things

- ❑ The risk response types for threats – dealing with *downside* or negative risk

- ❑ The risk response types for opportunities – dealing with *upside* or positive risk

- ❑ The fact that the response 'share' appears on the response lists for both upside and downside risk

- ❑ The five elements of the PRINCE2 Risk Procedure – identify, assess, plan, implement, communicate

- ❑ How the risk budget works – money is set aside to offset the financial impact of individual risks that can be controlled with cash, which isn't all of them. [**P2FD** Ch15 Managing the Risk Budget]

- ❑ The meaning of *risk owners* and *risk actionees* – and the fact that one person can be both the owner and actionee for a particular risk

- ❑ The 'anatomy' of a risk with the cause, risk event and then effect (impact) [**P2FD** Ch15 Identifying causes, events and effects – within the section Managing Risk with the Risk Procedure]

- ❑ How risk tolerance works – the points at which the Project Manager will have to escalate something to the Project Board because it goes beyond his delegated authority to deal with it

- ❑ The place of the Project Board in approving risk exposure and how this is affected by the members' 'risk appetite' – whether they're very cautious, very gung-ho, or something in between

- ❑ The risk measures of probability, impact and proximity

Revision checklist – Practitioner

Turning now to things you need just for Practitioner revision, have a look at these additional items:

- ❑ The detail of the Risk Management Strategy and the Risk Register – do you understand what information goes in each section in each product? Can you confidently allocate items of risk information to the correct heading? Can you spot errors in a faulty strategy or register?

- ❑ The idea of inherent risk (a poor choice of name, but it's the risk before any action has been taken to control it), then secondary and residual risk.

- ❑ The Risk Management Procedure again, but this time to put into practice the five elements in the context of a given project scenario.

- ❑ Risk identification – can you spot risks and especially watch out for positive risk, which can be harder to see than the negative risks? Can you spot secondary risks and identify residual risk?

- ❑ The risk action categories such as share, accept, exploit. Given a list of actions, are you familiar enough with the categories to quickly and accurately identify which category a particular action falls into?

Clarifying Some Key Points

As you revise the Risk theme, have a look at the points in this section. For each item, if you read a sentence or two and are sure that you're already clear on the point and know it, just skip the rest and move on to the next item.

Seeing risk as positive and negative

A dictionary definition of risk is 'the adverse consequences of future events'. In other words, it's negative. Risk is normally seen as something bad than can happen. There's been a move in risk management, which PRINCE2 has reflected, to also consider positive or 'upside' risk, which is about good things that can happen. That may sound a bit odd at first. 'You're at risk of winning a major prize' just doesn't seem to sound right.

A key to understanding positive and negative risk is the word 'uncertainty'. That word makes it easier to see that something good can happen as well as something bad. The trick in risk management now is to try and limit or prevent the bad stuff, and increase or make certain the good stuff. That's where the lists of risk actions fit in, one for the downside risks or 'threats' and one for the upside risks or 'opportunities'.

Learning the risk actions for the Foundation

PRINCE2 is horribly complicated when it comes to risk actions – unnecessarily complicated actually, although that's small comfort when you've got to learn them all for the Foundation exam anyway. Different people have different ways of remembering lists of things, but acronyms can be helpful. Here are a couple that may help.

Drowning is bad news, really it is; it's very negative. To avoid drowning, you need a buoyancy aid such as an inflatable raft. So, then, negative risk actions are AS RAFT:

- ✔ **A – Avoid:** Can you stop the risk happening? Can you avoid it altogether? There's a risk of a gas explosion from a gas heater, but if an electric one is installed instead, then the possibility of a gas heater explosion is eliminated. There may now be a danger of an electric shock, but that's a different risk and one that's arisen due to the action taken to control the gas explosion risk. You win a bonus point if you quickly recognised that a shock from the electric fire constitutes a secondary risk.

- ✔ **S – Share:** Get someone else to share the negative impact, perhaps for a share of the benefits of the project.

- ✔ **R – Reduce:** Okay, so perhaps you can't stop the risk happening, but can you reduce the chances of it happening and/or reduce the impact if it does happen?

- ✔ **A – Accept:** You choose to note the risk but not to do anything about it, at least at the moment. Perhaps the action would be too costly, for example, or be too distracting.

- ✔ **F – Fallback:** I hate this term, not least because so few people use it. Most use the word *contingency*. Basically contingency or fallback is allowing for the risk to happen – you can absorb the impact, completely or partially. So because you have a dodgy supplier, you put in some time contingency against the risk that supply will be delayed . . . again. If the supply is then a bit late, you can accommodate it.

- ✔ **T – Transfer:** Give it, or at least part of it, to someone else. A classic example is insurance, by which financial risk is transferred to an insurance company (albeit at some cost). Another classic is sub-contracting, where you may pay a fixed cost and if, say, a risk is realised that the work is much more complicated than anyone thought, well the sub-contractor will have to find the additional staff to put onto the job and pay the extra, not you.

Some positive things may affect the project, and it's usually wise to try and increase the chances of such beneficial impact. You need wisdom like that of a seer – so, for positive risk actions, SEER:

S – Share: Yes, again. Remember that this action is common to both lists; an action for positive, upside risk as well as for negative, downside risk. Here you may involve another organisation, for example, to invest in the project to bring about this happy result and to share in the benefits of it.

E – Exploit: Okay, so there's a chance that the positive risk may be realised. However, can you take an action to make it certain, or nearly certain, that it will happen?

E – Enhance: The impact of the positive risk may be really good. However, can you take an action which will make it even better?

R – Reject: If the positive risk is realised, then that'll be good and everyone will be pleased. However, it's not worth any action to try and increase the chances and effect of realising the positive risk. Such effort would, perhaps, just distract from getting on with the main work of the project.

Quick quiz on risk response types

So, AS RAFT and SEER. Now, all you have to do is remember what the letters of those acronyms stand for. Got all that? Great. How about a quick quiz to prove it then? Have a look at each risk action and decide what type of action it is within the AS RAFT and SEER response sets.

1. The news reports are saying it's increasingly likely there will be a train strike, so we're flying to Edinburgh instead to be sure that we make the meeting on time.

2. Our teams have limited experience in this highly complex area, so we're going to outsource this part of the work to an experienced company. If that company hits problems, it'll have to find more experts at its own cost to deal with them.

3. We may be liable for large costs if our advice to customers is incorrect, so we're taking out professional indemnity insurance for all staff with direct customer contact.

4. The new headquarters building will be great, and we think it would be fantastic to have a staff restaurant. A restaurant should be very popular, but that's not guaranteed. We don't have the funds for all of it, but we're inviting a catering company to set up and run a restaurant once we've put the basic facilities in place, and we'll split the profits.

5. Our staff will have to do technical work that's beyond anything they've done before. Things could go wrong, with consequent project delay, but we're sending staff on training courses to boost their knowledge and skill levels.

6. Customers are likely to buy more of our products, simply because ordering will be easier through the new website being developed by the project. However, we're going to offer a 10 per cent discount for online orders compared with orders placed through other sales channels to make certain of it.

7. The new warehouse stores some heavy goods, and we've had a lot of cases of back injury in the past. We're going to put all the really heavy stuff in one zone, with warning signs around the perimeter to remind warehouse staff to use proper lifting equipment.

8. Bad weather could affect the launch display to the point of it being cancelled. However, because holding the display in a large indoor arena would be very expensive, and because it'll be mid-summer, when there's less chance of rain, we've decided not to take action to change the venue and just hope that the weather's okay. If, nearer the time, forecasts indicate a high probability of really bad weather, we may think about this again.

9. We may face problems in the office move with the lifts breaking down. That would cause severe problems with the schedule for the move. We've arranged preventative maintenance though to have the lifts thoroughly checked and serviced before the move takes place. It won't guarantee that we'll avoid problems with the lifts, but it'll make it less likely.

10. Customers are likely to buy more of the product when they see the better information in the catalogue which is part of this marketing project. We could have an electronic catalogue with animated views of the products, which might boost sales even further. However, we've decided not to pursue that, at least for the time being, because the time and resources needed to do it would postpone the product launch date. We may pick up the idea in a future project.

Understanding the risk budget

Sometimes, but not always, a suitable way to deal with a risk is to throw money at it. For example, you're planning to buy a piece of equipment from a cut-price shop that does really good deals. However, the shop doesn't always have supplies and products can be out of stock for some time while the shop sources another cheap batch. The shop up the road is much more expensive for everything, but it always has stock. So, the risk is that when you go to the cut-price shop to buy the equipment (and you can't reserve it in advance), it won't have any. If that risk is realised, the plan is that we'll handle it by going to the more expensive shop and buying the equipment there. The additional money is put on stand-by as part of the *risk budget*. If the risk happens, the Project Manager can immediately spend the money set against that risk and which is pre-approved by the Project Board. The Project Manager can immediately send someone up the road to buy the equipment from the more expensive shop. However, if the cut-price shop does have stock and the risk isn't realised, then the Project Manager can't divert the unused money in the risk budget to somewhere else.

The risk budget can be set up differently, but the equipment example in the previous paragraph serves to show the underlying concept. The 2009 PRINCE2 manual is too simplistic on this, but that works in your favour for the exams.

One final element to take on board for the risk budget is that it's approved, initially at least, along with the Project Initiation Documentation (PID), because it's specified in the Risk Management Strategy (the last section of that strategy). Some new risks may be identified later in the project, so the budget could, therefore, include an additional amount to help deal with any risks that haven't been identified yet.

Appreciating that the process isn't a cycle

The PRINCE2 risk management procedure looks like a cycle, but it doesn't really work that way; you may have found it confusing as a consequence. The four parts that appear to cycle are identify, assess, plan and implement. However, having implemented an action to control a risk, you don't start all over again to identify it.

To make sense of the apparent cycle, think of it as covering all risk in the project. You identify the risk, assess it, plan actions and then implement them. Then you identify any new risks (perhaps when planning the next stage) and add them to the existing ones. You'll then assess new risks and the current state of existing risks before going on to plan actions. The cycle still doesn't work well, however, because if things are looking good with existing risks and the countermeasures are working, you're not going to plan and implement further actions.

The warning here is not to try to make sense of the model as a cycle in the normal sense. Just take it as a high level overview and you'll be fine.

Practising With Some Questions

The last section of this chapter has some practice exam-style questions for you to have a go with, preferably to time so that you get used to the pace of the exams. The questions have two purposes: the first is to give you some additional practice, but the second is to make particular points on exam strategy. Those strategy points are explained in the answers that you'll find at the end of each chapter.

Because books in the *For Dummies* series are designed for you to dip in to rather than read from cover to cover, I'm going to repeat some advice here in case you've not come across it already in the book. That advice is to get hold of the official sample papers available from the exam board, and use them alongside the examples in this book. The sample papers are free, and I'd have been giving you very poor value for money simply to fill this book with them. If you're attending a training course or doing a distance-learning course, your training provider should give you copies of the official sample papers. If you're studying alone, look on the APMG website or contact APMG, who run the exams on behalf of the UK Government (which owns PRINCE2).

For the Practitioner exam, you can use the official sample papers as you revise each part of the method, because they cover one section at a time. For the Foundation exam, it's difficult to use the official sample papers until you've learned all of PRINCE2, because questions are random and not grouped by subject. For the Foundation then, I suggest you do the questions in the book as you work through the subject areas, and then do a full sample Foundation paper at the end to get a feel for a full-length exam.

Okay, on with the questions then. You'll find 10 Foundation-level questions and 12 questions which reflect a couple of the Practitioner styles. You'll find help in Chapter 2 on dealing with the question styles as well as on overall exam strategy.

Foundation-level questions

Set your timer to eight minutes and try to complete the ten questions within that period. Try to answer the questions without looking at your PRINCE2 manual or any other reference material. If you don't know an answer to a question, just take your best shot at it and move on to the next one. You'll find the answers at the end of the chapter, together with a bit of explanation.

1. Which of these is NOT a PRINCE2 risk response?

❏ a) Fallback

❏ b) Transfer

❏ c) Share

❏ d) Refuse

2. Which of the following statements is correct?

❏ a) For a given risk, the risk actionee may be the same person as the risk owner.

❏ b) Risk management is optional in PRINCE2 for small and very low risk projects.

❏ c) No risks can be recorded until the Risk Register is opened.

❏ d) Team Managers are not involved with identifying risk.

3. Which term is used in PRINCE2 to describe something that could initiate a risk with a negative impact on objectives?

❑ a) Opportunity

❑ b) Trigger

❑ c) Cause

❑ d) Threat

4. If a team member notices a new risk when working on a Work Package, how does that team member normally report it?

❑ a) Make an entry in the next Checkpoint Report.

❑ b) Make an entry in the next Highlight Report.

❑ c) Raise an issue.

❑ d) Raise a Risk Report.

5. For risk management to be effective, three things are necessary. Two are that risks need to be identified and controlled. The third need is that risks are:

❑ a) Mitigated

❑ b) Recorded

❑ c) Assessed

❑ d) Avoided

6. What are the missing words from the following PRINCE2 definition of risk?

A risk is [?] that, should it occur, will have an effect on the achievement of objectives.

❑ a) A future threat or opportunity

❑ b) An uncertain event or set of events

❑ c) An identified issue

❑ d) A positive or negative circumstance

7. Which of the following is *not* part of the PRINCE2 risk management procedure?

❑ a) Identify

❑ b) Plan

❑ c) Resource

❑ d) Communicate

8. Which of the following statements are correct?

A. Risk tolerance is the level of risk exposure that, when exceeded, will trigger an Exception Report to bring the situation to the attention of the Project Board.

B. In PRINCE2, the Risk Register for a project is created during the process Starting Up a Project.

C. The Project Manager may be designated as the risk owner for one or more risks.

D. The Risk Management Strategy is created and maintained by the Project Manager.

❑ a) A, B and C

❑ b) A, B and D

❑ c) A, C and D

❑ d) B, C and D

9. Which of the following are two commonly used measures of a risk?

❑ a) Impact and cost

❑ b) Probability and impact

❑ c) Likelihood and acceptability

❑ d) Appetite and impact

10. Which role is ultimately responsible for all aspects of risk management in a PRINCE2 project and to ensure that there's a Risk Management Strategy for it?

❑ a) Executive

❑ b) Project Manager

❑ c) Business Assurance

❑ d) Corporate or programme management

Practitioner-level questions

After reading the additional project scenario information, try to answer the questions in this section within 18 minutes. That will mean you're working at the right pace for the exam. The basic scenario information for the project is at the end of Chapter 2.

Additional scenario

A lot of the work of the project is to be done by the Works Team, a subset of the staff of the Works Department within Princess Projects Plc, and which includes several key people such as the electricians. A common pressure on Works Department staff is being called away from tasks to deal with emergencies. This is fairly common, because the headquarters building is old and prone to problems. Clearly, emergencies usually take priority over project work, because if, for example, there's an electrical failure, then parts or even all of the headquarters can be affected and everything stops until the problem is located and fixed. It's not realistic to think that dealing with such emergencies can wait for a day or two until Works Department staff have finished some part of their work on a project.

Classic style questions

	Answer the following question about the risk that works staff could be called away from the project to deal with emergencies at headquarters. Being an old building, some things regularly break down. Remember to limit your answers to the number of selections requested in each section	
1	Which **1** risk management action would be categorised as 'fallback'?	
	A	Contract out the work to an outside company in place of the works staff
	B	Get advance authority for overtime working for works staff if it's required
	C	Ask the Works Dept to do maintenance on known HQ problem items before the project
	D	Take no action and hope that there are no big emergencies during the life of the project
2	Which **1** risk management action would be categorised as 'avoid'?	
	A	Contract out the work to an outside company in place of the works staff
	B	Get advance authority for overtime working for works staff if it's required
	C	Ask the Works Dept to do maintenance on known HQ problem items before the project
	D	Take no action and hope that there are no big emergencies during the life of the project
3	Which **1** risk management action would be categorised as 'reduce'?	
	A	Contract out the work to an outside company in place of the works staff
	B	Get advance authority for overtime working for works staff if it's required
	C	Ask the Works Dept to do maintenance on known HQ problem items before the project
	D	Take no action and hope that there are no big emergencies during the life of the project

Assertion–reason style questions

Each row in the table below consists of an assertion statement and a reason statement. For each row identify the appropriate selection from options A to E that applies. Each option can be used once, more than once or not at all.

Selection	Assertion	Reason	
A	True	True	AND the reason explains the assertion
B	True	True	BUT the reason does not explain the assertion
C	True	False	
D	False	True	
E	False	False	

	Assertion		Reason
4	The Executive should be named as 'owner' of the risk that works staff could be called away	BECAUSE	the Executive is ultimately responsible for all risk management in the project
5	The Project Manager should only use the Daily Log, not a Risk Register, in this project	BECAUSE	all risks in projects which involve only internal staff will be minor and can be put in the Daily Log which is informal
6	The Executive would be a suitable owner of a risk that a change in business policy will mean that the e-business unit is no longer needed	BECAUSE	the Executive is in contact with business managers in the corporate management structure
7	A Team Manager who discovers a new risk that the structural work might more complicated than first thought should inform the Project Board immediately	BECAUSE	the Project Board is responsible for ensuring that the e-business unit accommodation is ready on time
8	A risk that furniture might not be delivered on time does not need to be recorded	BECAUSE	only risks affecting work within the project should be recorded, not those involving external supply
9	Like any project, all risks in the e-business project can be transferred by taking out insurance	BECAUSE	ultimately the impact of any risk can be eliminated by spending more money, albeit at increased project cost

Matching style questions

For each item of risk information in column 1, select the correct part of the Risk Management Strategy in column 2 where that information would be recorded. An option in column 2 may be used more than once or not at all.

	Column 1	Column 2
10	If 50% or more of the negative risks associated with benefits realisation worsen by two scale points or more, the Executive must be notified immediately.	A Introduction B Risk management procedure C Tools and techniques D Scales E Risk categories F Early warning indicators
11	Impact of over £1 million – very high Impact of £500k to £999k – high Impact of £250k to £499k – medium Impact of £100k to £249k – low Impact up to £99k – very low	
12	Ernest Wise, the Project Manager, is responsible for the creation and maintenance of this strategy.	

Answers to the quick quiz

1 **Avoid.** This response was previously called 'prevent', which actually made the action clearer. In this case, if we go by plane, then the train strike can't affect us.

2 **Transfer.** The risk impact is being passed to someone else. Sub-contracting is a typical risk transfer action.

3 **Transfer.** Another transfer, this time covering the financial impact and passing it to an insurance company – albeit at the cost of the premium. Insurance is another typical transfer action.

4 **Share.** The investment will be shared with a partner in return for sharing the benefit (profit), so it's a 'share' response for an opportunity-based risk.

5 **Reduce.** The training won't eliminate (avoid) the risk, but it'll reduce the chances of mistakes with the consequent impact of project delay.

6 **Exploit.** There's a good chance of increased sales, but we're going to try and make an increase certain with the 10 per cent discount.

7 **Reduce.** Staff may still lift things incorrectly, but the warning signs will reduce the chance of injury, by reminding staff to use the proper equipment.

8 **Accept.** The key words here are 'we've decided not to take action'. It's still in the Risk Register though, first to explain the current inaction, but also so that the risk remains under review; if circumstances change (expectation of good weather), so might the response.

9 **Reduce.** The lifts are less likely to break down with consequent impact on the schedule.

10 **Reject.** We still hope that we'll realise the upside risk, but we've judged that it's not worthwhile to go chasing after it to try to make it more likely.

Answers to the Foundation-level questions

You may have found the practice Foundation questions not tough exactly, but picky. Many questions focus on small points of detail or very exact wording. As you may suspect now as you read this, the approach is entirely deliberate to make a point not just about risk questions but about all Foundation exam questions. Some questions are very picky, to the point that they can be very annoying to some candidates who can't see why such detail needs to be memorised at Foundation level or how it helps manage projects any better. Indeed, you may be one of those who thinks exactly that – but I, of course, can't possibly comment. Just take on board the point that you need to be very precise and note the exact terms when you're revising for the Foundation exam. Forget other approaches to project or risk management and put aside your own organisation's approach or terminology. Remember that the PRINCE2 exam is about PRINCE2 and only PRINCE2, exactly as written in the manual.

On to the answers then, with some explanation where that might be helpful.

1   **d.** There's a response that's 'reject', and unfortunately, perhaps, that also begins with an 'R'. This is where acronyms such as AS RAFT and SEER serve only as memory joggers, because you still need to remember exactly what the letters of the acronyms stand for. A nasty question, but it's included here to make the point about being sure of the acronyms.

2   **a.** Risk management isn't optional in PRINCE2. Risks identified during Start Up are recorded the Daily Log, even where there's a clear need to manage them formally. The risks are then transferred to the Risk Register during Initiation, when the Risk Register is then available. Everyone is involved with identifying risk, including Team Managers. Team Managers may also spot risks when doing Team Plans.

3   **d.** Remember, threats for negative risks, opportunities for positive risks.

4   **c.** This question shouldn't have been a problem unless all of the PRINCE2 management products are swimming around in your head and you're starting to lose focus on what they're all about. Team members have no part in preparing Checkpoint Reports or Highlight Reports. There's no such thing as a Risk Report in PRINCE2. If products are starting to swim around, try to stand back a bit in your revision and think at an overview level what each one is for, who prepares it, and how it's used. You can use the list of products at the start of Appendix A in the manual as a checklist for that revision.

5   **c.** Sometimes, it seems, question writers are desperate for new material and instead of thinking about what someone at Foundation level needs to know, they just leaf through the manual looking for something – anything – to ask a question about. This time it's a short list in the manual. However, if you didn't know that list, you should still have identified the right answer, because the same three elements are in the purpose statement for the Risk theme. [**Manual** 8.2.3 and 8.1]

6   **b.** No short cut here. You need to be familiar enough with things like definitions to be able to pick out the correct words quickly and accurately. The key word for risk is 'uncertainty', so that's a good clue here if you weren't sure.

7   **c.** Again, rote learning I'm afraid. Watch out for any short list of items such as the risk management procedure used here, for 'spot the wrong one' type questions.

8   **c.** The Risk Register is created during the process Initiating a Project, not during Start Up, and at the time that the Risk Management Strategy is being formulated.

9   **b.** Another measure is proximity, but that isn't mentioned in the question. Probability and impact are common measures in risk management generally, not just PRINCE2, hence the P–I Matrix.

10   **a.** The Executive is ultimately responsible, although others may do risk-related work and have an input. [**Manual** Table 8-3 Executive responsibility]

Answers to the Practitioner-level questions

Classic-style questions

1. **B.** Outside PRINCE2, fallback is sometimes called *contingency*. Either way, it's allowing for the risk to happen and absorbing the impact, or at least some of it.

2. **A.** *Avoid* means that the action will eliminate the risk. If no works staff are on the project because it's all being done by outside contractors, then works staff being called to deal with emergencies can't affect the project staffing any more.

3. **B.** There are two dimensions to risk reduction, and an action may hit on one or both. The first is to reduce the probability of the risk occurring, and the second is to reduce the impact if it does occur. In this case, if 'preventative maintenance' is carried out, perhaps the troublesome items will behave themselves, at least mostly, during the project and reduce the number of emergency call outs of the Works staff. It's certainly worth a try.

Assertion–reason questions

4. **D.** Team resourcing is the domain of the Senior Supplier on the Project Board, not the Executive, so even if you wanted a board 'owner', you shouldn't go for the Executive.

5. **E.** Projects need a Risk Register – it's a key product – and anyway it's not true that risks related to internal staff will always be minor.

6. **A.** Even if you don't know the names of the people in the scenario project, whoever is the Executive is usually a good choice for business risk ownership.

7. **D.** Team members should normally submit an issue to the Project Manager.

8. **E.** All genuine risks need to be recorded, and delay to the furniture is indeed a risk.

9. **E.** You can't buy your way out of all risk. For example, if the concrete in the building project is faulty and has to be dug out and re-laid, then money isn't going to make the new concrete set in three minutes flat and so meet the project deadline. Throwing money (risk budget) at them may be a possible action for many risks, but it certainly won't cover everything.

Matching-style questions

10. **F.**

11. **D.**

12. **A.**

If you're still a bit unclear on the contents of the Risk Management Strategy, have a look at *PRINCE2 For Dummies* or Appendix A of the manual – or both. [**Manual** A24, **P2FD** Ch15 Understanding the sections of the strategy]

Chapter 16

Change

*T*he Change theme isn't named very well, because although it's about change management, it's about rather more than that. In fact, the theme covers:

✔ Change management

✔ Configuration management (not quite the same thing as change management)

✔ Issue handling (and issues can be about anything, not just change)

The main target of change control in any approach to project management is to tackle scope creep, a major project killer. *Scope creep* is unauthorised change where someone asks for 'just' this little thing to be added in, and then another little thing, and then another, but without any extra allowance of time or resource in the project. These little changes are supposed to be absorbed somehow. The problem is that a large number of changes build up, cumulatively representing considerable change, and so damage or even kill the project, which can't now deliver within its allocated time and budget.

The main thrust of change control then is exactly that, to control change. Now, please note carefully that this is about change control, not change prohibition. PRINCE2 allows for change in the project, even very considerable change. It's just that change is done in a controlled way, and with extra time and resource being given to do the work.

Configuration management is basically version control, or versioning. It's important to take on board that configuration management is closely connected to change management because, if a change is made to a product, it's likely to be given a new version number and the details of the change recorded. However, configuration management isn't exactly the same as change management, because if under change control the change is refused, then there isn't going to be any change of version.

Issues, also covered in this theme, can be about anything at all. A particular issue may be to ask for a change – a *Request for Change* (RFC) – but it may be about something else such as to report a new risk, put forward a good idea, or ask a question. This is where the Change theme covers rather more than change management.

Revising the Change Theme

When revising the Change theme, make sure that you understand the areas set down in the checklists below. If you can't confidently put a tick against any item, go and have a look at that area again.

Revision checklist – Foundation

Have a look at this list as you prepare to revise for the Foundation exam. For each item on the list, are you confident that you know it? If not, target it for more revision until you can tick it confidently.

- ❑ The purpose statement for the theme – make sure you can recognise it to be able to identify missing words and know which theme the statement belongs to

- ❑ Issues and the three sub-types – Request for Change, Off-specification, Problem/concern – and who can submit an issue (anyone with an interest in the project or its outcome)

- ❑ Concessions (for Off-specifications) and the need for Project Board authority to agree them

- ❑ Formal and informal handling of issues – either a Daily Log entry or an Issue Report and Issue Register entry for each one

- ❑ The content and use of an Issue Report and the Issue Register – and who's responsible for them

- ❑ The five steps in the issue and change control procedure – what the five steps are, what's happening in each one and who's doing what [**Manual** Figure 9.1, **P2FD** Ch16 Handling an issue]

- ❑ Levels of authority for change – Project Board and Change Authority (which may be at any level between the board and the Project Manager)

- ❑ The change budget – and its use as a trigger for escalating issues to a higher level of authority (for example, if a requested change would cost more than the Project Manager's delegated change budget for a stage)

- ❑ Why an issue may be escalated – the fit with exception management such as problem resolution estimated to breach the cost or time tolerance for a stage

- ❑ The use of exception planning with change management – for large scale change beyond the limit of the change budgets

- ❑ The five elements of the configuration management procedure

- ❑ Configuration Management Strategy – where it's created (Initiation), who's responsible for it (Project Manager) and how it's used in Initiation and then through the project

- ❑ Configuration Item Record – why it's needed and the sort of information it contains

- ❑ Status accounting and the Product Status Account (the only report without the word 'report' in its title)

Revision checklist – Practitioner

Turning now to things you need just for Practitioner revision, have a look at these additional items. However, if you've already passed Foundation and come straight to this list, do look also at the Foundation checklist in the previous section. You need to be sure that you're still up to speed on those elements.

❑ Where issues are dealt with in the process model – Controlling a Stage to capture and examine issues, with advice from Project Assurance then action by the Project Manager or by escalating the issue to the Project Board

❑ The contents and use of the Issue Register – from its creation in Initiation during work on the Configuration Management Strategy, through to its closure at the end of the project in the activity 'Recommend project closure'

❑ The contents and use of the Issue Report – to record the detail of a formally managed issue

❑ The required characteristics of those appointed as Change Authorities [**Manual** Appendix C.8.2]

❑ The contents and use of the Configuration Management Strategy and who's responsible for it (Project Manager) – including where it may be updated, notably on a stage boundary

❑ The scope of configuration management in a project – what's in and what's out

❑ The contents and use of Configuration Item Records – where they may be created and used and by whom

❑ The contents and use of the Product Status Account – where this report may be called for, the fact it can be applied to different sets of products, and who may use it

Clarifying Some Key Points

Here are a few notes on some of the items in the checklist to help you revise. As in all the chapters in this book on processes and themes, this section focuses on a few of the areas which can be the source of misunderstanding or concern.

Being clear about the Change Authority

It's easy to get confused with the Change Authority within the PRINCE2 organisation structure. Not for the first time, the PRINCE2 language is somewhat at odds with normal use of terms in business and common practice in projects.

According to the PRINCE2 manual, the Project Board should deal with all Requests for Change and all Off-specifications. However, if the board members don't want to do that, they can delegate authority to make changes to a lower level.

The Project Board will have authorised the Stage Plan for a stage, but if someone then wants a change, by definition it isn't going to be on the plan and therefore won't have been approved by the board. Unless the Project Manager is to go back to the Project Board for every change, no matter how trivial, it makes sense to delegate some authority to the Project Manager to make decisions. Only if the change is more substantial or an accumulation of smaller changes hits the change budget limit will the Project Manager then need to go back to the Project Board for approval.

If the Project Board members anticipate a considerable number of changes above the level that they are willing to delegate to the Project Manager, then a *Change Authority* can be considered with an intermediate level of authority. The Change Authority as a separate body is set up where the Project Board doesn't want to – or doesn't have time to – deal with all of the changes that will be heading its way.

The structure which has the Change Authority as a separate body placed between the Project Board and Project Manager is shown in the organisation diagram of the roles in the PRINCE2 manual. The Change Authority function is then reinforced by having a description of the authority as a separate role in Appendix C of the manual. And that's exactly how many organisations use it.

Getting complicated

Things get complicated and confusing for many people learning PRINCE2 where the manual describes giving authority to the Project Manager to decide some changes. The manual says such delegation makes the Project Manager a part, or all, of the Change Authority. That description is at odds with the organisation diagram and at odds with how many people set up Change Authorities within their projects and organisations. Giving the Project Manager some discretion to agree changes is not normally thought of as the Project Manager being a Change Authority – it's just a standard management arrangement that's similar to normal business management.

In short, then, the PRINCE2 view is that the full Project Board should decide on all Requests for Change and all Off-specifications. However, if the members don't want to do that, perhaps because of the number of changes anticipated, they can:

- ✔ Appoint one or more members of the Project Board to function as Change Authorities so decisions will just be made by that subset, not the whole board, or
- ✔ Recruit different people into the project to act as a Change Authority, or
- ✔ Delegate authority to the Project Manager to decide on changes, which then makes the Project Manager the Change Authority, or
- ✔ A combination of all three, which then spreads out the Change Authority between the management levels

Defining the types of authority

The authority levels are often defined by cost, but they can also be defined by time or organisational authority. For example, any change that would add more than two days to the stage may need to be referred upwards for approval. Or any change that would have an impact outside the department where the project is being run, no matter how fast or cheap it is to implement. So the Project Manager of a small project to refit the stationery cupboard doesn't have the authority to commit the whole of a government department to a policy change on stationery supply, even if it only cost 5p and took three minutes to put into effect.

Understanding issues

You should be familiar with the three types of issue and the circumstances under which each one is used.

Requests for Change, Off-specifications and Problems/concerns are simply types of issue and are recorded in the same way using either the Daily Log (informal control) or an Issue Report and the Issue Register (formal control).

Avoiding confusion with a Problem/concern

Don't get confused by the title of the third type of issue, which is *Problem/concern*. This is badly named, because the word 'concern' is used negatively in day-to-day language. If some-one has a concern, the normal interpretation is that the person is worried about something. However, as the text of the manual makes clear, this third type really means 'other' and can include good things such as a team member putting forward a great idea for improving a product without increasing project costs – it isn't just about bad things.

Quick quiz – what sort of issue is it?

For each of these descriptions of an issue, should it be recorded as a Request for Change, an Off-specification or a Problem/concern? Answers are at the end of the chapter.

1. A Team Manager has reported that because of the cancellation of another project, her team can start work on product 3/24, the Outer Flange Casing, eight days earlier than scheduled and so deliver eight days earlier.

2. The wiring plan passed its check and was signed off two weeks ago. However, the IT Department has now identified a problem in that one of the planned routes for new mains cabling is too close to a computer cable run and will cause electrical interference. The wiring plan needs to be changed so that the mains circuit route involved is further away from the computer cables.

3. Two of the sales staff have identified the fact that holding additional data on customers, as planned for the new system, will save them looking up separate records before doing routine monthly calls to account customers. This was not previously realised and will save an additional five staff hours per week in the Sales Department.

4. Because the brochure advertising the new service will go to very senior staff in customer organisa-tions, it was to have been printed on heavy grade, acid-free Japanese chamois paper, as recorded on the Product Description. However, because of production problems in Japan after flooding in the factory, this paper cannot be obtained in sufficient quantity in the time available. Other options are a lighter grade chamois, which is available, or a different type of heavy-grade paper.

5. The Finance Director has asked that the moving plan, already agreed and signed off, should be changed so that the finance staff are moved to the new office building first rather than last. The staff have end-year accounts to prepare, and the recent delay in the project means that their planned move will now coincide with this busy period.

It's not the case that every time something fails to meet the requirements set down in its Product Description it's Off-specification. Many products fail tests for one reason or another during their development; if they didn't, there'd be need to test them. If a product does fail a test, the team simply works on it again to put the error right and then puts the product through the test again, hopefully successfully the second time around. If every minor test failure resulted in an Off-specification being sent to the Project Manager, the Project Manager would have a full-time job just reading them all. An *Off-specification* occurs if something doesn't meet its Product Description requirements, or it can be seen in advance that it isn't going to and this can't easily be corrected. In that event, there are usually wider implications (such as timing, cost or change of specification) and a decision needs to be made on how to handle it. That makes the matter something which should be recorded as an issue, and specifically an Off-specification.

Using change budgets and exception plans

PRINCE2 can accommodate change in two ways, and you need to be clear on both.

The first way is by using a *change budget*. Some of this change budget can be delegated to the Project Manager, so that he or she can decide on low-level change without having to consult the Project Board every time. I've already covered that mechanism in this chapter in the section 'Being clear about the Change Authority'.

If the required change is substantial and means that the stage, or even whole project, needs to be re-planned, then PRINCE2 can handle that too. It's like going into exception deliberately. As always, the key point is to check that this level of work is justified.

Suppose a junior team member comes up with a bright idea that would cost £10,000 to implement and add 200 staff hours and three weeks to the stage, and the Project Manager only has a change budget of £5,000. However, a conservative estimate is that this idea would save the company £1 million a month, starting even before the end of the project. Because the Project Manager doesn't have the authority to approve the change, the decision must be escalated to the Project Board. The board members are delighted (it's their project, so they can claim the glory . . . and a huge annual bonus) and happily agree to provide the money and staff resource as well as extend the stage to include the new work. The existing Stage Plan is no good now because things are going to be done differently. So the board instructs the Project Manager to force a stage boundary, produce an Exception Plan showing the additional work effort and time, and bring the plan back for approval. Oh yes, and it also authorises a reward for the team member whose idea it was, to the maximum allowed by company rules for junior staff – a £10 gift voucher.

The mechanism, then, for accommodating large-scale change is exactly the same as for an ordinary exception caused by a problem: escalation of the issue and then exception planning.

Getting to grips with configuration management

Many people struggle with the whole area of configuration management. The problem usually starts with the name, which sounds very technical. The underlying concept, however, is straightforward enough. If you're changing something, then you usually need to keep track of the latest version. Imagine having several copies of the Project Plan, each of which is different. Which is the latest copy and the one that everyone should refer to? The plan needs to carry a date, or better still a reference number in case there are two significant changes on the same day. That's configuration management.

Configuration management is a bit more than just version control, although that fact probably won't concern you too much outside the PRINCE2 examinations. Configuration management also covers how things fit together, such as parent–child configurations where, for example, a product that's being version controlled is made up of sub-components all of which are also being version controlled. Equally, one sub-component may be used in a number of larger products, such as a particular carburettor being used in several types of car engine. In considering a change to the shape of the carburettor, it's important to know which engines it's used in to check that it will still fit them all. It's this sort of information that's stored in the *Configuration Item Record*.

Appreciating the need for configuration management

There's a tendency to think that a stable product won't subsequently be changed and doesn't need to be controlled. There are two reasons, however, why the CM information on a stable product might be very important.

The first is in the case of something bought in from the outside, such as door handles. If, years after the refurbishment project is over, a door handle is broken and a matching replacement needs to be obtained, where did the handle originally come from and what make and model was it? That configuration management information is needed despite the fact that the door handles did not go through any 'versions' during the project. The handle example also illustrates the important point that configuration management is one of the follow-on actions that will continue after the end of the project and into the working life of the products.

The second reason is because of status accounting. Knowing and keeping track of progress through the states such as an 'outline', 'draft', 'final' and 'approved' design document can be very helpful.

Understanding the Configuration Item Record

For the Practitioner exam in particular, you should be familiar with the headings in the Configuration Item Record and aware of how the information helps prevent confusion and problems in the project. For example, it's really helpful, obviously, to know where a completed product is – a lot of time can be wasted looking for missing products. So, the 'Location' heading in the record comes into play. Or perhaps two team members are arguing about who has the up-to-date version of a specification document. One has a copy which says 'Version 4', while another has a copy that says 'Version 6'. So who has the up-to-date version? The answer is neither of them, because the Configuration Item Record shows under the 'Current version' heading that the latest version is Version 15, so both team members have copies that are long out of date.

Knowing the use of the Configuration Management Strategy

Configuration management can get very complicated, and sometimes it needs to be. Equally, it can often be carried out very simply. How configuration management will be done in a particular project is set down in that project's *Configuration Management Strategy*. The strategy will include specifying procedures, such as the booking in and booking out of products to team members so that changes to products can be carefully controlled.

Configuration management is needed for management products as well as specialist products.

Differentiating between baselines and releases

Regarding baselines and releases, PRINCE2 again trespasses into technical rather than business terminology with the potential to be a bit hard to follow if you don't have that technical background.

A *baseline* is a product at a known state, usually quality checked and signed off. If something goes wrong with the product, that baseline has been saved (if the product is suitable, such as with a document or computer program) and can be restored for work to start afresh from that baseline. The baseline can also be used for comparison, and that's true of the Project Plan. A project activity may be expected to take a particular amount of time. As the project develops, the forecast of the duration of the activity may change, but that changed duration can now be compared with the original expectation in the baseline. Project management computer tools often show the original, or baseline, position of each activity as well as the latest position to give a visual impression of any time saving or delay.

A *release* is a set of products that work together, each with a recorded version number. So in IT, a release may be a computer system of, say, five programs: version 4.5 of program 1, version 4.2 of program 2, version 6.8 of program 3, version 1.7 of program 4 and version 2.9 of program 5. A future release may only have some of the member programs updated, with the remainder being the same as in the previous release.

Understanding verification in the configuration management procedure

The manual sets down five elements in the configuration management procedure:

1. Planning

2. Identification

3. Control

4. Status accounting

5. Verification and audit

Check that you're familiar with all five areas. The last one often seems to cause confusion, but actually is straightforward enough. Configuration management is a precise business, and it's essential to check from time to time that the records are correct. So, the records may show that Mary Chan has the product 3/14 – Technical Specification – at the moment and is working on it. The records also show that the specification is still in a draft state and hasn't yet been finalised. So, you go to Mary and say 'Can I check please that you have the Technical Specification 3/14, that you're working on it and it's still a draft?' She confirms that's the case, so you've now *verified* that the information on the Configuration Item Record for product 3/14 is correct.

There's no set frequency for configuration management verification and audit checks in a project and that will vary from project to project. For a specific project, the required frequency will be set down in the Configuration Management Strategy (see the second heading in the Configuration Management Strategy description in Appendix A of the manual, Configuration Management procedure). A typical time for such checking is end stage to be sure that the records are all in order before work starts on the following stage.

Practising With Some Questions

To give you a feel for change-related questions in the exams, the following sections provide practice questions in both Foundation and Practitioner styles. You'll find the answers on the grey-edged pages at the end of the chapter.

Foundation-level questions

Here are ten questions in Foundation style. Set a timer for eight minutes, but if you can answer confidently in less, great. Remember, don't use your manual or any other reference information to help; it must all be from memory.

1. What's the name of the type of issue that records that a product does not meet its requirements and can't easily be made to do so?

    ❏ a) Non-compliance Report

    ❏ b) Off-specification

    ❏ c) Request for Change

    ❏ d) Baseline

2. Who can submit an issue?

    ❏ a) Only members of the Project Board

    ❏ b) Only Team Managers from within the customer organisation

    ❏ c) Only people outside the project

    ❏ d) Any member of the project, corporate or programme management, or other stakeholders

3. What's the first action to be taken when an issue is received by the Project Manager?

❑ a) Escalate it to the Project Board immediately.

❑ b) Escalate it to the Project Board in the next Highlight Report.

❑ c) Decide whether to handle it formally or informally.

❑ d) Decide whether to delegate it to Project Support.

4. An issue and a risk are the same thing – the only difference is in the timing. A risk is before something has happened and an issue is to report it after it's happened.

❑ a) True

❑ b) False

5. When is change control used in the project?

❑ a) Only during Starting Up a Project when the scope is being decided for the Project Brief

❑ b) Only during Initiation while the Project Initiation Documentation (PID) is being drawn up to define the project

❑ c) Only during the delivery stages, after the PID has been agreed

❑ d) Throughout the project

6. What's the purpose of the Product Status Account?

❑ a) To provide information about the state of a defined set of products

❑ b) To report progress to the Project Manager on products under construction

❑ c) To calculate costs and forecast the remaining spend

❑ d) To record who's accountable for ensuring products meet their quality criteria

7. In PRINCE2, what's a Request for Change?

❑ a) An alternative name for an issue

❑ b) An issue that specifically asks for adjustment to the project scope

❑ c) A request to exchange a bank note for coins to the same value

❑ d) An issue asking for a change to a baselined product

8. Which of the following is a heading in the Configuration Management Strategy?

❑ a) Issue and change control procedure

❑ b) Organisational configuration management standards

❑ c) List of products requiring configuration control

❑ d) Configuration Item Records

9. Four of the elements of the issue and change control procedure are capture, examine, propose and implement. Which is the other one?

❑ a) Delegate

❑ b) Escalate

❑ c) Decide

❑ d) None of the above; there are only four elements in the procedure

10. Which of the following is a requirement for any appointed Change Authority?

❑ a) To be made up of one or more members of the Project Board in order to have the required level of authority within the project

❑ b) To be from the Quality Assurance function to have the required understanding of relevant organisational standards

❑ c) To be made up of one or more people with sufficient specialist knowledge of the business, user and supplier stakeholder areas

❑ d) To be made up of people who are also working on a project team, to ensure a thorough understanding of the project's deliverables and the impact of changes

Practitioner-level questions

For the following Practitioner questions, set your timer for 18 minutes, but if you can answer more quickly, so much the better (provided you get the answers right, of course). As with the other chapters, there are a couple more Practitioner level questions here than you'll face in a section in the exam, so you get a bit more practice. Answers are on the grey-edged pages at the end of the chapter. You'll find advice on dealing with the different styles of Practitioner question in Chapter 2.

Assertion-reason questions

Each row in the table below consists of an assertion statement and a reason statement. For each row identify the appropriate selection from options A to E that applies. Each option can be used once, more than once or not at all.

Selection	Assertion	Reason	
A	True	True	AND the reason explains the assertion
B	True	True	BUT the reason does not explain the assertion
C	True	False	
D	False	True	
E	False	False	

	Assertion		Reason
1	The Executive is responsible for producing the Configuration Management Strategy	BECAUSE	the Executive is responsible for producing all the strategies as a means of instructing the Project Manager how the project should be controlled.
2	Once agreed as part of the Project Initation Documentation (PID) the Configuration Management Strategy cannot be changed	BECAUSE	it is essential for consistent project control that all four strategies remain stable and unchanged through the life of the project.
3	An issue may be submitted at any time during a project	BECAUSE	an issue may be handled informally, and if so it is recorded in the Daily Log.
4	Configuration Management will cover management products, not just as specialist products	BECAUSE	it is important to control change to some management products such as the Business Case.
5	All issues should be recorded on an Issue Report, then either in the Daily Log or Issue Register	BECAUSE	the Issue Register should be monitored regularly by the Project Manager.
6	Configuration Item Records should be created during stage planning	BECAUSE	PRINCE2 requires that the status is known of all products in the project.

A classic style question

	Answer the following question about responsibility for the handling of escalated issues.		
	Remember to limit your answers to the number of selections requested in each section		
7		Within the decision making process for an issue escalated by the Project Manager, which **1** role should ensure that the expected benefits of the project are safeguarded?	
	A	The Executive	
	B	The Senior User	
	C	The Senior Supplier	
	D	Project Assurance	
	E	Those identified as stakeholders in the Communications Management Strategy	

Matching style questions

For each item of information in Column 1, please select the correct section of the Configuration Management Strategy in Column 2 in which this information would be recorded. An option in Column 2 may be used more than once or not at all.

	Column 1	**Column 2**
8	Configuration management auditing will be carried out between one and three weeks before stage end.	A Introduction
9	Configuration Item Records will use the standard PRINCE2 headings, but omitting the 'Item type' and 'Item attributes' sections which are not needed.	B Configuration management procedure
10	Project Assurance will check the Issue Register at three weekly intervals during each stage.	C Issue and change control procedure
11	Configuration management (CM) in this project will use our 'VerCon' CM computer software.	D Tools and techniques
12	Because of the large number of staff involved in the project, team members will submit issues to their Team Manager in the first instance. The Team Managers will pass on only those issues with an impact outside their current Work Package.	E Timing of configuration management and issue and change control activities F None of the sections above

Answers to the quick quiz – what sort of issue is it?

1. **Problem/concern.** Remember that this third category of issue means 'other' and may be good news, like the early delivery of the outer flange casing, not just bad news.

2. **Request for Change.** It's asking for a change to a product, the wiring plan, that has already been quality checked and signed off – for which the configuration management term is *baselined*.

3. **Problem/concern.** Still more good news with a staff time saving increasing the project benefits – just like you get all the time on your projects.

4. **Off-specification.** An Off-specification is used if the product doesn't comply with its Product Description and can't easily be made to do so. Or it can be seen in advance that the product's not going to comply with its Product Description, which is the case here with the specialised paper.

5. **Request for Change.** Another change to a product that's already been baselined – this time the moving plan.

Answers to the Foundation-level questions

1. **b.** Off-specification

2. **d.** Just about anyone, provided the person has a genuine interest in the project

3. **c.** Decision on formal or informal handling. [**Manual** 9.3.3.1]. It's a common reaction to say that issues should immediately go to the Project Board. Remember that the Project 'Manager' is appointed to manage and will be able to deal with many issues without escalating them to the board.

4. **b.** False. Issues and risks are not the same thing at all. An issue can be about anything and isn't necessarily risk related. A team member having a good idea during week 16 of the project and submitting it as an issue wouldn't have been foreseen and put in the Risk Register. Usually in the exam you will get a number of true/false questions rolled into one, so this question is very kind; I hope you appreciate it.

5. **d.** Change control is needed throughout the project. Even in Initiation, for example, controlled change may be needed to important management products such as Product Descriptions and the Project Plan.

6. **a.** The Product Status Account is a report which, as the name suggests, can be called for to report the state of a set of products. A typical use is for the Project Manager to ask for the report towards the end of a stage to ensure that all the stage products (apart from the ones just being finished) show up with a status of 'complete'.

7   **d.** It's not an alternative name for an issue, because it's one of three types of issue.

8   **a.** Issue and change control procedure. Organisational standards may be consulted, but they're not reproduced in each project's strategy. The exact list of products needing configuration control won't be known at the time the strategy is produced (early in Initiation and before even the Project Plan has been created), and indeed new products will be defined as the project continues and stage planning is done for successive stages. Similarly, the Configuration Item Records will be set up when products are identified which come under the scope of configuration management in the project. The scope of configuration management is set down in the strategy, then, but not the details of individual products. A strategy is about 'how' something will be done, not the actual doing of it.

9   **c.** Decide, which is step four and comes before 'implement'

10   **c.** Having sufficient knowledge of the stakeholder areas. You'll find the requirements for the Change Authority in Appendix C of the PRINCE2 manual, which sets down all the roles and responsibilities in the project management team.

Answers to the Practitioner-level questions

Assertion–reason questions

1   **E.** Both statements are false. As with producing the other parts of the Project Initiation Documentation (PID), the configuration management strategy is the responsibility of the Project Manager, not the Executive. The Executive doesn't produce any of the strategies. Instead the Executive will discuss any control requirements with the Project Manager, and these will be reflected in the strategies. The Executive and other Project Board members approve the controls in their acceptance of the PID, which contains the four strategies.

2   **E.** Both false again. It's extremely important that the strategies are kept up to date throughout the project, reflecting any change in control requirements. Often the need for changes to one or more strategies will come to light during stage planning on the stage boundary. One of the jobs to do in the activity 'Plan the next stage' in the process Managing a Stage Boundary is to review the PID, and this includes a check on the relevance and suitability of the strategies and controls. [**Manual** 17.4.1]. The check is carried out at the same time as those to see whether any changes need to be made to the project management team (the roles and responsibilities) and whether any change is needed to the project approach.

3   **B.** Both statements are true, but the second statement is not the reason that the first one is correct. The fact that issues can be handled informally is not the reason that anyone can send one in.

4   **A.** Both statements are true, and this time the second statement is the reason that the first one is correct, so it's an 'A' answer rather than a 'B' answer. Some management products, such as the Business Case, are highly likely to change during the project and do need to be version controlled. These are in the 'Baseline' management product list on the first page of Appendix A of the PRINCE2 manual.

5   **D.** The first statement is false, while the second is true. Informally controlled issues are not recorded on an Issue Report, just in the Daily Log. Formally controlled issues have an Issue Report and an Issue Register entry. The Issue Register should indeed be monitored regularly by the Project Manager, as noted against the product in Appendix A of the manual. In passing, this doesn't mean that the Project Manager should ignore issues in the Daily Log, or that other people won't also check the Issue Register. Project Assurance will also need to check the register, for example, to ensure that issues – once recorded – are not then overlooked.

6   **C.** The first statement is true and the second is false. When planning a stage and taking the relevant part of the Project Plan to a lower level of detail, the more detailed products will be defined. Those which fall under the scope of configuration management will then have Configuration Item Records made so that they can be configuration managed. This is the responsibility of the Project Manager as part of stage planning. [**Manual** Table 17-1]. The Project Manager doesn't need to know the status of all products. This is consistent with the point that only some management products are on the 'Baseline' list on the first page of Appendix A in the manual. Also, setting down the scope of configuration management within the project indicates that some specialist products will fall outside that scope. If a product won't change once it's created, if it's not going to go through different states that need to be monitored during its creation, and if reference information doesn't need to be held about it, then it won't normally need to be configuration managed.

Classic-style question

7   **B.** The Senior User. You'll find information on responsibilities within a theme in a table on the last page of each of the theme chapters in the PRINCE2 manual. [**Manual** Table 9-3]

Matching-style questions

8   **E.** This entry refers to the timing of a configuration management activity (audit).

9   **F.** Although this information belongs in the Configuration Management Strategy, it doesn't belong in any of the sections listed in column 2. It belongs in another section, 'Records', which defines the composition (and format) of records, including the Configuration Item Record.

10   **E.** Another example of the timing of an activity, this time related to change and issue control rather than configuration management. This question also illustrates the point that more than one question may require the same selection from column 2.

11   **D.** This refers to the use of a computer system, which is a tool, for configuration management. Appendix A of the manual makes specific reference to computer systems for configuration management under this heading in the strategy.

12   **C.** This information records a variance in the normal procedures for issue handling, and so falls into the section 'Issue and change control procedure', which includes such departures from normal corporate practice.

For the matching question block, the options A and B are not the correct answer for any of the questions. D and F are the correct answer once, while E is the correct answer twice. That pattern of answers illustrates the information in the question block header that 'an option in column 2 may be used once, more than once or not at all'.

Chapter 17

Progress

*I*f you're revising the themes in order, I've got some good news for you. This is the last one – you're nearly done, so hang on in there. The Progress theme has some important parts for you to check up on in your revision, but you'll be pleased to know that the content is limited, so this last bit shouldn't be too onerous. Indeed, if you made sure that you were clear on things like reporting, stages and exception management in earlier parts of your revision (such as when looking at the Controlling a Stage process), you may find there's little more to cover in this theme now.

Appreciating It's More Than Just Progress

Just in case you thought you were misunderstanding something, the Progress theme covers a lot more than progress. Before the 2009 edition of the PRINCE2 manual, the theme used to be called 'Controls', and I can't begin to imagine why the authors changed the name for the 2009 edition. I mention that because 'controls' is a better description and it gives you a much clearer picture of what's involved. The theme does indeed cover progress control, but more besides. The full content is as follows:

✔ Progress control

✔ Types of stages – management stages and technical stages

✔ Management stages as the key PRINCE2 control

✔ Factors to consider when choosing management stages – including risk, planning horizons (how far can you see clearly ahead), Project Board preference, maximum limits on time and cost (for example, no stage to be longer than three months)

✔ Exception management (a control that has much wider application in PRINCE2 than just progress)

✔ Reporting (again, more than just progress reporting) – what each report is, what its sections are and why it's needed

✔ The Work Package as the Project Manager's control for work flow

✔ The use of logs in the method

Revising the Progress Theme

To check on the detail as you plan your revision, have a look through the checklists to see where you feel confident and where you may still be a bit unsure. If you can't tick an item with confidence, mark it down to have another look at it. The checklists cover the exam syllabus, but a bit more detail in addition to help you make sure that you've got the important areas locked in.

Revision checklist – Foundation

Have a look at this list as you prepare to revise for the Foundation exam. Make sure that you know each item thoroughly. If you don't feel confident on any item, 'give it a bit more wellie' with some further revision (thank you Wallace and Gromit).

❑ The purpose statement – what jolly fun; makes you really glad you're learning PRINCE2 at exam level doesn't it?

❑ The four management levels

❑ Reports in PRINCE2, what they're for and how they work between the management levels

❑ Progress reporting with the Highlight Report and Checkpoint Report

❑ The two logs – Daily Log and Lessons Log – what they're for and how they work

❑ Work Packages and how they work – the Work Package is counted as a control, because the Project Manager uses it as an authority, and as a work definition, to regulate the flow of work to teams

❑ Exception management – what it is and how it operates, and in which products it's specified (for example, project level tolerances in the Project Initiation Documentation, or PID)

❑ How exception management works between the management levels

❑ The Product Checklist and its use in progress control

❑ Time-driven controls (to a set frequency) and event-driven controls (things that kick in when something happens)

❑ The concept of a management stage and a technical stage, and how the two types relate

❑ Key factors when choosing management stage boundaries – including risk, Project Board preference, planning horizons (how far you can see ahead clearly) and maximum limits (for example, no management stage to be longer than three months)

Revision checklist – Practitioner

If you haven't already had a look at the Foundation checklist above, do so now before going on to the Practitioner checklist, just to be sure that you're still up to speed with the Foundation areas. Then have a look at these additional Practitioner points. As a handy hint in passing, do make especially sure that you're familiar with the Work Package, because it's a frequent visitor to the shores of the Practitioner exam.

- ❑ Reports in PRINCE2 – do you understand each section in each report, and can you identify which section particular project scenario information should go in?
- ❑ The two logs – Daily Log and Lessons Log, and again do you understand the contents?
- ❑ Work Packages – the content, how they are used, by whom (Project Manager and Team Manager roles) and where in relation to the activities within the processes of Controlling a Stage and Managing Product Delivery
- ❑ Exception management – can you see how to apply this within a project, and can you see quickly whether it's been applied incorrectly?

Clarifying Some Key Points

Here are a few revision notes on some of the items in the checklist. As with the other chapters on processes and themes, this section focuses on a few of the areas which can be the source of misunderstanding or concern. For each subject area if, when you've read a few sentences, you're sure you're already clear on the point, just skip the rest and move on to the next heading.

Understanding exception management

The problem with exception management is that it's easy! You may be looking for something really difficult that's a unique PRINCE2 concept, but actually exception management is normal everyday management.

I've done a lot of work over the years with police forces, and I often like to use police examples to illustrate things. So, is the Commissioner of the Metropolitan Police visiting every police station in London today to check everything is okay? No, of course not. The Commissioner is busy (we hope) doing important police management stuff, not trudging around the police stations. The Commissioner expects that everything is going okay and that he or she will be told quickly if something significant happens, such as a major crime. So, too, with the project. At stage level, the Project Board has approved the plan and appointed a Project 'Manager' to run things on a day-to-day basis. The Project Board members now assume everything is going okay – to plan – and have told the Project Manager to report back to them quickly (with an Exception Report) if anything goes significantly off track. They've specified exactly what 'significantly' means, too, and those limits (upper and lower) are the tolerances.

Some people learning PRINCE2 struggle a bit at first with lower tolerance limits, especially with tolerances on time and cost. They can see why you need to tell the Project Board quickly if a stage is going to be very late or cost much more, but can't see why there's a need to report immediately if something is cheaper or faster. The reason for the reporting is that the board may need to tell others. For example, if the stage and then the whole project are going to finish early, other business areas may need to be warned so that they can take advantage of it. Equally, if the stage or perhaps the whole project is going to come in significantly under budget, then the Finance Director may need to be told the good news and that money will now be freed up for other things.

Underspends and early delivery are not normally as sensitive as being late or over budget, but do note carefully the 'normally' in that statement. Consequently the tolerance may not be as tight on the lower end of the band. So, for the stage budget, a projected overspend may be subject to a limit of 5 per cent before it's notified, but a project underspend has to be 15 per cent before it needs to be reported. [**P2FD** Ch17 Setting unequal tolerances]

Finally, on exception management, you need to be particularly clear on the management levels. Tolerance can be set at three levels and is always set by the level above. Those words, 'level above', should spring into your mind as soon as you see the words 'exception management' or 'tolerances'. The tolerance is the limit the level above has set to instruct the level below when to report something. You can see tolerances as delegated authority, because that's exactly what they are. To take stage tolerance as an example again, the Project Board (level above) is saying to the Project Manager, 'Go away and get on with this stage, and you can do that management within these limits. If you forecast at any time that you're going to exceed a limit in either direction, you must come back to us immediately.'

To emphasise the 'level above' idea, project tolerance is not set by the Project Board; you need to be clear about this. Project tolerance is set by corporate or programme management and is an instruction and authority to the Project Board. Stage tolerance is set by the Project Board and passed on to the Project Manager, while Work Package tolerance is set by the Project Manager for the Team Manager. Similarly, exceptions are notified back up to the level above. If a Team Manager detects that a tolerance is going to be exceeded, he or she notifies the Project Manager (usually using an issue). The Team Manager doesn't jump a management level and notify the Project Board. If the project goes into exception, the Executive will inform programme or corporate management – the level above the project. [**P2FD** Ch17 Using Tolerance at Different Levels]

Knowing your time- and event-driven controls

Most PRINCE2 controls are *event driven*; the control kicks in when something happens. For example, the exception procedure is event driven and will be initiated if a projection indicates that a tolerance limit will be exceeded. The End Stage Assessment (ESA) is event driven and happens when the event of end stage occurs. If the stage is slightly delayed, then a planned ESA will be slightly delayed, and if the stage completes slightly early, then the Project Board will meet early for the ESA.

There are just three *time-driven* controls. Two are the progress reports, which are produced at set intervals – the Highlight Report (Project Manager to Project Board) and the Checkpoint Report (Team Manager to Project Manager). The Project Manager may choose to hold regular meetings with Team Managers, and such meetings are the third time-driven control.

Practising With Some Questions

To test your knowledge of the Progress theme, have a go with some practice questions. This section has Foundation- and Practitioner-level questions, and you'll find the answers, together with a bit of explanation, at the end of the chapter.

Foundation-level questions

To get used to the pace of the Foundation exam, try to see these questions off in eight minutes.

1. What's the major control in PRINCE2 that means that the Project Board doesn't have to authorise all of the money and staff resource for the project in one go?

❑ a) Work Package

❑ b) Management stages

❑ c) Project Initiation Documentation (PID)

❑ d) Technical stages

2. A management stage is:

❑ a) The time needed to produce a Work Package

❑ b) A financial period (monthly, quarterly or annual) defined by corporate or programme management

❑ c) A collection of activities and products whose delivery is managed as a unit by the Project Manager on behalf of the Project Board

❑ d) The PRINCE2 term for a technical stage

3. Progress is measured in the context of six control factors. Five of them are time, cost, quality, scope and benefits. Which is the sixth factor?

❑ a) Risk

❑ b) Performance

❑ c) Economy

❑ d) Environmental impact

4. At which management level(s) can tolerance be specified?

❏ a) Project level

❏ b) Stage level

❏ c) Work Package level

❏ d) All of the above

5. Which of these is an influence on the Project Board's decision on the number of management stages in a project?

❏ a) The complexity of the configuration management

❏ b) The level of risk

❏ c) The number of Team Managers

❏ d) The number on a dice thrown by the Executive

6. What's the minimum number of management stages in a PRINCE2 project that goes through to its planned completion?

❏ a) One: a single delivery stage in a simple project that needs little or no planning

❏ b) Two: Initiation and at least one delivery stage

❏ c) Three: Start Up, Initiation and at least one delivery stage

❏ d) Four: Start Up, Initiation, at least one delivery stage then closure

7. PRINCE2 uses two types of control. One is time-driven controls, what's the other?

❏ a) Ad-hoc controls specified by the Project Board

❏ b) Financial controls specified by corporate or programme management

❏ c) Delivery-based controls using key products

❏ d) Event-driven controls

8. Tolerances on the project are set by:

❏ a) Corporate or programme management

❏ b) The Project Board

❏ c) The Project Manager

❏ d) Project Assurance

9. Which of the following is *not* one of the tolerances used within PRINCE2?

❏ a) Cost

❏ b) Time

❏ c) Productivity

❏ d) Benefits

10. What would the Project Board do if a stage level Exception Plan had been produced?

❏ a) Do nothing, because it's within the delegated authority of the Project Manager.

❏ b) Hold a meeting (Exception Assessment) to consider and approve the plan.

❏ c) Refer the plan to corporate or programme management for approval.

❏ d) Declare an exception.

Practitioner-level questions

After reading the additional scenario, try to answer the 12 questions in 18 minutes. It really helps to work to the same pace that you'll need for the exam.

Additional project scenario

One Work Package in the project is to produce the draft office plan and the approved office plan. These are vital for the project and will show the layout of the four rooms in the e-business unit, including such things as electrical sockets, phone points and new doorways. These two products will be the first to be created in the project. The products are critical because if this Work Package is delayed, the product dependencies are such that the rest of the project will also be delayed.

You should use this information in this section, along with the main scenario information at the end of Chapter 2.

Matching-style questions

Some of the sections of a Work Package are listed in column 2. For each element of Work Package information in column 1, please select the correct Work Package heading in column 2 under which that information should be given to the Team Manager. An option in column 2 may be used once, more than once or not at all.		
	Column 1	**Column 2**
1	Because any delay in production of these products will impact the whole project, any projected overrun of more than one day must be reported. If the products will be finished more than two days early, this should also be reported.	A Work Package description
2	The draft office plan is due to be finished two weeks into this three-week Work Package. Completion of this draft office plan 'milestone' should be notified to Ernest Wise, the Project Manager.	B Techniques, processes and procedures
3	Progress on the Work Package should be notified to Ernest Wise at the end of each week.	C Joint agreements
4	This Work Package covers the two products of draft office plan and approved office plan. Any comments received from staff on the draft will be considered for possible amendment of the layout to be shown in the approved office plan.	D Tolerances
5	Cost is subject to limits of plus 7.5 per cent and minus 15 per cent.	E Constraints
6	Information should be included in the latest projection on the completion date of this Work Package in relation to the given tolerances.	F Reporting arrangements

Assertion–reason style questions

Each row in the table below consists of an assertion statement and a reason statement. For each row, identify the appropriate selection from options A–E that applies. Each option can be used once, more than once or not at all.			

Selection	Assertion	Reason	
A	True	True	AND the reason explains the assertion
B	True	True	BUT the reason does not explain the assertion
C	True	False	
D	False	True	
E	False	False	

	Assertion		Reason
7	The Project Board will approve the Work Package to create the draft office plan and approved office plan	BECAUSE	the two office plans are time critical and any delay in their production will affect the delivery of the whole project, for which the Project Board is accountable to the management of Princess Projects Plc.
8	The Project Manager will specify any tolerances on the Work Package	BECAUSE	the Team Manager must know at what point any deviation from the plan must be reported.
9	If the Team Manager detects that the office plans Work Package will not finish within its specified cost tolerance, he or she will raise an Exception Report	BECAUSE	in PRINCE2, it's required that all exceptions are notified with an Exception Report giving the reasons for the exception and making a recommendation on how the matter should be handled.
10	The Work Package will include only the Product Description for the approved office plan	BECAUSE	only the final product of the Work Package needs to be defined, not all of the products in the package.
11	The management stages in the project must have the same boundaries as the technical stages	BECAUSE	the term 'management stages' is simply the PRINCE2 alternative name for technical stages.
12	The Project Board must specify the upper and lower limits of benefits projections for the e-business project beyond which the Project Manager will report the benefits projections to the board	BECAUSE	as part of its progress control approach, PRINCE2 requires that all six types of tolerance, reflecting the six control factors, are specified for every stage in every project.

Answers to the Foundation-level questions

1 **b.** You can't think 'control' within PRINCE2 without immediately thinking 'management stages'. They're *the* big Project Board control.

2 **c.** The management stage is a block of work that the Project Board is willing to delegate to the Project Manager to be done in one go.

3 **a.** It's about rote-learning the six control factors, and there's no short cut to that.

4 **d.** Tolerance can be set at different levels, so don't get locked into stage-level tolerance.

5 **b.** In reality there are quite a few factors, but the PRINCE2 manual is very narrow and refers specifically to just four, one of which is the level of risk. [**Manual** 10.3.2.2]. By the way, answer 'd' was intended as a joke and to provide some light relief in your revision, but if you didn't realise that then I worry about your organisation's projects. Sadly there are no signs of humanity in the Foundation exam now, but in the good old days there used to be a couple of questions in the pool with a tinge of humour in them.

6 **b.** Remember, Start Up isn't a stage – it happens before the project and so pre-dates the project stages, and the project may not have a closure stage.

7 **d.** Event-driven controls, which include things like end stage and exception. These kick in when the relevant event occurs.

8 **a.** Remember, tolerance is set by the level above. It's a common error to think that project tolerance is set by the Project Board.

9 **c.** Tolerances relate to the six control factors: costs, timescales, quality, scope, risk, benefits. [**Manual** 1.5.2, **P2FD** Chapter 2 Appreciating the Six Control Variables]

10 **b.** Although the name 'Exception Assessment' is hard to find in the manual. [**Manual** Glossary]

Answers to the Practitioner-level questions

The Practitioner practice questions in this chapter are mostly centred on the Work Package, although this brings in other elements of the Progress theme, such as exception management. In the exam, if you see a block of questions focused on a particular management product, it pays to flip your manual open to the relevant page in Appendix A immediately, before you tackle those questions. The product details are then in front of you. Otherwise, when you're deep in the section and dealing with a minor point, you may be tempted to try to remember what's in the product, with the possibility that you'll get it wrong. But if you've already opened the manual at the page, you can take a mere moment to glance at it and make sure of the mark.

1 **D.** Tolerances are the limits which define the delegated authority of the person receiving the work which in this case is a Work Package. Tolerances always specify an upper and lower limit.

2   **C.** The joint agreement specifies key milestones.

3   **F.** The requirement for progress reporting using the Checkpoint Report.

4   **A.**

5   **D.** Tolerances again, this time on cost. Remember, an option in column 2 may be the answer to more than one question.

6   **F.** Reporting requirements again. This answer 'F' is to hammer home the point that an option in column 2 can be the answer to more than one question and, because this is the last question in the panel, you can also see that some of the options in column 2 weren't needed at all. Don't make the mistake of thinking that these questions are like children's puzzles where you draw lines from one side to the other and every question on the left-hand side has a corresponding and different answer on the right-hand side so that all the answer options are used.

Assertion–reason style questions

If you were confused by the assertion–reason style (and many people find it tricky), do have a look at Chapter 2. There's help in that chapter for understanding all of the question styles, and for assertion–reason there's a simple three-step approach.

7   **D.** The Project Board is not involved in approving individual Work Packages. As a job it's too low-level, being down in the depths of the process of Controlling a Stage, the delegated work of the Project Manager.

8   **A.** Yes, tolerance is set by the level above, and the person doing the work must know the limits of his or her delegated authority to control that work. So, the assertion statement on the left is correct because of the reason given on the right.

9   **E.** Be careful if your organisation is still using an earlier version of PRINCE2, because the use of Exception Reports at the different management levels has yo-yoed between different versions. In the 2009 edition, the Exception Report is only used by the Project Manager, and then only to report a stage level exception. A Work Package exception is notified using an issue unless the Project Manager has specified an alternative procedure. The Executive reports a project exception to programme or corporate management, as instructed, but that's beyond the project now and so outside the scope of PRINCE2.

10   **E.** The Product Descriptions of all products included in the Work Package should be included. The Product Description contains vital information not only to define the products, but also to give information on how they're to be tested. It's not down to Team Managers to re-invent some of the products in the Work Package.

11   **E.** The names 'management stage' and 'technical stage' are not interchangeable. Some management stage boundaries may be aligned with technical stage boundaries, but it isn't mandatory that all of them are. It's important in this question to notice the word 'must' in the assertion statement. [**P2FD** Ch17 Thinking 'management' stages not 'technical' in the section 'Controlling the project with stages']

12 **E.** The assertion statement refers to project tolerance not stage tolerance. Take care to read questions in the exam very carefully and take on board every word, and not least as you approach the end of a section when you may be under a bit of time pressure. Project tolerances, including one on benefits if it's been set, are specified by the level above, which is corporate or programme management. Notice too that this is the fourth occurrence of 'E' as a correct answer. That's unlikely in the exam, but is here to emphasise that you need to focus on determining the correct answer from your knowledge of PRINCE2, not by trying to second-guess the probability of correct answers from the structure of the paper.

Finally, this selection of Practitioner questions mostly covers the Work Package, because it gives a good example of product-oriented questions, which in turn bring in other elements such as exception management. Don't forget to cover all aspects of the theme in your revision, though, as set down in the checklists near the start of this chapter.

Part IV
Revising the Method as a Whole

The 5th Wave   By Rich Tennant

THE CUSTOMER/SUPPLIER ENVIRONMENT

©RICHTENNANT

"Let's consider revising the process."

In this part . . .

While Part II covers the PRINCE2 processes and Part III the themes, this part – Part IV – switches attention to the integration of the method to help you make sure that you can join everything up. You'll find information here on the support of the PRINCE2 principles which loom large in the exams. There's also a chapter on the management products to help you check that you understand them all and can answer exam questions with confidence.

Chapter 18

Revising the Management Products

Some people think, and indeed many are wrongly taught, that PRINCE2 is all about documenting projects. It's not true that PRINCE2 is a documentation method, but having said that, quite a few things needed to control the project may well turn out to be documents. Try relying on your memory for all the risks and risk actions in a large, complex project if you're not convinced. The problem when you're learning the method is that there are quite a lot of 'documents' and many are very detailed. An even bigger problem is that you really need to know about these 'documents' to be successful in the PRINCE2 exams. In fact, your revision and knowledge are so crucial here that the 'documents' justify a whole chapter. If you're not reading this late at night with eyes bleary from revision, you may have noticed that the word 'documents' earlier in this paragraph was in inverted commas. When you're first learning PRINCE2, it can help you to think of the management products in this way. As you progress, you'll realise that they needn't always be documents, but there's more on that point in the next section.

Understanding Management Products

PRINCE2 takes a product-based approach to planning, but that product emphasis extends further than planning. The first thing to appreciate about *products* – what people will produce – is that there are two sorts: specialist and management.

Specialist products are, primarily, what the teams are building. Specialist products on a project may include things such as a design drawing, a computer program, a brick wall and a strategy report. You may think of them as 'technical', but in PRINCE2 the word is 'specialist'.

In contrast, *management products* are the things being used to manage the project. Management products include things like the Project Plan, the Project Brief, the Daily Log and the End Project Report. The management products are the focus of this chapter. It's very easy to know what the management products are in the method because they're all listed in Appendix A of the PRINCE2 manual.

Many management products turn out to be documents, albeit electronic ones most of the time. However, picking up the point in the first paragraph of this chapter, bear in mind that a product in a particular project needn't necessarily be a document. For example, when PRINCE2 was first being written, the name Highlight Report was chosen carefully. Note, it's a Highlight *Report* not a Highlight *Document*. In a more informal project, much of the reporting may be verbal and not written down at all. The decision on what must be written down and what can be verbal for a particular project is decided during Initiation and is then recorded in the Communications Management Strategy. Other management products may be delivered in the form of emails and presentations at meetings.

Knowing the Three Categories of Management Product

If you look at Appendix A of the PRINCE2 manual, you'll see that the management products are defined and explained in turn and in alphabetical order. On the first page of the appendix, you'll find them listed in a different order, though, and grouped in three categories according to whether the products are baseline products, records or reports.

Baseline products

The word *baseline* is a configuration management (version control) term. It follows that baselined products are those for which you want to keep track of versions, perhaps to look back at an earlier version. The baseline products are those which are highly likely to change or are certain to. It's because of the changes that you may want to look at an earlier version.

Records

Records are kept up to date all the time and so aren't version controlled. An example is the Quality Register. The Quality Register contains a list of quality actions to be taken in a stage. When an action is performed, such as a test of a specialist product, then the appropriate entry is signed off in the Quality Register with the date the test was done; it acts as a sort of checklist. You don't need to version control the register, because the entries are dated anyway.

Reports

A *report* is a snapshot at a particular point in time and won't be changed. If a Team Manager sends a Checkpoint Report to the Project Manager to set down the progress that's been made in the past week, then that report is dated for that point in time. The Team Manager won't alter the report three months later and send in a revised version.

Reports are fairly quick to produce; that's another reason why, normally, you don't want to have versions and so treat the reports as baseline products. A Checkpoint Report shouldn't take the Team Manager much more than about 45 minutes to put together, and probably rather less, so it isn't going to go through several versions in that time.

Reports are easy to spot in PRINCE2 because, apart from one, they all have the word 'report' in their title. The exception is the Product Status Account, for which the title doesn't include the word 'report' – so be careful to remember that it is a report.

Setting About Your Revision of Products

Whether you're about to tackle the Foundation or Practitioner exam, or one straight after the other, you need to be crystal clear on management products. Scan down the list in Table 18-1 and check whether you feel confident about each product. To help with your revision, the table also shows in which process the product is created and who creates it.

Table 18-1		PRINCE2 Management Products	
Reference	*Product*	*Process*	*Created By*
A1	Benefits Review Plan	Initiating a Project	Project Manager
A2	Business Case (Outline)	Starting Up a Project	Executive
A2	Business Case (detailed)	Initiating a Project	Project Manager
A3	Checkpoint Report	Managing Product Delivery	Team Manager
A4	Communication Management Strategy	Initiating a Project	Project Manager
A5	Configuration Item Records	*See Note 1 below*	Project Manager/ Support
A6	Configuration Management Strategy	Initiating a Project	Project Manager
A7	Daily Log	Starting Up a Project	Project Manager
A8	End Project Report	Closing a Project	Project Manager
A9	End Stage Report	Managing a Stage Boundary	Project Manager
A10	Exception Report	Controlling a Stage	Project Manager
A11	Highlight Report	Controlling a Stage	Project Manager
A12	Issue Register	Initiating a Project	Project Support
A13	Issue Report	Controlling a Stage	Project Manager (usually)
A14	Lessons Log	Starting Up a Project	Project Manager
A15	Lessons Report	See Note 2 below	Project Manager
A16	Plan	See Note 1 below	Project or Team Manager
A17	Product Description	See Note 1 below,	
A18	Product Status Account	on demand	Project Support
A19	Project Brief	Starting Up a Project	Project Manager
A20	Project Initiation Documentation (PID)	Initiating a Project	Project Manager

(continued)

Table 18-1 *(continued)*

Reference	Product	Process	Created By
A21	Project Product Description (PPD)	Starting Up a Project	Project Manager
A22	Quality Management Strategy	Initiating a Project	Project Manager
A23	Quality Register	Initiating a Project	Project Support
A24	Risk Management Strategy	Initiating a Project	Project Manager
A25	Risk Register	Initiating a Project	Project Support
A26	Work Package	Controlling a Stage	Project Manager

Notes on the table

Note 1. The manual is strange for Configuration Item Records in terms of showing who's responsible for what, but this is probably just down to poor writing. In Initiation, Project Support creates the Configuration Item Records, but on a stage boundary apparently it's down to the Project Manager. The process involved depends on the product being created (management or specialist) and the plan level (project or stage).

Note 2. Lessons Reports can be created at end stage and also at the end of the project. However, there's also a 'Lessons Report' entry in the Highlight Report so that a significant lesson can be passed back into the organisation without delay to benefit other projects immediately and without waiting for the end of the stage.

For the Practitioner exam, predictably, you'll need to be especially clear on the contents of the individual management products – but then you'll have the advantage of being able to look things up in the PRINCE2 manual. Remember that for the Foundation, although you won't need so much detail on management products, it all has to be in your head for this closed-book exam. When revising for either or both exams, make sure you're familiar with the following aspects.

Knowing what the product is

Make sure that for each product you know what it actually is and what it's used for. With so many flying around, it's easy to miss out on some and find that actually you can't remember them too well. For example, do you know what the Project Approach is and what other product(s) it appears in? If you do know, well done! It may be that I've hit a nerve though, because the Project Approach often gets forgotten. To remind you if you're unsure, the Project Approach sets down anything affecting the nature of the final deliverable of the project and also things affecting how the project is to be run. The Project Approach forms part of the Project Brief in Start Up, but then in Initiation it goes on to be part of the Project Initiation Documentation (PID), where it's then maintained throughout the project. The use of the Project Approach to record things affecting how the project will be run is not apparent from Appendix A in the manual, although it's mentioned in the text of the Start Up chapter. [**Manual** 12.4.5, **P2FD** Ch4 Thinking through the Project Approach]

Knowing where the product's created and when it's used

Do you know where each product is created in terms of the processes and activities? For the Foundation, you need to know the processes at least. So, for example, the Issue Register is created in the process Initiating a Project and, within that, in the activity 'Prepare the Configuration Management Strategy'.

Make sure that you know where the product's used and where it's updated. Watch out particularly for the process of Managing a Stage Boundary, because a lot of things can be updated there. Don't be fooled by poorly named activities such as 'Update the Project Plan'; here, the activity actually involves updating a considerably wider range of products than just the plan. In fact, that makes a good point for your revision: exactly what products are created and updated in the stage boundary process? See whether you can come up with an accurate list before checking it out in the manual or in *PRINCE2 For Dummies*. By the way, at the end of each of the chapters in *PRINCE2 For Dummies* which covers a process you'll find a list of the main products involved in that process. [**P2FD** Ch6 Checking out the major stage boundary products]

Knowing who's responsible

Be sure that you know who creates each product, who updates it and who needs to look at it. Do watch out for the Business Case though. You may think that the Project Manager produces the Business Case, because it forms part of the Project Brief and then the PID. It's true that the Project Manager produces the detailed Business Case for the PID, but in Start Up the manual says that the Executive produces it. In just about every organisation I've seen, that's rather unlikely – but as in all other cases, be careful to answer according to the manual, not according to organisational practice. [**Manual** Table 12-4]

Knowing the sections – for the Practitioner

For the Practitioner exam, you should also ensure that you understand each section of each management product. As you revise, check out the headings in the 'Composition' section of each product in Appendix A of the PRINCE2 manual. Each heading has a brief explanation against it, and most of them are pretty clear. Don't make the mistake of thinking that because the explanations are there, you don't need to put much effort into going through them beforehand though. Remember that in the Practitioner exam you'll be under time pressure and you simply won't have time to start reading lots of the manual to find out what the products are about – you need to know already. Now that's not to say that you won't consult Appendix A but rather that you may refer to it quickly to confirm something, not to in order to start finding things out.

Management products come into the Practitioner exam in a number of different ways, all needing familiarity with those products. You may be given an example of a product that has errors in it. You need be able to spot quickly what is wrong and pick the right replacement option to put it right. Or, in a matching question, you may be given different items of information and asked to say which product they belong to. You can see that both of these question types require a good level of familiarity with the detail of the products involved.

Practising With Some Questions

Have a go with the questions in the next sections to check your understanding of PRINCE2 management products. Because the products cover the whole method, you should tackle these questions towards the end of learning PRINCE2, when you have covered everything or nearly done so. You'd find it a bit hard to get the right answer to a question on products in project closure if you were on the first day of your PRINCE2 studies and had only learned as far as Initiation.

For the Practitioner exam, you won't get a whole section of the paper on management products. Instead, product-based questions can appear anywhere in the exam in a subject area that uses them. The Practitioner-level questions I provide here are to help in your revision of management products, no matter what theme or process they relate to.

Foundation-level questions

Try to answer these questions in eight minutes. Remember, read the questions carefully.

1. Which of the following is a progress report produced by a Team Manager?

❑ a) Team Progress Report

❑ b) Product Status Account

❑ c) Highlight Report

❑ d) Checkpoint Report

2. Which of the following is a report that the Project Manager may ask for at any time during a project, rather than at set, timed intervals?

❑ a) Checkpoint Report

❑ b) Exception Report

❑ c) Product Status Account

❑ d) Highlight Report

3. Which of the following forms part of the Project Brief?

❑ a) Daily Log

❑ b) Outline Business Case

❑ c) Risk Management Strategy

❑ d) Configuration Management Strategy

4. Which of the following may be generated by a Team Manager?

❏ a) Lessons Report

❏ b) Issue

❏ c) End Stage Report

❏ d) Exception Report

5. Which of the following products is *not* produced during the Initiation Stage of a PRINCE2 project?

❏ a) Daily Log

❏ b) Benefits Review Plan

❏ c) Project Plan

❏ d) Communications Management Strategy

6. Which of the following statements are correct?

A. An Exception Report is produced by the Project Manager.

B. Highlight Reports are produced at regular time-based intervals.

C. Lessons Reports may be produced during a project as well as at the end of it.

D. The End Project Report is produced by the Executive.

❏ a) A, B and C

❏ b) A, B and D

❏ c) A, C and D

❏ d) B, C and D

7. Which of the following products is created on a stage boundary?

❏ a) Lessons Log

❏ b) Risk Management Strategy

❏ c) Risk Register

❏ d) Configuration Item Record

8. Which of the following statements is correct? The Lessons Log:

❑ a) Is updated only on stage boundaries and then at the end of the project

❑ b) Includes lessons to be applied to the current project

❑ c) Is created during the first delivery stage

❑ d) Must be maintained by the Senior Supplier

9. Which of these products is created in the process of Starting Up a Project?

❑ a) Risk Management Strategy

❑ b) Project Initiation Documentation (PID)

❑ c) Project Product Description (PPD)

❑ d) Work Package

10. Which PRINCE2 report is produced towards the end of a project?

❑ a) End Project Report

❑ b) Project Brief

❑ c) Benefits Review Plan

❑ d) Risk Register

Practitioner-level questions

There are two sets of questions in the area of management products to help you practise for the Practitioner exam. The first set contains examples of the sort of question mentioned earlier in the chapter, in which you're presented with an item of information and you have to say which management product it belongs in. The second set gives examples of a style that's quite hard work. You're required to say whether each part of the product is correct and, if not, which of the options is the correct one to deal with the problem.

After reading the additional scenario for the project, allow 18 minutes for these questions.

Additional scenario

For the Practitioner questions in this chapter, please take into account the following additional project scenario information as well as the original information at the end of Chapter 2.

Set out below is a copy of an Exception Report for the project to prepare a suite of offices for a new e-commerce business unit. The report has just been prepared by the Project Manager, who's about to send it to the members of the Project Board to inform them of a problem with equipment – a broken high-power hammer drill.

1. Exception title

002

2. Cause of the exception

Unforeseen spend for hire of a high-power hammer drill with an 'SDS+' feature for drilling and cutting into very hard brick and concrete.

3. Consequences of the deviation

Even though it will cause an overspend beyond tolerance on the stage, I had no choice but to hire a high-power SDS+ hammer drill to replace the Works Team's SDS+ drill which broke beyond repair. The consequences of the deviation are a spend of £35 a day on the hire. A new high-power SDS+ hammer drill is being purchased by the Works Team out of its own budget, but the long Princess Projects Plc procurement process means that it'll be a while before it arrives. Hiring a hammer drill meant that the structural alteration work could continue uninterrupted.

4. Options

The following hire options were considered, and we went with option 3:

1. Brinkworthy Tool Hire Shop: £40 per day, but a drill was not available for two days

2. ABC Builders Hire Department: £38 a day, but a drill not available for three days

3. FIX-IT-FAST Tool Hire Ltd: £35 a day, and a drill was available immediately

5. Recommendation

That the SDS+ drill hire continues with FIX-IT-FAST, because it's cheaper.

6. Lessons

When planning the project, we didn't think about equipment failure, because we were focused on the design of the new offices. It would be sensible to have a contingency budget allocation in projects to allow for equipment hire in the event of breakdown.

Warning: There may be errors in this Exception Report

Matching style questions

Answer the following questions about the New Business Suite project. For each item of information in Column 1, select the correct PRINCE2 product in Column 2 where that information would be recorded. An option in Column 2 may be used more than once or not at all.

	Column 1	Column 2
1	2 May. In a phone call at 3 p.m. this afternoon, the Executive authorised the addition of £85 to the stage budget to cover the cost of extra paint needed because of the accident where several paint tins got crushed when a desk which had been stood on end fell on them.	A Highlight Report
2	Priority – Must have.	B Lessons Report
3	Product A15, mains power circuit. Earth test by a qualified electrician. Planned date: 16 May.	C Exception Report
4	The projected stage overspend is due to the need to replace the new carpet that was damaged in the paint spill accident. If approved, it will take the stage £300 beyond maximum cost tolerance.	D Daily Log E Risk Register F Issue Register G Quality Register
5	RFC – approved Furniture Plan to be modified to allow for 2 additional side tables to take extra computer screens for monitoring web site hit volumes.	
6	Additional test on Product A15. The earth test is to be repeated after the failure of the first test on the new electrical mains circuit. Planned date: 18 May.	

Classic style questions

		Using the additional scenario information, answer these questions about the supplied Exception Report. The sections of the report in the additional scenario information have been numbered.
		One answer is required for each question.
7		Section 1 gives the exception title. The title given . . .
	A	is a good one since a number provides a simple and unique reference.
	B	is incorrect and should be replaced by the words 'Exception Report'.
	C	is incorrect and should be replaced with 'Problem/concern'
	D	is incorrect and should be replaced with the words 'Risk exception'.
	E	is incorrect and should be replaced with 'Cost exception due to need for drill hire'.
8		Section 2 is to set down the cause of the deviation. Which is the correct action to take with this section as currently worded?
	A	Leave the paragraph in place as it is a sensible explanation.
	B	Replace the paragraph with 'Additional expenditure for tool hire'.
	C	Replace the paragraph with 'Tool breakdown caused by very hard brickwork'.
	D	Replace the paragraph with 'Cumulative cost overruns in the stage'.
	E	Replace the paragraph with 'Project Board instruction to report tolerance breach'.
9		Section 3 is about the consequences. Which action should be taken with this section?
	A	The section should be left as it is written as it correctly describes the consequences.
	B	The section should be re-written to explain the impact(s) of the drill problem on the project before any action is taken to manage the situation.
	C	The section should be deleted as it is not relevant to this particular situation.
	D	The section should be extended to explain exactly how the problem arose and why it could not have been forseen and prevented.
	E	The section should be deleted and replaced with the words 'The consequences are increased risk to the project. The new risk has been recorded in the Risk Register.'

These questions continue on the next page

Classic questions continued

10	Section 4 gives options for the exception. The options …	
	A	are correct since these give different options for hiring replacement equipment.
	B	are incorrect and should outline the options for dealing with the problem of the broken hammer drill, not options for shops hiring a replacement.
	C	should be extended to show that all local hire shops have been checked for price and equipment availability to ensure that the best value was obtained.
	D	should be extended to give the full cost of hire over the expected hire period until the new replacement drill arrives through the company's procurement procedure.
	E	should be deleted because in this instance there was no option other than hiring equipment and the board does not need to know the fine detail of the hire shops.
11	Section 5 gives a recommendation. Which of the following correctly describes this section as currently worded?	
	A	It is a correct recommendation since stopping the hire would delay the stage.
	B	It is a correct recommendation because FIX-IT-FAST is the cheapest hire option and therefore gives the lowest overrun of the stage cost tolerance.
	C	It is a wrong recommendation because the Project Manager should be thinking more widely of the lesson learned and recommending fast-track ordering to be set up in the company for urgent purchases affecting time-critical projects.
	D	The wording shows misunderstanding of the PRINCE2 exception mechanism since the recommendation should come before action is taken, not to continue action started without the Project Board's permission.
	E	The section should have been left empty, to be filled in by the Senior Supplier on the Project Board once he or she had taken specialist advice on the best solution.
12	Section 6 is about any lessons learned. Which action should be taken with this section?	
	A	The section should be left as it is written. It correctly describes a lesson that might be applied to later projects.
	B	The section should be deleted as lessons recorded should be about how improvements can be made in using PRINCE2 for project management, not the technical detail of equipment provision on a particular type of project.
	C	The section should be deleted as it is now too late for this project since the budget would have been agreed in Initiation, before any of the delivery stages got underway.
	D	The section should be extended to explain in much more detail why the problem was not forseen and which specialists are to blame for this oversight.
	E	The section should be deleted and the content transferred to the Lessons Report to be submitted at the end of the project.

Answers to the Foundation-level questions

1 **d.** Be careful not to confuse the Checkpoint Report with the Highlight Report. They are similar beasts – progress reports – but the management level is different.

2 **c.** The Checkpoint and Highlight Reports are both produced at set intervals. The Exception Report isn't, but it's produced by the Project Manager, not asked for.

3 **b.** You should know this, but even if you don't, you should be clear that the strategies are produced in Initiation, not Start Up when the brief is being done. Logs and registers are stand-alone products and don't form part of the brief or Project Initiation Documentation (PID). Putting those together, you may have been able to deduce that 'b' is the correct answer by ruling out the others. Such an approach is a perfectly valid strategy if you're not sure of an answer, and part of the function of this question is to give an example of that elimination strategy.

4 **b.** Anyone can generate and submit an issue, and that includes Team Managers. The three reports are all produced by the Project Manager. The Team Manager can note a lesson on a Checkpoint Report, but doesn't write a Lessons Report.

5 **a.** Remember, both logs – Daily and Lessons – are produced in Start Up. The other options in this question are all far too detailed for the rapid work of Start Up.

6 **a.** I always think that this is an unkind question style, because effectively you're faced with four questions not one. Be careful not to lose track; to help prevent that you might like to write 'T' (true) or 'F' (false) against each statement as you work through the list. Remember, you can write on the exam paper.

7 **d.** The significant word here is 'created'. The others may be updated but are not created on a stage boundary. Configuration Item Records are created as part of stage planning for the next stage where new products are defined at stage planning level. [**Manual** Table 17-1]. One of the functions of this question is to remind you to be very aware of every word in the question. It's easy, especially when under time pressure, to miss the significance of words such as 'created' and 'updated'.

8 **b.** In Start Up, entries are made in the Lessons Log for things from past experience which may be of value in the current project. In Start Up, the log is retrospective. From that point on, it's used mostly to record lessons learned in the present project which may be of use to future projects.

9 **c.** If you've got as far as product planning when you're reading this, you may correctly associate Product Descriptions with plans and so with Initiation onwards. However, this isn't an ordinary Product Description but the *Project* Product Description (PPD). The PPD may be modified in Initiation and indeed later in the project as well, but it's created in Start Up and forms part of the Project Brief.

10 **a.** Well, you've been working so hard on some fairly tough questions that I had to drop in an easy one. A report at the end of the project: the End Project Report. It's a pity the Foundation exam isn't as kind hearted. Actually though, once again there's a learning point behind this question as well as kindness. The learning point is that some exam questions are very straight-forward and, if you happen to know the answer, easy. Don't expect everything to be difficult and go looking for some deep complexity when the answer is straightforward and staring you in the face.

Answers to the Practitioner-level questions

Matching-style questions

1 **D.** This is a good use of the Daily Log to reduce formal documentation.

2 **F.** A Request for Change (RFC) is a type of issue and has a priority. None of the other products listed in column 2, as defined in Appendix A of the PRINCE2 manual, have priority headings. The Lessons Log does, but the product in column 2 is a Lessons Report.

3 **G.** This is a quality action to be taken, so it's listed in the Quality Register.

4 **C.** A projection that the stage will exceed tolerance is an exception. It would be escalated to the Project Board using an Exception Report.

5 **F.** Again, an RFC is a type of issue. The correct selection is Issue Register. It would also appear on the issue itself, but that isn't an option in column 2.

6 **G.** The Quality Register again, this time for a new quality action that comes to light during a stage rather than one that was planned during stage planning.

Classic-style questions

The Exception Report example is completely wrong. The report should be submitted if the Project Manager does not have power to act (because to do so would exceed tolerance) and needs authority to take action. The report is not to recommend continuing action which is unauthorised. With any set of questions on a specific management product, it helps to look quickly at Appendix A of the PRINCE2 manual so that the right use of the product is fresh in your mind. The mistakes in the example then often jump out at you, and hopefully they did here. Having opened the manual at Appendix A, keep it open at the page while answering, so that you can glance back at it whenever you need to.

7 **E.** The title should *describe* the exception in overview – in this case a cost exception, although it can also include time exception. The error becomes very obvious if you have the manual open at the product and are looking at the explanation for the 'Exception title' section of the report. [**Manual** A10.2]

8 **C.** The cause of the deviation was the tool breakdown. The key word is 'cause'. This breakdown will lead to delay, extra cost, or perhaps both, but that delay or overspending is a consequence, not the cause.

9   **B.** The section as written does not explain the consequences of the problem as it should, but rather is reporting the consequences of the unauthorised action already taken by the Project Manager.

10   **B.** This section should give the Project Board different options for dealing with the deviation. One option, for example, is to delay the project by waiting for the new drill to arrive through the procurement system rather than hiring one. That may not be an option that the Project Manager would recommend, but it's an option nevertheless.

11   **D.** Answer D correctly explains the misunderstanding evident in the product.

12   **A.** The lesson is valid, although perhaps not very well thought through or worded. It's rather better than the rest of the report though – but that's not saying much. Clearly the Project Manager wasn't trained by Nick Graham and Inspirandum Ltd!

Chapter 19

Knowing How PRINCE2 Fits Together

*L*earning PRINCE2 is tough, really it is, and piecing it all together in a short period of time is especially tough. I've spent many years teaching PRINCE2 courses, and I often tell those attending my courses that learning the method is a bit like learning to drive a car. At first it seems impossible. I grew up in Birmingham and lived on an extremely long road. I remember getting into the instructor's car for my first lesson and driving off. I was well pleased, I can tell you. I went through the gears and then drove along smoothly. Then we finally got to the end of the road and a T-junction. 'Brake,' said the instructor, 'Mirror, signal, move more to the left, brake more, you're going much too fast, clutch . . . ' I remember thinking to myself 'This is impossible, how can I ever do all of this at once?' Now, years later, I regularly drive into Central London through heavy traffic without a second thought. So, too, with PRINCE2. If you're finding it hard to learn the detail to exam standard, and then to fit it all together, don't worry. Eventually you'll drive PRINCE2 without a problem.

You may be looking at this chapter before you've revised all of the themes and processes, because you're already concerned that you can't see how the method fits together. The integration isn't easy, but in any case it's hard to appreciate how 'it' (the method) works before you fully understand what 'it' is. If you have a copy of the companion book to this one, *PRINCE2 For Dummies*, you'll find that Chapter 2 gives an overview of the structure, which you may find helpful. When you've learned the detail of the method, you'll reach a point where it should click together and you'll 'get' it. Hopefully, you'll reach that point before the exams, although all is not lost if you don't. This chapter is to help you a bit, but also to give you some reassurance that it'll all eventually make some sort of sense.

If you've already covered the processes of Starting Up a Project and Initiating a Project, you may be starting to find it difficult to relate the different elements, but here I have an advantage over you in that I know the whole method. So you may be thinking, 'Where on earth does the Project Brief come? Is it in Start Up, or Initiation? Or perhaps it's neither; I can't remember.' However, I can sit back smugly. The Project Brief is a sketchy document, so it must be done in Start Up. Where else could it come? When the whole method becomes logical like that – believe me, it does get a whole lot easier. At that point, the underlying logic and structure of PRINCE2 helps drive your memory, and you're no longer learning isolated islands of seemingly unrelated things.

Appreciating the Four Integrated Elements

PRINCE2 talks of four integrated elements. These are simply the:

- Processes
- Themes
- Principles
- Tailoring PRINCE2 to the project environment

When you fully understand the method, you'll see how the four fit together. It's actually rather important that you do see how the elements fit together, because you're expected to know that for both exams. For the Foundation exam especially, be sure also to take on board the phrase 'four integrated elements'.

The Processes

The *processes* are the suggested 'when' you do something. They cover the sequence of the project from Start Up to closure. In anything other than a small project, you're likely to have several delivery stages, so the processes used for the delivery stages will repeat for as many stages as there are. A variation occurs in the last stage, however, since at the end of it you'll be closing the project rather than preparing for a following stage.

It's a common mistake to think that each stage in the project involves a single process. While it's true that each stage is *driven* by a single process, that process will 'call' other processes to do parts of the work. Figure 19-1 shows Start Up and the project stages and illustrates where the processes are involved.

You'll have seen from the PRINCE2 manual that every process has a process diagram. In each case, the diagram shows a series of activities for the process, with those activities linked by arrows to show the default sequence in which you do them. In the Practitioner exam, the exact activities and sequences are not going to present a problem because the exam is open book and you can have the manual open in front of you to look at the diagrams whenever you want to. For the Foundation exam, which is closed book, you need to be aware of the activities in each process to know what that process is doing, and of the overall sequence in which the manual suggests that the activities are done. You do not, however, need to learn the diagrams by heart.

Going down a level, the method then has recommended actions within each activity. The recommended actions are listed as bullet points under each activity heading in the PRINCE2 manual. Unless you have a photographic memory, you'll never remember all the actions for all the activities in the method, but you do need to be aware of what the activity is about and particularly who's doing it and which management products (such as the Business Case, the Daily Log and the Project Plan) are in use.

There are seven processes, and for the Foundation exam you should be able to list them from memory.

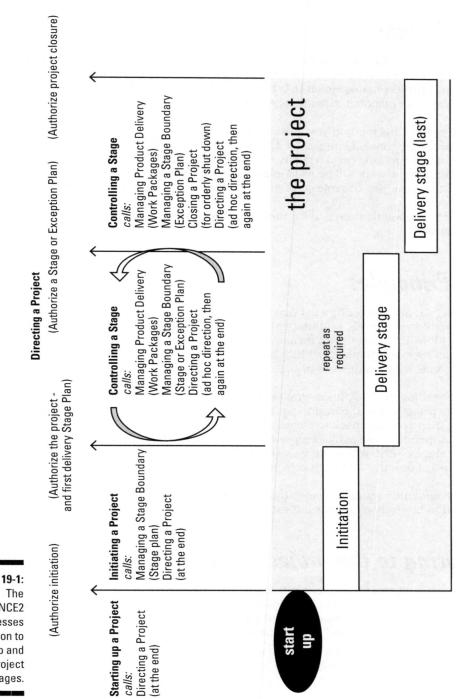

Figure 19-1:
The
PRINCE2
processes
in relation to
Start Up and
the project
stages.

The Themes

In contrast to the processes, which give the suggested 'when' (the points at which you do things), the *themes* set down advice on 'what' you do in project management – or at least in the parts of project management that the method covers, which isn't all of it. So the themes cover things like planning, risk management and progress control.

In some parts of the method you'll use particular themes intensively, while in other parts you'll hardly use those themes at all. Other themes are pretty much in continuous use throughout. Progress control will obviously be happening right through the stages, while the Organization theme will be used mostly in Start Up, with a bit in Initiation and at the end of each stage to adjust the roles and responsibilities if that proves necessary.

PRINCE2 has seven themes, and for the Foundation exam you should be able to remember what they are.

The Principles

The *principles* are, allegedly, what makes a project a PRINCE2 project. The authors of the manual have very bravely said that unless a project is following all seven principles, then it isn't a PRINCE2 project. That means there are considerably fewer PRINCE2 projects out there than everyone thinks. So, PRINCE2 expects the project to be fully justified throughout, and this is set down in the first principle, that of 'continued business justification'.

If you're reading this chapter as you're starting to learn PRINCE2, don't worry too much about the principles at the beginning. They'll make more sense as you go through the method; then you can check to ensure that you understand each one at the end. For example, the principle 'manage by exception' isn't going to make complete sense until you see how the stages work. When you've learned all the themes and processes, you should be fully aware of exactly what each principle is, so check this out to make sure.

For the Foundation exam, you need to know the list of seven principles, and for both exams you need to be really clear on what each one is about.

Tailoring to the project environment

It may seem a bit strange to include the project environment in the 'integrated elements' since it isn't something with distinct PRINCE2 content, unlike the other three elements. Rather, it's more like a backdrop behind the other three elements. PRINCE2 states clearly (at long last) that the method must be fitted to the needs of the project.

Because the project environment and tailoring doesn't have content you have to learn, it's easy to forget that it's one of the four elements, so watch out for that when revising for the Foundation exam. You may find that you can reel off the first three elements from memory easily enough, but then struggle to remember what the fourth one is.

There are three important viewpoints in PRINCE2: business, user and supplier (BUS). The viewpoints fit into the customer/supplier environment, with the business and user interests on the customer side, and the supplier, predictably, on the supplier side. Figure 19-2 illustrates the fit of the three views and may help you remember them.

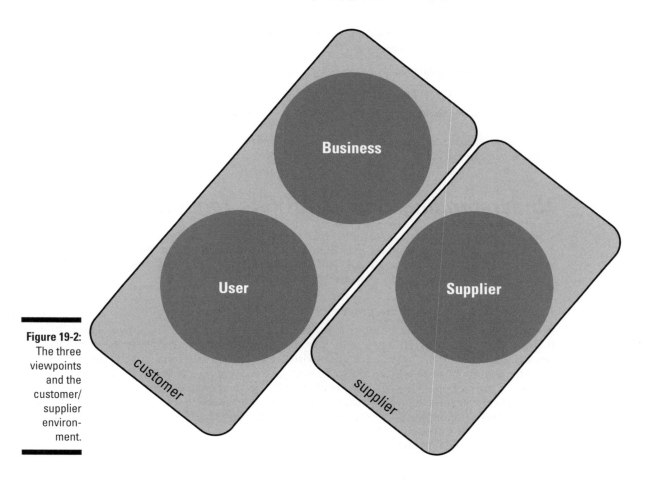

Figure 19-2:
The three viewpoints and the customer/ supplier environment.

Perusing purpose statements

All the processes and themes have a purpose statement. Unfortunately, these purpose statements are the subject of some questions in the Foundation exam question pool. Knowing the method and how the parts fit together includes knowing the purpose of each part, so you need to be able to recognise which purpose statements go with each theme and process. So, once you've looked at all the themes and processes, do you think you can recognise the purpose statements? For each statement in the quiz, say which theme or process it belongs to:

1. To establish mechanisms to judge whether the project is (and remains) desirable, viable and achievable

2. To enable the Project Board to be accountable for the project's success by making key decisions and exercising overall control

3. To assign work to be done

4. To identify, assess and control uncertainty

5. To establish mechanisms to monitor and compare actual achievements against those planned

You'll find the answers at the end of the chapter. One of the tricks here is to identify key words that associate the purpose statement with a particular theme or process; the answers give examples of that too.

Understanding How It All Fits Together

Having learned the various bits of PRINCE2, it can be hard to see how they fit together. The introduction to this chapter may have helped by explaining that the processes are the 'when' and the themes are the 'what' you do. However, for the exams, you're going to need to take that forward to specific knowledge.

How the themes fit with the processes

Knowing where the themes fit into the process is both intuitive and, when you know the themes, sort of obvious. However, the fit is also complicated. My son Peter, to whom this book is dedicated, has always been great with graphics, and when he worked for my company for a while he built a bit of software that gave an overview of PRINCE2. Part of it was a picture of the high level process model alongside the 'pie chart' of the themes. It was ingenious. When you selected a process, the themes that are used by that process lit up. When you selected a theme, the processes that use it lit up. The trouble was that nobody was ever going to remember those combinations, and sadly we ended up dropping that part of the software. It's that same complex matching that you're facing right now.

You may find it helpful as part of your revision to write two lists to mimic Peter's software model. Write down a list of the seven processes. For each one, then think through what's going on and list the themes that are involved. For example, in the process of Starting Up a Project, the first activity is 'Appoint the Executive and the Project Manager'. The work involves roles and responsibilities then, so write down 'Organization' in your list of themes used by the Start Up process.

When you've finished with the processes, write another list, this time of the seven themes. For each theme, look at the process model again and think which processes use that theme. So, when working on the Organization theme, you'll write down 'Starting Up a Project'. The Organization theme is used by Start Up in its first activity of 'Appoint the Executive and Project Manager', as noted in the previous paragraph, but then again for the activity 'Design and appoint the project management team'.

Tracking the principles through the method

The PRINCE2 examiners are quite keen on putting in questions to test your knowledge of how the processes and themes 'support' the principles. You can take the same approach to revising the support of the principles as with the interaction of themes and processes – by writing lists. Don't try to memorise the lists, or your brain will be in grave danger of exploding, but rather use the list as a means of recording your understanding of the interaction as you revise. It's that understanding which will then lead you to the correct answers in the exams.

Understanding how the PRINCE2 principles are supported by the rest of the method involves you in some careful thinking, so here's an example to show what your list might look like as you start to consider the principle of 'learn from experience'.

Learn from experience:

✔ **Starting Up a Project:** Lessons Log created. Lessons from the past that need to be considered for this project entered into the log.

✔ **Directing a Project:** Passing on lessons learned in this project, as reported by the Project Manager, into the organisation. Making sure that plans and the Project Initiation Documentation (PID) for this project take on board lessons from the past.

✔ **Initiating a Project:** Applying past lessons from the log when preparing the PID. Noting any new lessons learned during Initiation into the Lessons Log.

✔ **Controlling a Stage:** Looking for lessons, logging them and putting them in Highlight Reports. Logging lessons being learned when dealing with issues and risks. Taking note of lessons information recorded by Team Managers in their Checkpoint Reports.

✔ **Managing Product Delivery:** Team Managers looking for lessons and putting them on Checkpoint Reports.

✔ **Managing a Stage Boundary:** Lessons Report included in the End Stage Report.

✔ **Closing a Project:** Lessons Report, from Lessons Log entries, included in the End Project Report. Also some lessons may lead to follow-on action recommendations to be passed back into the organisation, for example recommending a change in project standards because of something learned. Lessons Log closed.

Practising With Some Questions

On the following pages you'll find some practice questions to help check your understanding of the elements of the method and their integration. Aim to do them to time, so that you get accustomed to the pace of the exams.

Foundation-level questions

Have a go at these questions and try to answer within eight minutes. If you get a question wrong, try to work out why. Was it because you simply didn't read the question carefully enough, and actually you know the PRINCE2? Or was it because you don't properly understand that point and you need to look at it again in your revision?

1. Which option shows how the method supports the principle of 'focus on products'?

❑ a) Lessons are recorded in the Lessons Log.

❑ b) The Project Product Description (PPD) is created in the process Starting Up a Project.

❑ c) Products brought in from outside the project are known as 'external' products.

❑ d) The Project Manager is responsible for issuing Work Packages to Team Managers.

2. Which of the following is *not* a PRINCE2 theme?

❑ a) Business Case

❑ b) Plans

❑ c) Roles and Responsibilities

❑ d) Change

3. Which of the following supports the PRINCE2 principle of 'manage by stages'?

❑ a) Work Packages

❑ b) Management stages

❑ c) Technical stages

❑ d) Financial periods

4. Which of the following processes is *not* involved in supporting the PRINCE2 principle of 'continued business justification'?

❏ a) Directing a Project

❏ b) Initiating a Project

❏ c) Managing a Stage Boundary

❏ d) Managing Product Delivery

5. Which of the following supports the PRINCE2 principle of 'tailor to suit the project environment'?

❏ a) Including a tailoring statement in the Project Initiation Documentation (PID)

❏ b) Requiring Team Managers to state in each Team Plan how PRINCE2 is being implemented for the Work Package

❏ c) Checks by Project Assurance at the end of the project that PRINCE2 has been applied correctly to work to carry out the follow-on action recommendations

❏ d) Regular financial reporting to corporate or programme management

6. Which of the following PRINCE2 processes *does not* make use of content in the Plans theme?

❏ a) Initiating a Project

❏ b) Managing a Stage Boundary

❏ c) Managing Product Delivery

❏ d) Closing a Project

7. Which of the following PRINCE2 processes is outside the project?

❏ a) Starting Up a Project

❏ b) Directing a Project

❏ c) Managing Product Delivery

❏ d) Closing a Project

8. Which of the following statements is correct?

A. The contents of the Risk theme are used during project initiation.

B. The Project Product Description (PPD) is created in the process of Initiating a Project, ready to be included in the Project Initiation Documentation (PID).

C. The updating of the Business Case on a stage boundary supports the principle of 'continued business justification'.

D. The method supports the principle of 'defined roles and responsibilities' by including the project management team structure in the Project Initiation Documentation (PID).

❑ a) A, B and C

❑ b) A, B and D

❑ c) A, C and D

❑ d) B, C and D

9. Which of the following are included in the integrated elements of PRINCE2?

A. Principles

B. Controls

C. Themes

D. Processes

❑ a) A, B and C

❑ b) A, B and D

❑ c) A, C and D

❑ d) B, C and D

10. Which of the following are management levels within the PRINCE2 project management structure?

❑ a) Senior management, middle management and operational management

❑ b) Accepting, executing and delivering

❑ c) Management, specialist and technical

❑ d) Directing, managing and delivering

Practitioner-level questions

In the Practitioner exam, you'll be pushed harder to demonstrate that you understand the integration of the method and how the processes and themes support the seven PRINCE2 principles.

Try to do the Practitioner questions in this section in 18 minutes or less. There's no additional project scenario information to read, but don't forget the original scenario information at the end of Chapter 2. Chapter 2 also has guidance on dealing with the different question styles, including the three-step approach for the assertion–reason format.

Assertion-reason style questions

Each row in the table below consists of an assertion statement and a reason statement. For each row identify the appropriate selection from options A to E that applies. Each option can be used once, more than once or not at all.

Selection	Assertion	Reason	
A	True	True	AND the reason explains the assertion
B	True	True	BUT the reason does not explain the assertion
C	True	False	
D	False	True	
E	False	False	

	Assertion		Reason
1	The Project Board should only check the cost of the e-business unit project during project Initiation	BECAUSE	the justification of the project is 'compulsory' and is being done on the direct instruction of the Board of Directors
2	Previous HQ projects involving structural changes should be checked at Start Up	BECAUSE	experience from earlier projects may be valuable in the e-business unit project
3	The e-business unit project can only have one delivery stage	BECAUSE	there's no need for regular checks of the Business Case by the Executive
4	The Project Product Description for the project will not be updated	BECAUSE	the requirement for an e-commerce unit is in the company's five year plan
5	PRINCE2 must be applied in full to the project with no parts of any theme or process left out	BECAUSE	PRINCE2 is the chosen standard for the e-commerce unit project and must therefore be used in the standard way
6	Other than Executive and Project Manager, no formal roles are needed for the e-business unit office project	BECAUSE	the people involved in the project are likely to change and so work and responsibilities should be determined as required as the project continues

Matching style questions

	For each statement about the 'e-business unit' office refurbishment project in Column 1, please select the correct option in Column 2. An option in Column 2 may be used more than once or not at all.	
	Column 1	**Column 2**
7	As more business functions are due to be moved into head-quarters in the next two years, the Project Board will be careful to refer information on any useful experience from the project back to organisational managers.	A Continued business justification B Learn from experience C Defined roles and responsibilities D Manage by stages E Manage by exception F Focus on products G Tailor to suit the project environment
8	The Project Board has set an upper and lower limit on costs for the stage of the project where structural alterations are to be done to make the new doorways. Provided that the Project Manager can deliver within the limits, there's no need for Project Board involvement in day-to-day management.	
9	Project and Stage Plans for the project to refurbish offices for the new e-commerce unit will include Product Descriptions and the Project Board have asked for the stage level Product Checklist to be included in the Highlight Report.	
10	For this project only, all risks will be reported to the Princess Projects Plc Risk Manager by sending a copy of the Risk Register as approved in the PID and then any updates. This is so he can be fully aware of risk in the project and check to see if there are wider implications that could affect the launch of the e-business unit and related operations. The company risk standard does not normally require all project risks to be reported in this way.	
11	In a previous office refurbishment project, some extremely hard, black coloured material was found in many of the old bricks in the walls. The HQ building is very old and nobody in the Works Department knew what the black substance was, but it proved very hard to cut into and equipment was damaged.	
12	Mary Li, the project Executive, has agreed with corporate managers that the Princess Projects Plc central Project Office will provide administrative support for this project.	

Answers to the quick quiz

1. Business Case (theme) – key word 'viable'

2. Directing a Project (process) – key words 'Project Board' and 'overall control'

3. Controlling a Stage (process) – key words 'assign work'

4. Risk (theme) – key word 'uncertainty', part of the PRINCE2 risk definition

5. Progress (theme) – key word 'monitor'

Answers to the Foundation-level questions

1. **b.** A clear, and immediate, focus on the 'project product' in Start Up. Answer 'c' refers to products, but doesn't show support of the principle as well as 'b'.

2. **c.** The roles and responsibilities are covered by the Organization theme.

3. **b.** PRINCE2 works with management stages, some of which may align to technical stage boundaries, but some may not.

4. **d.** Team Managers just get on with the work they've been instructed to do. They're not involved in justifying that work or with checking the Business Case.

5. **a.** The Project Initiation Documentation (PID) has a tailoring statement. [**Manual** A.20.2]. Some Team Managers may not even be using PRINCE2 for their Work Packages if they are suppliers from outside the customer organisation.

6. **d.** Initiating a Project covers the Project Plan. Managing a Stage Boundary delivers Stage and Exception Plans. Managing Product Delivery covers Team Plans. All of these processes use the planning approach set down in the Plans theme.

7. **a.** The project begins with the Initiation Stage, after Start Up has been run and the Project Board has completed its first activity, 'Authorize Initiation'.

8. **c.** The Project Product Description (PPD) is produced in Start Up and goes, initially, into the Project Brief. This question is to help counter a common misconception that the PPD must be produced during Initiation, because it becomes part of the Project Plan. If you weren't aware that the PPD becomes part of the Project Plan, don't be too hard on yourself, because the manual isn't very clear on the point. You'll find a brief reference to it in Appendix A, though. [**Manual** A.16.2 Product Descriptions section]

9. **c.** The four elements are the processes, the themes, the principles and tailoring to the project environment.

10. **d.** Answer 'b' summarises the activities in the process Managing Product Delivery, while 'c' lists types of stages and 'a' has general management, not PRINCE2, terms.

Answers to the Practitioner-level questions

Assertion–reason style questions

1 **D.** The costs are part of the Business Case, which must be checked at end stage. This supports the principle of 'continued business justification'. If the costs escalate considerably, even though the project is by direct instruction of the Board of Directors, the Project Board may conclude that it's no longer justified and suggest that the Board of Directors withdraws its instruction and so allow the project to be stopped.

2 **A.** This supports the principle of 'learn from experience'. In this instance, it's retrospective: experience from past projects helping with this project.

3 **E.** There's no requirement for a single delivery stage, and the Executive, as the person responsible for the Business Case, must keep an eye on that case. But there's no connection between the number of stages and the need to have continued business justification anyway. If the Business Case collapsed mid stage, the project should still be stopped and doesn't have to wait until the end of the stage.

4 **D.** The Project Product Description (PPD) is kept up to date throughout the project, helping fulfil the PRINCE2 principle 'focus on products'.

5 **E.** The last of the PRINCE2 principles is 'tailor to suit the project environment'. The method must be fitted to the project, not used en-bloc in some 'standard' way.

6 **E.** All of the roles should be filled, except the optional Team Manager role, although in this project that role will be needed too. Yes, staffing does change, particularly on longer projects, but that's why the project management team structure should be kept up to date; it doesn't mean that the structure should be abandoned. This fulfils the principle 'defined roles and responsibilities'.

Matching-style questions

7 **B.** This time, forward looking to pass on lessons learned in this project so that future projects will benefit.

8 **E.** Exception management, in this case referring to stage cost tolerances. Don't forget that tolerances can be applied in addition at project level and also at team (Work Package) level. Tolerances are mostly commonly applied to time and cost, but can cover any or all of the six control areas of time, cost, scope, quality, benefits and risk.

9 **F.** The product focus is strong in PRINCE2, both for the whole project (Project Product Description – PPD) and at stage level, down to progress control with the Product Checklist. Brush up on the Product Checklist if you can't remember it – and don't forget it for your real projects after the exams, because it's very powerful. Yes, life and projects will continue after the exams. [**P2FD** Ch17 Measuring progress with the Product Checklist]

10   **G.** It isn't normal in PRINCE2 to pass on details of every risk to the corporate or programme level, but in the case of this particular project, it's a requirement of the company. So then, the normal PRINCE2 approach needs to be adjusted – tailored – to fit, hence supporting the last of the seven PRINCE2 principles. For a bonus point, where would it be recorded that all risk information should be copied to the company's Risk Manager? You'll find the answer at the end of these answers!

11   **B.** Learning from experience again. As you'll see in other parts of this book, they didn't do too well picking up on this lesson and had a problem with a broken drill – a problem that could and should have been foreseen.

12   **C.** Project Support is a defined role. You need to be familiar with all the roles on the project management team for the Practitioner exam, but don't forget that they're all set out in Appendix C of the PRINCE2 manual, and you can quickly turn to it if you need to confirm a point of detail on the exact responsibilities. One of the keys to success in the Practitioner exam is to know where things are in your manual so that you can quickly refer to the information when you need to. You'll find this tip, along with some others, in Chapter 21 in the Part of Tens, which describes ten things to remember before taking an exam.

Practitioner question 10 – bonus point

The need to copy all risk information in the project to the company's Risk Manager would be recorded in the Risk Management Strategy, in the 'Risk management procedure' section. [**Manual** A.24.2]. Risk information may also be put into the Communications Management Strategy. For a bonus point to the bonus point . . . no, you've worked hard enough.

Part V
The Part of Tens

In this part . . .

Every *For Dummies* book has a Part of Tens, a handful of concise chapters that really pack a punch.

These chapters give you some advice when getting ready for the exams, but one is a bit special and is some additional help in getting to grips with product-based planning. This approach to planning is rather unusual even now in project management. Even if you are attending a training course with an accredited company (other than mine!) you might find that it isn't taught too well. So there are ten points to help you ensure that you understand the approach and get great marks in planning questions in the exams as a result.

Chapter 20

Ten Things for Your Revision

Since you've bought this book, I can assume that you're already convinced about the need to revise for the PRINCE2 exams and practise with sample questions. This chapter provides a few guidelines which you may find helpful in structuring your preparation.

Scheduling Revision In With the Learning

When you've revised in the past, it's probably been for school or university exams, or at least for something that's taken a relatively long time to learn. You're probably used to scheduling your revision at the end of that long learning period and in time for the exam. With PRINCE2, it's more likely that you're going to be learning the method quickly – over a period of a few days up to three or four weeks – before taking the exams. Because the learning period is shorter, it's better to schedule revision time during the learning as well as at the end of it. Actually, that will also help you learn as well. If you're crystal clear on the bits of PRINCE2 you've learned so far, then you'll find that it's much easier to take on board the remaining parts.

Keeping Up With Revision

In line with previous revision experience, you may still think that it's preferable to get the learning under your belt first and then revise everything at the end. If you're attending a face-to-face, classroom-based course that includes the exams as part of the event, you'll have a problem if you stick with that approach. The PRINCE2 method is very big, as the thickness of the official manual immediately reveals. If you finish the learning on one day and take the first of your exams on the next day, you simply won't have time to revise the whole method in sufficient detail. So, as suggested in the previous point, schedule your revision during the learning process and then make sure you keep up to date. On the last day of your course, you'll then have a limited amount to brush up on and some spare time to have a go with a practice exam paper.

Leaving yourself a big revision load just before the exam, and then working late into the night to cover it and do a practice paper, is asking for trouble. Going into an exam room really tired after working until 3 a.m. is not the best start or likely to contribute to your success. It *is* likely to lead to you getting answers wrong, even where you know PRINCE2, because in your tiredness you may misread the questions.

Being Systematic

As you're planning your revision, be systematic and make sure that you schedule in revision of all parts of the method. You need to be fluent across the whole of PRINCE2 to be successful in the exams. Don't make the mistake of looking only at selected parts and missing the finer points which are the subject of exam questions – questions which you'll then have difficulty answering. In the Foundation exam you'll end up guessing, and in the Practitioner you're likely to waste time looking things up which really you should have known. If you have to look a lot of things up in the Practitioner, you run the very real risk of timing out, not being able to finish the paper and so failing.

Going Large On the Tricky Areas

The last point emphasises the need to be systematic in your revision and cover the whole method. However, as you allocate time to revision it makes sense to allow slightly more time for those areas where you're a bit unsure. That's where the practice questions in this book and in the practice papers available from the exam board may help you. If you have difficulty answering a question, take that as a warning that you're not sufficiently fluent on that point in the method.

An important exception to this is in the area of quality. Because the 'quality' chapter in the official manual is rather strange – focusing on definitions and procedures rather more than on the implementation of quality – many people feel uncomfortable with it, even when actually they have sufficient grasp of the content to tackle the exams. If you have professional quality experience you may feel even more uneasy, because it all seems slightly off beam. Don't worry about that and just be sure that you understand the meaning of quality terms in the way that PRINCE2 uses them, and for the time being simply forget your previous experience.

Getting Help If You're Still Unclear

If you're unclear on a part of the method covered in your training, and you've already gone over your training material, check out other sources for help; don't just give up. If you don't have a copy of *PRINCE2 For Dummies*, then you might like to get hold of one, because the nature of the book allows a more down-to-earth explanation than the manual. But also, if you're on a course, then ask the course tutor. If you're with a good training company, then the tutor can explain the point another way, perhaps with a few examples from live projects he or she has worked on, so you can understand. If the trainer can only repeat what's in the manual (too often the case) and doesn't seem to have any practical experience to fall back on for meaningful examples, then at least you now know why that course was cheaper than the others you considered!

Practising With Exam Questions

Include practice with questions, to time, including the official practice papers. Allow some time in your schedule for follow-up where questions show a gap in your knowledge and understanding.

Being Familiar With Objectives and Purpose Statements

For the Foundation, make sure that you go over the purpose statements to be sure that you're familiar enough with them to know which bit of PRINCE2 each purpose statement belongs to and to be able to replace any missing words with the options in the answers.

Knowing How It All Fits Together

For both exams, but especially the Practitioner, make sure you understand how the parts of the method fit together, because there are frequently questions on how the seven principles are supported by other parts of the method.

Annotating Your Manual

For the Practitioner, write reference stuff in your manual, but only where it's helpful. If, as you revise, you realise that something in the manual isn't particularly clear and you're likely to be confused in the exam if you consult it, write a brief explanatory note in your manual. Don't overdo the notes though; if they're so dense that you can't see the wood for the trees, you won't find the one you're looking for.

Knowing Where Stuff Is

Finally, again for Practitioner level, know where stuff is in the manual – use tabs to help find things quickly. The revision time is a great time to do this, because as you look at a particular topic you'll often realise that a particular section will be useful – such as the Quality Review panels in the Quality theme chapter.

Chapter 21

Ten Things to Remember Before Taking an Exam

This chapter in the Part of Tens summarises advice given earlier in the book. It's here because you may find it helpful as a quick checklist on the practicalities before you tackle an exam.

For Both Exams

The first seven things to remember apply to both the Foundation and Practitioner exams.

Being confident

Most people pass the exams. In the Foundation, it's rare for anyone to fail if they've prepared thoroughly. In the Practitioner, most people pass. So, provided you've done your homework, be confident. Okay, so it may go wrong for you, but cross that bridge if – and only if – you come to it. Try not to go into the exam room fearing the worst and so face more pressure than you need to. That additional pressure can cause poorer performance, for example if you need to re-read a question two or three times because you're busy worrying rather than concentrating.

Remembering to RTFQ

It's hard to overstate this point. You really do need to RTFQ (Read The Flipping Question), as they told you for school exams. In the Foundation especially, the whole meaning of the question can hang on a single word, and at the time of writing this book, a significant number of questions are still poorly phrased. Especially if you're under time pressure, focus hard on taking in every word, for example whether a product is 'created' or 'updated'.

Remembering to ATFQ

Next, ATFQ (Answer The Flipping Question). If you have several possible answer options and need to think about one or two (or even check out the manual in the Practitioner exam), it's surprisingly easy to lose track of the exact wording of the question and start answering something else. In the Foundation, watch out for negatives such as: 'Which one of these is *not* . . .'. While going over the possible answers, it's easy to forget the 'not'.

Arriving in good time

Do some risk management and plan your journey. Plan to arrive in good time and don't add travel panic to the pressure of the exam.

Getting your exam stuff together

Getting your basic exam kit together can make a big difference to your confidence and hence performance. Make sure you have the following gear:

- **Sharp pencils:** Most people prefer wooden pencils because they have stronger leads than automatic pencils, and you're going to be filling in lots of ovals. You don't want the hassle of a constantly breaking pencil lead. And have a spare or two. Ever had a wooden pencil that's been dropped, and when you sharpen it the new bit of lead just falls out – and you sharpen it again only for the same thing to happen? Don't hit that avoidable problem in an exam.

- **Pencil sharpener:** Your training company may have provided some sharpeners, but it's better to have your own right in front of you, so you know you've got a good one that actually works.

- **Eraser:** Unless, that is, you don't ever make mistakes. Again, have a good one that will rub out pencil thoroughly and cleanly. A plastic eraser is better than one made of rubber. And it's better to have a proper eraser than to rely on a small, perhaps poor one on the end of your pencil.

- **Photo ID:** You need to produce photo ID to sit the exam. Don't go and forget it and so not be able to sit the paper. A driving licence or passport is ideal, but some security passes are okay. If you intend to use something other than a driving licence or passport, check in advance that the ID is acceptable.

- **Sweets and water:** You may like to have some refreshment during the exam, but if you do take sweets into the exam room, make sure that they haven't got noisy cellophane wrappers!

- **PRINCE2 manual:** For the Practitioner exam only, you can take in your PRINCE2 manual, but only your PRINCE2 manual. No other reference material is permitted unless you have special permission – see the next point.

✔ **Dictionary and PRINCE2 glossary:** If you're taking the exam in your second language, you're allowed to have a dictionary to help with translation, and a PRINCE2 glossary in your first language if one's been produced. Check this out beforehand. Don't think you won't bother, because you're already familiar with the PRINCE2 terms. It's good risk management to prevent a problem, not hit one with an unexpected word that makes you miss a mark.

Getting some rest

Don't revise late into the night the day before the exam. It's better to get an early night and arrive in the exam room fresh and alert.

Practising with sample papers

This book has questions to practise with, but it's also important to get the official sample papers so you can have a go at doing a whole paper at once, or at least a substantial part of it in the case of the Practitioner level. If you're taking a course with a PRINCE2 training provider, you should be given sample papers as a matter of course. If the training provider doesn't provide them, ask for them.

In this book, I could have got permission to include two official sample papers, but that wouldn't have left space for any other questions, and it wouldn't have given you as much practice in each of the subject areas. It would also have been poor value for money if we filled a large part of the book with something that you can so easily get for free! But that doesn't mean you should skip the free official sample papers. Use the book as well as the sample papers, not instead of them. Recently obtained official sample papers also have the advantage that they'll be right up to date with the latest question formats. Things do change occasionally in the exam, and the trouble with books is that they only get updated with new editions from time to time.

For the Practitioner Exam Only

For the Practitioner exam, don't forget these three additional preparation points.

Tabbing your manual

You can put sticky tabs on the page edges of your manual to help you find things quickly. Remember though that you can't add extra information, just the name of the item. So, a tab on the page that lists the risk actions may be helpful. You'll be able to find things in the manual anyway by flipping through, but if you can save a few seconds each time you need to find something, that mounts up to a worthwhile amount of time over the course of a two and a half hour exam. That time can be used for scoring marks, not trying to find things and discovering that they've been left out of the index to the manual (sad, but true – they really should have got John Wiley and Sons to publish it!).

Tabbing is a very personal thing. Some people use a single colour and tab up just a few essential items. Others visit the supermarket and get kits with different colour tabs, and then have the tabs running along the top and bottom of the manual as well as down the side. Someone on one of my courses did this recently, and I think the manual could have been submitted as modern art for the Turner Prize – it was certainly more attractive than a sheep cut in half or an unmade bed. In short, do whatever works best for you.

Knowing where stuff is

A really key point for Practitioner: know where stuff is. Don't waste time trying to work something out or trying to remember detail when you can have the manual open at the page. Some things are general and some are specific and worth a tab on the page edge. So on specifics, the risk actions page and the Quality Review information are good for tabs. On general stuff, remember that at the end of every theme chapter in the PRINCE2 manual, there's a list of the roles involved in that theme. At the end of each activity description within each process, there's a table showing what products are in use in that activity and who's involved.

Making notes

Under the current rules, you can write notes onto the surface of the pages of your manual – which is as it should be. Make notes alongside anything that you may need to refer to in the exam that isn't already explained in the manual. That includes brief explanations on things where you think you may forget and the manual wording is less clear than it could be. However, don't go to the opposite extreme of writing so many notes that you can't find the one you're looking for because of the mass of writing covering every square centimetre of white space.

You can also annotate your manual, so highlighting or underlining particular key points can be helpful too. As with the notes, though, don't overdo it. If you highlight everything, you'll just have a bright yellow manual, and you'll be no better off finding a particular key point. Pretty, perhaps, but not very useful.

Remember, too, that while you can write onto the surface of the page of your manual, you're not permitted to write reference notes on separate sheets of paper and slip them into your manual, or to write them on sticky notes and fix them onto the pages. A location tab simply saying 'Risk Register' stuck on the edge of the appropriate page in Appendix A is fine. Having extra information on the tab such as 'set up by the Project Manager in Initiation' is not okay.

Chapter 22

Ten Points To Be Clear About On Products

In This Chapter

▶ Knowing that there are two types of product

▶ Being clear on what a product actually is

▶ Distinguishing between 'internal' or 'team' products and 'external' products

▶ Seeing how to adjust the PRINCE2 products to meet the needs of the project

*P*roducts are a core part of PRINCE2 planning, and cover not just what the teams are building but what's being used to project manage the project. Other approaches to project management include a product-based focus, including those used by NASA, the US military and another project management method, PRIME, where products are even more integrated. However, the focus is still new to many people, because most project management computer tools and books are still dominated by an activity-led approach. Consequently, you may feel more unsure about products than about other elements of PRINCE2. This Part of Tens chapter is to help you check that you understand what products are all about.

Knowing What a Product Is

It's easier to get to grips with the idea of products if you forget the PRINCE2 project management stuff for the time being and focus on what the teams are doing. Projects are primarily about delivering things, so the main work of the project teams is production. What the teams are *producing* are the *products*. A product is something that you can hold in your hand or, if it's too big for that, something you can kick. When a Team Manager goes to the Project Manager and says 'We've finished it!' what is 'it'? A product is something physical. Exceptionally, occasional products are needed that aren't physical, and if you're interested you can read about them in *PRINCE2 For Dummies*. However, such exceptions have never yet come into an exam, because the exams are aimed at a more normal type of project.

Appreciating the Two Product 'Flavours'

In the previous point, I said to forget all about the PRINCE2 project management stuff for the time being. Well, now it's time to remember it again, because PRINCE2 recognises two categories of product. The products being built by the teams are known as *specialist products*. You need to get familiar with the PRINCE2 language for the exams, but if you're struggling to get your head around the idea of products, it may help at first to think of specialist products as *deliverables*, if you're more familiar with that term.

What the teams are building is extremely important, but for the project to be successful you're also going to need some things for planning and control. You'll require things such as a Risk Register, a Project Plan and a Daily Log. These things are also products, but ones that are being used for project management. For that reason they're known as *management products*. Knowing whether something is a management product is dead easy, because all the management products are covered in Appendix A of the manual. So, brick walls, computer programs, new office designs and installed machines are all specialist products – things being produced by the teams – while the Project Initiation Documentation (PID), End Project Report, Issue Log and Business Case are all management products.

Knowing What a Product Isn't

Specialist products are what the teams are producing; they're usually physical things. You may be tested in the Practitioner exam on what products are and aren't. You'll find more on this in Chapter 14, but in short, if you're presented with a diagram or a list of products which 'may contain errors', then be on the lookout for non-products such as:

- **Activities:** Watch out for any verbs in the product names
- **Sources of supply:** Where the product has come from, notably when it's from outside the project, rather than what the product actually is
- **Resources:** Particularly people rather than the products which those people are generating, but resources can be financial resources too

Zooming In On Management Products

Within the category of 'management products' there are three subcategories. You'll find a management product list grouped according to these categories on the first page of Appendix A in the PRINCE2 manual.

Baseline management products

The baseline management products are ones which will change, or which are highly likely to change, and for which you'll want to keep earlier versions. The key to remembering this is the word *baseline*, which is a configuration management (version control) expression.

If something is changing, you're going to need version control to know how and when it's changed and whether you've got the latest version. The Project Plan is included in this category. The Project Plan will definitely change during the project. For a start, things never go exactly to plan, and the plan will need adjusting, but anyway you're going to want to enter *actuals* of time and money actually spent in order to do further forecasts. It's no surprise then to find plan (Project Plan, Stage Plan and Team Plan) on the baseline list.

Records

Records are dynamic products in constant use and being updated with the latest information. However, it's not the case that you'll normally want to roll back the product to a previous state. The Daily Log makes a great example here. The Daily Log acts primarily as a diary. If you note something today then find out in two days' time that circumstances have changed, you won't go back and alter the earlier entry. Instead you'll just add another dated note explaining the new situation.

Reports

Reports are snapshots at a point in time, and consequently are not normally version controlled. The Project Manager will report progress to the Project Board at set intervals – normally monthly or two-weekly. The Highlight Report for a particular month should be prepared in under an hour, so it's not going to go through several versions. If something happens in December that affects the forecast for the project, the Project Manager will explain that in the end-December Highlight Report. He or she won't go back and alter the end-November report and re-issue it. The November report was a snapshot of the position at that time, and because there's only one November report for that project in that year, there's no need for configuration management.

All reports have the word 'report' in their title, except for the Product Status Account.

Understanding Product Diagrams

When looking at the product diagrams, you may wonder why they don't normally show things like the Project Brief, the PID and the Highlight Reports (progress reports). It's normal to show only specialist products on the planning diagrams. A workable limit to the number of products on a plan is 30 (that's up to 30 on the Project Plan then up to 30 lower-level products on each Stage Plan), and in most projects you need all that space to show the specialist products. That doesn't mean that the management products are forgotten, though; they're simply not put on the diagrams. In the case of progress reports which are at set time intervals, you can't put them on a sequence diagram anyway, because they come in lots of places.

Knowing Your PBS From Your PFD

The two product diagrams used in PRINCE2 show the two views of structure and sequence, so they're very different. Both diagrams are simple in concept. You can't be asked to draw the diagrams in the exams, because both papers use a multiple-choice question format. However, in the Foundation exam you can be asked general questions about them, and in the Practitioner exam you may be given diagrams and have to answer questions which reflect the project scenario, including finding any errors in the diagrams given and perhaps identifying the correct snippet of diagram to replace the wrong part. Or you may have a diagram with just numbers in the boxes and have to show which products go in which place.

The Product Breakdown Structure (PBS)

The *Product Breakdown Structure* (PBS) is simply a list. It's a list of the specialist products but grouped according to their categories and subcategories. The most powerful use of this diagram is when you're first identifying products. You can just produce a random list of products as they came to mind. It often helps, however, to give some structure to your thinking and to go through the product categories one at a time. If you're considering a house-building project, for example, you might think about the brickwork products first, then the woodwork products, then the electrical products and then the decorating products. As you think more about the electrical products, you might find it helpful to break them down into two subcategories according to whether they belong to the power circuit or the lighting circuit.

The Product Flow Diagram (PFD)

In contrast, the *Product Flow Diagram* (PFD) is a sequence diagram. It shows the order in which products will be created during the life of the project. That's not going to be the same order as the categories in the PBS. Taking the example of the house building again, you might have thought about the brickwork products first, but, looking at the sequence, you wouldn't develop all brickwork products first in the project. The brickwork for the foundations will indeed be early on in the project, but building the garden wall will come almost last when there's no more need to bring lorries onto the site.

Fitting the diagrams together

The lowest level of the PBS is the list of products, grouped by the higher level boxes which are merely category labels. The PFD shows those same lowest level boxes, but put in project order. Then the final box on the PFD is the same as the top box of the PBS and represents the whole project. [**P2FD** Ch14]

The products in the PBS and those in the PFD are exactly the same. It's just that one diagram shows them grouped in categories and subcategories, while the other shows them in the order in which they'll actually be created during the project.

Knowing What's In and What's Out

Most products in the project will be built by the teams. Some, however, may come from outside the project. Unless you work in a company that makes computers, if you're running an IT project then the computer itself will be an external product – something coming over the project boundary from outside. Now, be careful not to fall into the trap of thinking that external products are unimportant. I used to work in IT projects, and you can take it from me that in an IT project the computer is rather important. The point is that the computer, vital though it is to the project, came in over the project boundary from somewhere outside; it wasn't created by the team.

A common confusion when first learning about internal and external products is to mistake the project boundary for the organisational boundary. An external product is a product coming from outside the project, not necessarily from outside the customer organisation. For example, it may be coming from another project. Perhaps another project is developing a specification for a piece of equipment it's constructing, and your project needs a copy of the specification because a product being built in your project will have to interface with that other project's equipment.

It may help you to clarify which products are internal products and which are external if you look at a diagram. Figure 22-1 shows how a product from an outside supplier can be an internal product, while the product from somewhere else in your own organisation can be an external product. Remember, this is all about the project boundary.

Figure 22-1 shows an extract from a Product Flow Diagram for a project involving two suppliers from outside the customer organisation. Supplier A is providing a team in the project, and the work of that team is included in the Project Plans. Supplier B is just sending in a product and is not involved in the work of the project. The diagram uses the normal notation of a rectangle for internal or team products, and an ellipse for external products. The reasoning behind the symbols on the diagram is:

- **Products A and B:** These are being produced by project teams that are from within the customer organisation.

- **Product C:** This product is being produced by a team from Supplier A. The team is from outside the customer organisation, but it's inside the project because the team is a project team.

- **Product D:** This product is external. Yes, the product is coming from within the same customer organisation, but it's coming from outside the project – perhaps it's coming from another project.

- **Product E:** This product is also external. It's external not because the product is coming from outside the customer organisation, which actually it is, but because the product is coming from outside the project.

Another source of external products is where things already exist when the project starts. If a product already exists, then one of your teams on the project isn't going to be asked to build it so, by definition, that product is external. In the manual, and especially in the exams, products already in existence are called *pre-requisites*.

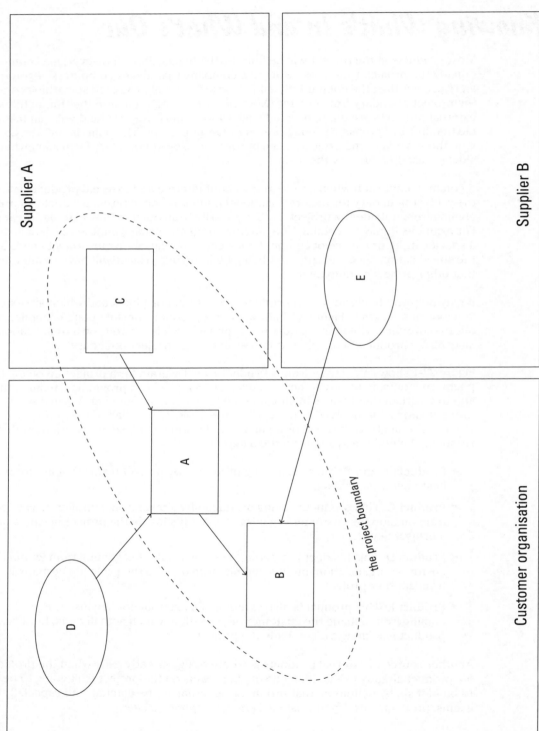

Figure 22-1:
Products
and the
project
boundary.

Describing Products

Product Descriptions, as the name suggests, simply describe the products. The default is that you'll have a Product Description for each product in your Product Flow Diagram – including external products. There's an option to miss out Product Descriptions where these are not necessary, such as if a team already fully understands the product. In real life that can be rather dangerous, but as this book is about exams you can ignore the point for now. *PRINCE2 For Dummies* has more on project reality.

The contents of the Product Description are pretty logical. If you're the Project Manager and you're asking a team to build a product, then you need to define the product so that the team members know what to do. Unfortunately, for historic reasons, some of the headings in the Product Description are a little obscure. Check out the explanations in the manual or in *PRINCE2 For Dummies* to be sure that you're clear on them. [**Manual** A17, **P2FD** Ch14 Writing Product Descriptions]

Following the Link to Quality

Products are closely associated with quality, although in the PRINCE2 manual this isn't brought out as well as it might be. Take note though that of the 12 headings on a Product Description, the last 5 are all quality related. That's important to know for both exams, together with knowing what those quality headings are all about.

Describing the Whole Project

One Product Description is slightly different from all the rest, and that's the Project Product Description (PPD). This defines what the whole project is to deliver, rather than an individual product within it – and consequently, while the headings are similar to a normal Product Description, they're not identical. The important thing to keep in mind with the PPD is that it's about the *whole* project. The PPD is created before the project begins and in the process Starting Up a Project where it forms part of the Project Brief. It does have a life beyond the brief, though, and will be maintained throughout the project, starting in Initiation, where it becomes part of the Project Plan, which in turn is part of the Project Initiation Documentation (PID). The PPD will be reviewed at the end of each stage and also checked at the end of the project to ensure that the project has delivered what it was supposed to.

Index

About the Author

Nick Graham is a project methods specialist and has been involved with PRINCE2 since before it was even called PRINCE. As a Project Manager he was trained in PROMPT II, the method on which the PRINCE versions have been based. He started originally with a systems method where he caught the bug for highly productive application of methods and moved on to project management methods. More recently he has been the joint author of PRIME, an alternative project management method which is designed to be wider in scope and more business focused than PRINCE2.

He remains an strong enthusiast of PRINCE2 used intelligently and applied appropriately. He is renowned for highly practical training so that those he teaches not only succeed in the exams but can also go back into the workplace to use PRINCE2 effectively, productively and with confidence. His training course delegates have described his style as energetic, lively, fun, very practical and very informative. In this book, Nick offers advice based on his long experience teaching PRINCE2 since the method was launched and in coaching candidates for the exams. Unlike his training courses, this publication is geared solely to passing the exams.

Nick is also the author of the companion volume to this book, *PRINCE2 For Dummies,* and in general project management he was the joint author of the UK edition of *Project Management For Dummies*.

In the PRINCE2 exams Nick held the record for many years for the highest pass mark achieved at Practitioner level. He no longer holds the record, but would be genuinely delighted if a reader of this book won it 'back'. His advice to delegates on courses is not to study to pass but study to excel, and that same advice is offered to you. Nick's own success with the PRINCE2 method is reflected in his consultancy work where he has taught and advised organisations ranging from individual consultants, up through small and big business to multi-nationals, in the third (charity) sector, in the NHS and police, in research organisations and in local and central government. His own background in both the public and private sectors allows him to communicate easily with staff in all areas and at all levels.

Nick is available for consultancy advice, project training and workshops which can all be so cost effective when they help speed projects towards completion and realisation of benefits. His own company is Inspirandum Ltd and you can contact him through the company's website.

Nick is a member of the Association for Project Management (APM) and of the Institute of Directors (IoD).

www.inspirandum.com

Dedication

This book is dedicated to my son, Peter Graham. Peter has moved away from his involvement in project management training to pursue his lifelong interest in politics. However, it is a real plus to have an elected politician who actually understands projects and project management. I wish him continuing success, mostly because he is my son but partly in the hope that his influence will ultimately be seen in rather better oversight of projects within government. His talents, and not least his flair with graphics, are nevertheless missed in Inspirandum Ltd.

Author's Acknowledgements

This is the third book I have had the privilege of writing in the John Wiley *For Dummies* series. As always, I am so very grateful for the encouragement I've received from John Wiley staff and, this time around, from the commissioning editor for the title Claire Ruston whose kindness and sustained enthusiasm has meant such a lot. On the practical side of the editing and preparation, it's been great to be working with Simon Bell once again. I so value talking things through with Simon before starting in earnest on the writing, and our time at Chichester talking through this book was as valuable as ever to be sure that things went along the right track. I'm so conscious that the work that I do in preparing the text is just one part of what is a long and complex process under Simon's experienced eye.

At home I have to thank my wife Kath who also works in our company, Inspirandum Ltd. Kath's patience in dealing with so many pressures to leave me in peace at the computer is precious indeed. I should also thank Apple Computers. Sitting at a computer screen for so very many hours at a time can be daunting indeed, but when that computer is an iMac then it's pure pleasure.

Publisher's Acknowledgements

We're proud of this book; please send us your comments at http://dummies.custhelp.com. For other comments, please contact our Customer Care Department within the U.S. at 877-762-2974, outside the U.S. at (001) 317-572-3993, or fax 317-572-4002.

Some of the people who helped bring this book to market include the following:

Acquisitions, Editorial, and Vertical Websites

Project Editor: Simon Bell

Commissioning Editor: Claire Ruston

Assistant Editor: Ben Kemble

Copy Editor: Kate O'Leary

Technical Editor: APMG Group

Proofreader: Mary White

Production Manager: Daniel Mersey

Publisher: Miles Kendall

Cover Photos:

Cartoons: Rich Tennant (www.the5thwave.com)

Composition Services

Project Coordinator: Kristie Rees

Layout and Graphics: Carrie A. Cesavice

Proofreaders: Susan Moritz

Indexer: Potomac Indexing, LLC

Special Art:

FOR DUMMIES®

Making Everything Easier! ™

UK editions

BUSINESS

Bookkeeping
FOR DUMMIES
978-1-118-34689-1

Pop Up Business
FOR DUMMIES
978-1-118-44349-1

Starting & Running a Business
ALL-IN-ONE
FOR DUMMIES
978-1-119-97527-4

MUSIC

Mandolin
FOR DUMMIES
978-1-119-94276-4

Ukulele
FOR DUMMIES
978-0-470-97799-6

DJing
FOR DUMMIES
978-0-470-66372-1

HOBBIES

Stargazing
FOR DUMMIES
978-1-118-41156-8

Keeping Chickens
FOR DUMMIES
978-1-119-99417-6

Beekeeping
FOR DUMMIES
978-1-119-97250-1

Asperger's Syndrome For Dummies
978-0-470-66087-4

Basic Maths For Dummies
978-1-119-97452-9

Body Language For Dummies, 2nd Edition
978-1-119-95351-7

Boosting Self-Esteem For Dummies
978-0-470-74193-1

Business Continuity For Dummies
978-1-118-32683-1

Cricket For Dummies
978-0-470-03454-5

Diabetes For Dummies, 3rd Edition
978-0-470-97711-8

eBay For Dummies, 3rd Edition
978-1-119-94122-4

English Grammar For Dummies
978-0-470-05752-0

Flirting For Dummies
978-0-470-74259-4

IBS For Dummies
978-0-470-51737-6

ITIL For Dummies
978-1-119-95013-4

Management For Dummies, 2nd Edition
978-0-470-97769-9

Managing Anxiety with CBT For Dummies
978-1-118-36606-6

Neuro-linguistic Programming For Dummies, 2nd Edition
978-0-470-66543-5

Nutrition For Dummies, 2nd Edition
978-0-470-97276-2

Organic Gardening For Dummies
978-1-119-97706-3

12-47776–210.8x274.3mm

FOR DUMMIES®

Making Everything Easier!™

UK editions

SELF-HELP

978-0-470-66541-1

978-1-119-99264-6

978-0-470-66086-7

LANGUAGES

978-0-470-68815-1

978-1-119-97959-3

978-0-470-69477-0

HISTORY

978-0-470-68792-5

978-0-470-74783-4

978-0-470-97819-1

Origami Kit For Dummies
978-0-470-75857-1

Overcoming Depression For Dummies
978-0-470-69430-5

Positive Psychology For Dummies
978-0-470-72136-0

PRINCE2 For Dummies, 2009 Edition
978-0-470-71025-8

Project Management For Dummies
978-0-470-71119-4

Psychology Statistics For Dummies
978-1-119-95287-9

Psychometric Tests For Dummies
978-0-470-75366-8

Renting Out Your Property For Dummies, 3rd Edition
978-1-119-97640-0

Rugby Union For Dummies, 3rd Edition
978-1-119-99092-5

Sage One For Dummies
978-1-119-95236-7

Self-Hypnosis For Dummies
978-0-470-66073-7

Storing and Preserving Garden Produce For Dummies
978-1-119-95156-8

Teaching English as a Foreign Language For Dummies
978-0-470-74576-2

Time Management For Dummies
978-0-470-77765-7

Training Your Brain For Dummies
978-0-470-97449-0

Voice and Speaking Skills For Dummies
978-1-119-94512-3

Work-Life Balance For Dummies
978-0-470-71380-8

12-47776—210.8x274.3mm

FOR DUMMIES®

Making Everything Easier! ™

COMPUTER BASICS

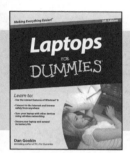

978-1-118-11533-6

978-0-470-61454-9

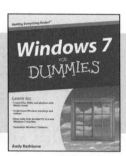

978-0-470-49743-2

DIGITAL PHOTOGRAPHY

978-1-118-09203-3

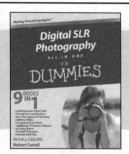

978-0-470-76878-5

978-1-118-00472-2

SCIENCE AND MATHS

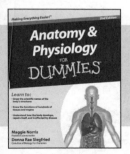

978-0-470-92326-9

978-0-470-55964-2

978-0-470-90324-7

Art For Dummies
978-0-7645-5104-8

Computers For Seniors For Dummies, 3rd Edition
978-1-118-11553-4

Criminology For Dummies
978-0-470-39696-4

Currency Trading For Dummies, 2nd Edition
978-0-470-01851-4

Drawing For Dummies, 2nd Edition
978-0-470-61842-4

Forensics For Dummies
978-0-7645-5580-0

French For Dummies, 2nd Edition
978-1-118-00464-7

Guitar For Dummies, 2nd Edition
978-0-7645-9904-0

Hinduism For Dummies
978-0-470-87858-3

Index Investing For Dummies
978-0-470-29406-2

Islamic Finance For Dummies
978-0-470-43069-9

Knitting For Dummies, 2nd Edition
978-0-470-28747-7

Music Theory For Dummies, 2nd Edition
978-1-118-09550-8

Office 2010 For Dummies
978-0-470-48998-7

Piano For Dummies, 2nd Edition
978-0-470-49644-2

Photoshop CS6 For Dummies
978-1-118-17457-9

Schizophrenia For Dummies
978-0-470-25927-6

WordPress For Dummies, 5th Edition
978-1-118-38318-6

Think you can't learn it in a day? Think again!

The *In a Day* e-book series from *For Dummies* gives you quick and easy access to learn a new skill, brush up on a hobby, or enhance your personal or professional life — all in a day. Easy!

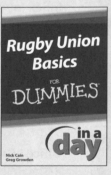